ADVENTURES IN EAST AFRICA

ADVENTURES
in East Africa

Archbishop MAKARIOS of Kenya

With a Foreword by His All Holiness,
Patriarch Bartholomew

Saint Tikhon's Seminary Press

MMXXI

Library of Congress Cataloging-in-Publication Data

Names: Makarios, Archbishop of Narobi and All Kenya
Title: Adventures in East Africa
Description: South Canaan, Penn.: St. Tikhon's Seminary Press, 2021.
Identifiers: ISBN 978-1-7328522-9-7
Subject: letters, pastoral; sermons, religious; church history, African Orthodox Church of Kenya.

Cover design based upon a shield of the Maasai people (of modern-day Kenya and Tanzania) in the collection of the Metropolitan Museum of Art, New York, New York (The Michael C. Rockefeller Memorial Collection, Gift of Joseph J. Shapiro, 1972).

Image on the back cover is courtesy of the author.

All footnotes have been added by St. Tikhon's Seminary Press.
All scriptural quotations have been adopted from the King James Version.

St. Tikhon's Seminary Press, South Canaan, Penn.
STS Press is an imprint of Saint Tikhon's Monastery Press

ISBN 978-1-7328522-9-7

Contents

Foreword

IT IS WITH GREAT DELIGHT that we welcome this fourth volume[1] by His Eminence Metropolitan Makarios (Tillyrides) of Kenya in the series entitled *Adventures in the Unseen*. Within this compelling collection of addresses and discourses lies an opportunity to engage first-hand with the vibrant Orthodox Christian presence in Africa. The author eloquently describes African culture from his personal encounters, the many ways in which it is complemented by the Orthodox faith, and the potential for their simultaneous flourishing together.

Other significant topics are covered in great depth throughout the book, one of the most prominent being the nature of missionary work and outreach. Archbishop Makarios provides us with a deeper and clearer understanding of mission and conversion in Africa from an Orthodox perspective. For him, it is not the missionaries who should be solely credited for the blossoming of Orthodoxy in Africa, but the sincere and devout relations of the African people with the Creator that have cultivated the strong Orthodox presence in Africa. As he has said, the success of Orthodoxy in Africa is not because of evangelization, nor proselytism, but because of the quest of African people seeking the One, Holy, Catholic and Apostolic faith.

1 Volumes I and II were published by The Orthodox Research Institute, Rollinsford, NH in 2004. Volume III was published by Cocheco Falls Publishing, Dover, NH in 2011.

Thus, the role of the Christian missionary is explained as one of service, of *diakonia*. The missionaries, then, are not simply propagators of a Christian denomination, but "instruments of God, honing and nurturing" the faith of those whom they serve. This would imply, of course, that for Archbishop Makarios and his flock, translations and the availability of more resources are part of the initial stage. He insists that the piety of the African people calls for more: for a living God. The rich, historic and living tradition of the Orthodox Church is therefore not only to be translated, but also to be learned by heart. In other words, what they learn about and experience—or rather *Whom* they learn about and experience—should penetrate their hearts and become a part of them.

Ultimately, for all Christians, it is never an institution or missionaries who are the source of transformation. The source of all that is good, of every good and perfect gift, is our Lord God and Savior Jesus Christ.[2] In congratulating Archbishop Makarios on captivating volume, we commend him above all else for his works of ministry, and for the building up of Christ's body in this region.[3]

+BARTHOLOMEW OF CONSTANTINOPLE

2 James 1:17.
3 Ephesians 4:12

Introduction[1]

A LEADING ROMAN AUTHOR who had a great deal to do with Africa gave to the world the well-known aphorism, *ex Africa semper aliquid novi.*[2] For those of you who have forgotten your Latin, the approximate translation is: "Always something new from Africa." Another saying I would like to quote is: "Africa is adventure." After many years of living, working, and ministering on the Dark Continent, I can confirm the complete truth of both sayings. Africa has always been an exciting continent and the excitement remains today.

I had the privilege of being born into a strongly Christian home on the island of Cyprus, which was evangelized by the apostles Paul and Barnabas. My late mother, who reposed at more than ninety years, remained what she had always been throughout her life—a faithful and dedicated Orthodox Christian. While still very young, I had the leading that religion would be my life's work. When I was a little older, I thought I would become a monk and I had thoughts of settling in one of the monasteries on the Holy Mountain.

Since many of you here will not know what I mean by the words "the Holy Mountain," I had better explain. In northern Greece, there are three peninsulas extending like fingers into the Aegean Sea. From the name of the mountain situated on it, the most northerly of these peninsulas is called

1 Introduction originally published in 2000.

2 Pliny the Elder, *Naturalis Historia*, 8, 42; a translation of the Greek, Ἀεὶ Λιβύη φέρει τι καινόν, likely originating with Aristotle.

Mount Athos. But we Orthodox call it "the Holy Mountain" because for more than a thousand years Mount Athos has been a quasi-independent monastic republic. Scattered along the length of the peninsula are many monasteries as well as the cells of a large number of hermits who feel called by God to live solitary lives. As I have said, my aspiration was to become a monk on the Holy Mountain.

But as another saying goes, "Man proposes, but God disposes." The heavenly Father had other plans for me. I must explain that there are different kinds of monks. At one extreme are men of the humblest origin who may be barely literate. But there are also monks who are university men and there are some who are very learned. The one definite requirement for monasticism is the clear calling of God upon the man's life, and that calling can be laid equally upon a peasant and a university professor. From an early age, I had that calling on my own life, for which I thank God. But those over me in the faith advised that I would be of greater value to God if I acquired a thorough education. I accepted this guidance and made plans to study at an Orthodox seminary in Paris. Before I began my studies, I went for a time of prayer and reflection in an Orthodox monastery near London.

He meets Archimandrite Sophrony

I was blessed with a life changing experience at this monastery. At that time—a youth of twenty—I met the man who became my spiritual father. His name was Archimandrite Sophrony, and he was a monk of such transparent holiness that I was attracted to him at once.[3] He had spent several years on the Holy Mountain where I hoped to go. From time to time, the Orthodox Church canonizes members of her communion—both men and women—who have attained to the highest levels of holiness. In other words, she declares them to be saints of God. Orthodox Christians ask the saints to pray for them in the same way that we might ask a living person to pray for us. Of course, in one sense, the saints in paradise are more gloriously alive than any of us here on earth.

During the years he was living on the Holy Mountain, my spiritual father, Archimandrite Sophrony, was himself privileged to have as his own spiritual father a monk named Silouan. Although the name of Father Silouan is unknown to the wider world, yet spiritually he was a giant.

3 "Archimandrite" is a title of honor given to senior priest-monks. Arch. Sophrony was glorified as a saint of the Orthodox Church in 2020. For an account of his life, see Nicholas Sakharov, *I Love Therefore I Am* (Crestwood, N.Y.: SVS Press, 2002).

Born into a Russian peasant family in 1866, he served as a soldier in the Russian army. His education was restricted to a few months in a village school where he learned to read and write and very little else. Like so many young men, Silouan did not always live a clean life. After a very real conversion experience, he felt the leading to become a monk. He arrived on the Holy Mountain in 1892 and remained there until his death on September 24, 1938, a period of forty-six years. He never became a priest but was blessed with a number of mystical experiences and the gift of unceasing prayer. In 1988, the Holy Orthodox Church accorded to Silouan the highest accolade she can grant to one of her sons: he was canonized and has thus taken his place as an acknowledged Saint of God.

I am sorry to have digressed in this way, but I must admit that I do take a certain sanctified pride in having a spiritual connection with a man of such outstanding holiness of life. I believe that my own spiritual father, Archimandrite Sophrony, most likely equaled his mentor, Saint Silouan, in holiness and spiritual achievement.

So as a twenty-year old, I came under the influence of Father Sophrony. He was to guide me with dedication and devotion until he entered into the higher life on July 11, 1993. Although I had the desire to be a monk on Mount Athos, my life as a young man was devoted to study. I studied in Paris, in Rome, in Oxford, and finally at the University of Louvain in Belgium. Then, I was offered the post of Principal of the Makarios III Seminary in Nairobi, Kenya, where priests of our Orthodox Church are trained. This was in January of 1977, and the seminary had not, at that time, been long in existence. I considered the offer and prayed about it, but was not very enthusiastic. The desire of my heart was still to be a monk on the Holy Mountain.

But then, as I always did in times of perplexity, I took counsel with my spiritual father, the holy monk Sophrony. "Go to Africa," he said. "It is there that you will find your life's work. And eventually, you will die in Africa." I could not fail to take this counsel as a command from Almighty God. And so I came to Africa, and was launched into a career of excitement and adventure that has not yet ended.

A brief history of the Church in Africa in the twentieth century

At this point, I am going to make another digression. We are now very nearly at the end of the century. If asked the question, "What was the most remarkable development involving Christianity during the twentieth century?" different people would no doubt give different answers. If I were to be asked this question, I think I should have no hesitation in knowing what my own answer would be: namely, the planting of the Holy Orthodox Church in East Africa, and its truly phenomenal growth over an area of Africa about the size of Western Europe. Although these have been amazing developments, it seems strange—at any rate to me—that they appear to be very little known outside the communion of the Orthodox Church. Let me briefly outline what has been achieved.

During the 1920s, two former Anglican priests in Uganda, entirely as a result of private studies and research, converted to Orthodoxy. At first, understandably, they were not sure how to proceed, but they built a simple church in the Orthodox style, furnished it with icons, and began to hold services of worship approximating as closely as they could to correct Orthodox patterns of worship. Naturally, they made mistakes, but they also made progress and congregations were built up of humble black people who regarded themselves as Orthodox Christians.

However, there is more to being a proper Orthodox believer than a correct mode of worship. To be truly Orthodox, the believer must be in fellowship with the great worldwide Orthodox Church, which acknowledges the Ecumenical Patriarch as its senior bishop.[4] In Africa, the entire Orthodox body on the continent acknowledges the Patriarch of Alexandria as its Father in God. In 1946, one of the two Ugandan priests who had planted Orthodoxy in his country went to Alexandria and met the Patriarch. The Patriarch then formally recognized the African Orthodox community in Uganda and took it under his pastoral care. From that time until the present day, the Orthodox Church of East Africa has experienced continuous growth and expansion.

From Uganda, Orthodoxy spread into neighboring Kenya and from there to Tanzania and Rwanda. The growth and expansion is still very much in evidence up to the present day. With the exception of the ancient Coptic churches in Egypt and Ethiopia, until the advent of Orthodoxy,

4 This statement should be qualified with the understanding that the Ecumenical Patriarch is, likewise, in communion with all the other local orthodox churches (Alexandria, Antioch, Jerusalem, Moscow, etc.). Orthodox ecclesiology does not reduce catholicity to communion with the Patriarch of Constantinople, as does the Roman Catholic Church with the Roman pontiff. See George Florovsky, "The Catholicity of the Church" in *Bible, Church, Tradition: An Eastern Orthodox View* (Vaduz, Europe: Buchervertriebsanstalt, 1987), 37–55.

Christianity was planted entirely by white missionaries. In sharp contrast, Orthodoxy is the product of black spirituality, black enterprise, and black effort. In recent years, this has been supplemented by certain foreign help; notably the Orthodox Church of Finland, which has manifested a fraternal love and interest in her "brethren in Africa." But this in no way detracts from the fact that Africans themselves planted the Orthodox faith in the soil of Africa.

In addition to the help given by the Finnish Orthodox, no work in East Africa can be complete without reference to Archbishop Makarios III of Cyprus. When he also held the post of President of Cyprus, the Archbishop was often in the headlines during the 1950s. Through his friendship with the first president of independent Kenya, Mr. Jomo Kenyatta, Archbishop Makarios III made two visits to Kenya. During one of these visits, he baptized several hundred Kenyan converts to Orthodoxy. On his second visit, President Kenyatta gave a piece of land as a site for an Orthodox seminary. It is in commemoration of the fatherly interest shown by Archbishop Makarios III of Cyprus that the seminary is named in his honor.

African Orthodoxy is not confined to the Paschan regions of the continent. It has also been planted in different countries of West Africa, notably Nigeria, Ghana, Cameroon, and Cote d'Ivoire. I cannot give any exact figure of the number of Orthodox in East Africa, if only because any figure I give today will be obsolete tomorrow, with the Church in that region continuing to experience remarkable growth. But the total number of faithful certainly runs into hundreds of thousands.

When I began my appointment at the seminary in Nairobi, there were twelve students. As I have mentioned, I began at the seminary in January 1977. At that time, and for over fourteen years beyond, I was a layman. This was a serious limitation on my usefulness and after a consultation with His Beatitude, the Patriarch of Alexandria, he decided that in the interests of the seminary and other work, I must be elevated not only to the priesthood, but to the episcopal order. In the space of less than a week, I was ordained deacon and priest and then, on Sunday, July 25, 1992, I was consecrated Bishop of Riruta, which is the name of a town near Nairobi.

The number of students in residence at the seminary progressively increased until there was an average number of between forty and fifty. Most were from Uganda, Kenya, and Tanzania, where the Church was already established. But, toward the end of my appointment in Kenya there were a number of students from outside the East African region, specifically

Madagascar, Cameroon, Ghana, Nigeria, and Zimbabwe. The course for the priesthood is three years. There is a separate course for catechists, which lasts two years.

He arrives in Kenya

When I first went to live in Kenya, there were already about one hundred African Orthodox priests serving the parishes. Although they were earnest Christian men, and canonically ordained, they were mostly lamentably lacking in education. Many of them were semi-literate. This state of affairs was most unsatisfactory. When I left Kenya to assume my Arch episcopal appointment in Zimbabwe, there were not less than three hundred priests in the country, with one hundred in Nairobi. By that time, the majority had passed through the seminary.

Some of our students were from Orthodox homes, while others had Roman Catholic or Protestant backgrounds. However, some had been converted from pagan religions. The academic training of students was obviously not neglected, but I have always felt that the more important aspect of seminary should be the spiritual. The training of our students at the Nairobi seminary was centered on the daily celebration of the Divine Liturgy. It was a thrill for me to see my students growing spiritually before my eyes. There were, of course, many disappointments, frustrations, and some heartaches. It was always a painful experience to have to dismiss a student when it became clear that, for one reason or another, he did not have a true vocation to the priesthood.

An examination of a political map of Africa shows that the continent is made up of a patchwork of countries, large and small. Most of these have no natural boundaries while the political boundaries, such as they are, all date from the colonial era when most of the major powers of Europe and some of the minor ones engaged in what, at the time, was called "the scramble for Africa." These boundaries bled out across national and linguistic lines in a most arbitrary way. For example, the trade language of East Africa is Swahili. This language is spoken over wide areas of six different countries: the Democratic Republic of the Congo, Rwanda, Burundi, Uganda, Tanzania and Kenya. The situation is further complicated by the immense variety of different ethnic groups and languages. In Kenya, which is somewhat larger than France, there are more than 117 ethno-linguistic groups and no less than fifty-eight languages. These languages are not mere dialects. The great majority of them are as unlike each other as French and Italian. It is an unfortunate fact of tribal history that there has been a great deal of inter-tribal hostility. It was distressing that it was not unknown for students to bring their tribal and other animosities with them to the seminary. It was with good cause that I was obliged to include in the seminary regulations a stern prohibition against fighting under pain of instant dismissal. Since English is the official language of most of the countries from which the students are drawn, English is the language of instruction at the seminary.

From the time of my arrival in Nairobi, I resolved, so far as this was possible, to share the living standards of the students. I ate the same food as the students, and since refrigeration was not available in the seminary kitchens, I sometimes found myself suffering from food-related ailments to which the students seemed to be largely immune.

In addition to my duties as Principal of the seminary, I undertook an enormous amount of additional work, especially after I became a bishop. Throughout East Africa, the Orthodox Church has attracted converts from many ethno-linguistic groups. I was determined that the main service of our Church, the Divine Liturgy, as well as other services should be available to the people in their own languages. After the expenditure of a great deal of time and effort, I can now tell you that the service of the Divine Liturgy is today available to our black Orthodox faithful in sixteen languages of tropical Africa. Among them is Shona, which is the main vernacular of Zimbabwe.

The critical nature of evangelism

Orthodoxy has never divorced the work of evangelism from man's social needs. From my first day in Kenya, I tried to do what I could to ensure that health and educational facilities were available to the Orthodox flock; although it goes without saying that we never excluded needy non-Orthodox from using these amenities. Today, as our network of parishes in Kenya ministers to the souls of the faithful, we have a parallel network of five hospitals, one hundred clinics, twenty schools, and one hundred day nurseries.

Without a dynamic work among young people, there can be no future for the Church. With this in mind, I gave much emphasis to youth work. It was a work, moreover, that had the important additional benefit of cutting across tribal and ethnic lines. We organized all manner of functions: seminars, festivals, competitions, and choirs. I also trained young people to be Sunday school teachers. The outcome was most fruitful. The youth work thrived and it was cause for great joy for me to see so many of our young people growing spiritually.

While I am not comparing myself with Saint Paul, which would be ridiculous, a verse written by the apostle does seem to sum up quite well many of the events I experienced during my twenty years in Kenya: "In journeyings often, in perils of waters, in perils of robbers … in perils in the city, in perils in the wilderness."[5]

Some of the adventures that befell me were really quite hair-raising. As in many other parts of Africa, crime has become a serious problem in Kenya; Three times I was assaulted by criminals; once I was shot at. Mercifully, the bullet whistled past my head leaving me unscathed. I was not so fortunate on another occasion when I suffered a knife-wound at the hands of a bandit. Sickness also took its toll. I had attacks of cerebral malaria and once came very close to death. During seminary vacations and at other times as circumstances allowed, I traveled extensively on church business. To avoid the heat of the day—Kenya straddles the equator—I used to travel at night. Many times during these travels, I was in danger from wild animals, in addition to the other perils of the road. I give heartfelt thanks to our heavenly Father that, through every contingency, he never failed to sustain me and bring me through.

Kenya today

Today, Kenya, and indeed the whole of tropical Africa, is in a sorry state. The two great problems are corruption and the AIDS pandemic. Throughout life, corruption is an all-pervading fact of the body politic of the continent. AIDS is a cancer of immorality. The old standards of fidelity —tribal ethics—have broken down in Africa in much the same way that Christian standards have broken down in European society. In Africa, the consequences have been catastrophic. I have been assured by doctors well acquainted with the facts that half of all the hospital patients are HIV positive, and the same is true of half of the babies born in Harare. AIDS is overwhelming the medical profession and swamping the health services throughout the sub-Saharan regions of the continent. Hundreds of

5 2 Cor. 11:26.

thousands of children have been orphaned by AIDS; the number is increasing daily.

The situation is an appalling disaster for the whole continent. An entire generation—in essence, those who are sexually active—are being struck down. My heart goes out especially to the untold thousands of innocent black women who are infected with HIV by their unfaithful husbands. What makes the situation particularly tragic is that it is all so completely avoidable. If the Christian ethic were to be observed of chastity before marriage and fidelity after marriage, the horrifying AIDS pandemic would be stopped in its tracks. When it comes to HIV and AIDS, there was never a truer statement than the biblical warning that "the wages of sin is death."[6]

The pandemic is now rife everywhere in sub-Saharan Africa. In Kenya, I found that I was continually being asked to officiate at funerals of AIDS victims. Whether the victims were Orthodox or not, there were always non-Orthodox present at the funerals, and this gave me many opportunities to propagate the holy faith of Orthodoxy. Although it is a terrible calamity for Africa, it nevertheless opens up innumerable opportunities for Christian witness. The AIDS patient is struck down in the prime of his life, sometimes in the flower of youth. Checked in his evil ways and brought face to face with the prospect of death, as often as not, he is receptive to the truth of the Gospel. I believe that in the providence of Almighty God, for many young sinners, AIDS has become an open door to the salvation of their souls.

As an Archbishop of the Orthodox Church, I am going to close my address with my assessment of what I believe the future might hold for my Church. I am frankly optimistic. Under God, I foresee a great flowering. With the demise of Communism, Orthodoxy is experiencing a tremendous renaissance throughout the former Soviet Union and in those former Soviet satellite states that were predominantly Orthodox. During the seventy years when the Evil Empire was dominant, Orthodoxy never, for one hour, lost its vitality or its sense of mission. So far as the future of Orthodoxy in Africa is concerned, my optimism is even more pronounced. I foresee that Orthodoxy will spread far and wide throughout the continent. With this in view, I cannot do better than to quote the Patriarch of Alexandria, His Beatitude, Petros VII. When asked, "How do the native Africans perceive Orthodoxy?" this was the Patriarch's reply:

6 Rom. 6:23.

> Africans perceive Orthodoxy with the simple sincerity of their gentle souls. They are such simple people, but yet so rich in sincere feelings of love and goodness. So when approached by the Orthodox clergy—provided that they themselves are ready for Orthodoxy—they accept the Faith of the apostles without hesitation. For them, Orthodoxy is the pure religion. It not only reaches out to them, but embraces them, not out of self-interest, but simply because it offers the truth of God.

It is for these reasons that Orthodoxy has spread so dramatically on the Dark Continent. As I have already outlined, a tremendous amount has been achieved in East Africa. I believe with all my heart that what has been done there will also be done in Central Africa. The first black Zimbabwean priest will soon be ordained and one of my priorities is the establishment of a seminary in Harare.

It is my fervent hope and prayer that as Orthodoxy spreads, it will make a growing social impact. As lives of men and women are transformed by sacramental grace, which is also none other than the grace of the risen and glorified Christ, society itself will be progressively transformed. The individual and the family are the microcosm. Society at large is the macrocosm. It is inevitable that the transformation of the one will result in the transformation of the other.

But while it has its social dimension, the main business of the Holy Orthodox Church is of course the salvation of souls. This has been the Church's preoccupation for over two millennia and she has not failed in her task. When our Lord returns at the end of the age, I am thankful to the triune God that the sons and daughters of Africa will not be lacking in that great gathering.

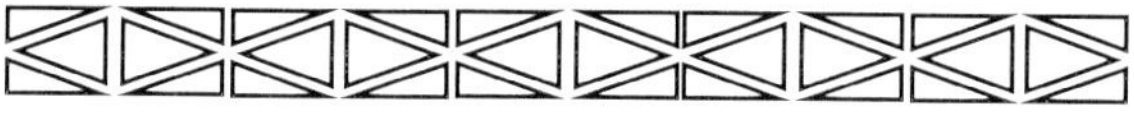

Festal Homilies & Encyclicals

PASCHAL ENCYCLICAL[1]
on the Sign of the Cross

April 4, 2010

My Co-Workers, dear Brothers and Sisters in Christ: Christ is risen!

BROTHERS AND SISTERS in Christ, today is a great day that we celebrate yet another Holy Pascha. First and foremost we give thanks to our Almighty God for enabling us to cross the fasting period successfully and to attain our highest peak, which is the celebration of Pascha. We have perhaps asked ourselves many questions concerning this feast, and why we anticipate it so, for it occurs only once in a year. We have celebrated it many times in the past. And it is a given that today's feast will also come to an end, for there is nothing in this present world that does not come to an end; everything is temporal and transitory. The days of our lives disappear like shadows and pass like a dream until we come to our own end. My point of concern here is not to say that Pascha is not desirable, but to say that our paschal celebration should not in fact end at all, but should be a daily affair. It should never be seen as a once-a -year event. The daily Pascha to which I am referring here is the cleansing of sins, gaining a contrite spirit and humble heart, bringing forth tears of compunction, obtaining a pure conscience, and the banishing of carnal passions, and the banishing of carnal passions: adultery impurity, lust, and all other sins and passions.

My dear brethren, if we succeed in the virtues mentioned above, we will

1 An encyclical is a letter, sent by the ruling bishop to his diocese on important days of the church calendar, or in response to an momentous occasion.

be filled with joy today in this radiant and greatly desired feast, and not just this one glorious day, but throughout our daily lives. We should always strive to be righteous, as this is the only way to make our joy in this feast a reality. For example, we cannot say that a man whose ship is damaged and is in danger of sinking is having a pleasant voyage because the ship will finally sink. The same applies to the person who is weighed down by sin. We cannot say that he or she is having a beautiful Pascha celebration. Our Pascha journey is nothing less than our preparation for this great feast. It is a preparation that involves much chanting followed by many readings and spiritual lessons, and prayers followed by other prayers. All these circles carry us along and help to unite us with the Lord. And in order for us to achieve this we must die to our passions, and with the help of the Holy Spirit, to resurrect our virtues. We must also keep remembering our Lord Jesus Christ, for he suffered for our sakes, leaving us as an example that we might follow in his way. We ought to also thank Almighty God for bestowing on us the good things of this present life, and his great assurance that those who labor in him until the end shall receive from his hand the joys of eternal life and shall inherit the heavenly Pascha.

Today brethren, as we celebrate the feast of Pascha, just allow me to reflect upon the Cross of Christ, which is for us a symbol of hope. St. Paul's advice in his letter to the Galatians was, "But God forbid that I should glory, save in the Cross of our Lord Jesus Christ, by whom the world is crucified unto me, and I unto the world."[2]

Throughout the whole world, men and women think and live by symbols. Symbols constitute a convenient way of expressing in a small compass complex and far reaching ideas. For example, the early Christians used a fish as their secret symbol, since the letters of the Greek word of fish furnished the initial letters for the expressions, "Jesus Christ," "Son of God," and "Savior." But the most meaningful symbol the world has ever known, or will ever know is the Cross. Crowded into this symbol lies the whole significance of the universe and the world of human life and destiny. Throughout the history of the Church, Christians have preached the Cross, displayed the Cross in their homes and on their altars, venerated the Cross in the Liturgy, and signed themselves with the Cross in worship of the Holy Trinity and during times of fear and temptation.

As Christians, we boast in the Cross because it is through the Cross that God tells us about himself in such an emphatic and conclusive way that

2 Gal. 6:14.

any man or woman zealous for truth, obedient and teachable in spirit, cannot fail to discover the grand intention of our heavenly Father. Through the Cross, it is revealed to us that God hates sin. He is an ethical God of uncompromising morality. He loves humanity with everlasting love, and he uses the Cross to encourage us, to help us through his Son in our sinful nature. By the Cross, God is here, the suffering loving God, the invisible Spirit working within us.

Brothers and sisters in Christ, the Cross tells us that we are not only sinners, but also that we are created and fashioned in the image and likeness of the Holy Trinity. And because of the uniqueness of our having been created in his image, God reveals himself in flesh in order that he may save our humanity. Today, my fellow Christians, the Cross also has a story of forgiveness and healing of the body and mind and soul for us men and women and children. It is a message of hope for all of us who are burdened by sin, obsessed by fear, for all who are sick and afflicted.

This message, brothers and sisters, is the message of forgiveness and a new start, a message that is backed by the invincible power, wisdom, and love of the Creator and the Father of all mankind. Therefore, my dear children in Christ, let us today, through Christ, venerate the Cross which is and has been the focal point of human history, marking a new order of events, and that proclaims a God of righteousness, love, and godliness to every single person, as well as the possibility of forgiveness—a new start for us. We look upon the Cross on which Christ was crucified for our sins and those of the world. And this is why during Holy Week we relive Christ's suffering, his passion and death; we lament for him, and ask for forgiveness, taking up our crosses with him.

One important mystery that will never cease to amaze all Christian generations is Christ's own faith in his Father. We see Christ trusting his Father until his last breath. Through this strong faith he becomes victorious over death, and we are finally spiritually saved. Christ's promise for us today is that he is going to dwell in all of us who are worthy. Jesus says, "If a man love me, he will keep my words: and my Father will love him, and we will come unto him, and make our abode with him."[3] And he also says, "He that hath my commandments, and keepeth them, he is that loveth me: and he that loveth me shall be loved of my Father, and I will love him, and will manifest myself to him."[4]

3 Jn. 14:23.

4 Jn. 14:21.

Brothers and sisters, inasmuch as Christ is promising us great gifts and great joy, we should persevere with gladness for his name's sake, in every grief, every affliction, every loss, and we should be mindful of the apostle Paul's words to the Colossians when he says, "[I] now rejoice in my sufferings for you, and fill up that which is behind of the afflictions of Christ in my flesh for his body's sake, which is the Church."[5]

Finally, my co-workers, dear brothers and sisters in Christ, the suffering, passion, death, and resurrection of Christ is not a ticket for total happiness, but it is rather the beginning of a new life. As we grow in this new life of love, we might be challenged by the world's oppression and persecution, which of course takes place by Gods permission. What really matters here, my dear brothers and sisters, is not our trials *per se*, but our response to them. It is important to know that properly received trials reveal where our hearts are. They help to increase our faith, which must grow. The godly reaction to trials is joy and perseverance. Though at times difficult circumstances are from the evil one, to be angry at circumstances is to be angry with God who permits them. May the precious Cross of Christ and his forgiveness continue to give us strength to endure all the sufferings and trials that come along our path of salvation.

Christ is risen!

May the risen Christ be with you and guide you throughout your lives and bless you always. Amen.

In His service,
+ ARCHBISHOP MAKARIOS

5 Col. 1:24.

HOMILY
on the Feast of the Dormition of the Theotokos

August 15, 2010

I greet you in the Name of the Father, the Son, and the Holy Spirit.

My spiritual children in Christ, the context of our Lord's command to make disciples of all the nations and to baptize them in the Name of the Father, and of the Son, and of the Holy Spirit means that making disciples cannot be done through human strength and skill, but only through the power of God. This is the reason why Christ is commissioning the apostles by his authority to go into the world and preach the Gospel. The reality of the Resurrection is important not only because of its historicity, for the verification of apostolic witness and its necessity for faith, but also for its power in our Christian life and mission. The resurrected Son of God is living with us and also giving us his power to spread the good news of the Kingdom. He makes possible salvation for all mankind—for those who are willing to listen to him and follow his teachings.

Christ's apostles followed faithfully the words of their master, both taking his words forth into the world and passing them on to their own disciples. Saint Paul later sent an epistle to the Corinthians, in which he set out the particular duties of apostolic service. Paul says:

> Giving no offense in anything, that the ministry be not blamed: But in all things approving ourselves as the ministers of God, in much patience, in afflictions, in necessities, in distresses ... By honor and

> dishonor, by evil report and good report … as deceivers, and yet true … As sorrowful, yet always rejoicing; as poor, yet making many rich; as having nothing, and yet possessing all things.[6]

The apostle Paul here is not only addressing his disciples in the Church of Corinth, but today's Church as well. Paul is writing to all of us who call ourselves Christians and who come to church in order to learn to live a Christian life. We are all missionaries who have been *sent out there* to preach the Gospel of Christ—that is, the Resurrection. We are all in the service of the resurrected Christ, and in our current life we must follow the path trodden by him, fulfilling the commandment that he left us, and living so as to avoid those temptations that would dishonor Christ in the world, so that no one can reproach us Christians with the accusation that we do not practice what we preach. Thus, like the apostle Paul, we seek to follow Christ—in much patience, by honor and dishonor, by evil report and good report.[7]

"And he said unto them, Go ye into all the world, and preach the gospel to every creature."[8] These particular words were not only said to the disciples of Christ but are directed even to us, the contemporary Christians today. Our Lord and Savior Jesus Christ gave out this instruction in order for us to follow it diligently and use the riches of the Church for the salvation of our fellow men. In the previous chapter Paul says that we possess all things because Christ our God left a great deal of treasure in the world: his holy Church. The riches that I am talking about here pertain to the Church and include her faith, her patience, her courage, and her prayers. These are the riches that are very important to us, and they are the riches that we need in order "to go into the world and preach the gospel" of Christ. They are the riches that do not spoil or disappear, but increase in the hearts of Christians from year to year and day to day. The Church shares her riches with the whole world, not in hope of praise or rewards, but because such is the commandment of Christ, and such is the nature of love, for love carries its own reward and does not need recognition.

The heart of a person who is pure and full of love—with the deeds of compassion—and who does not expect a return, but simply gives both riches and good deeds, all of his or her loving acts fill the heart and can never, ever be hidden.[9] The pure heart warmed by divine love and steeped

6 2 Cor. 6:3–10.
7 See 2 Cor. 6:8.
8 Mark 16:15.
9 See Luke 6:45.

in grace is incapable of hiding the riches it has received. Instead, a person with such a heart will generously share them, creating a broad spiritual atmosphere of brightness and peace.

Brothers and sisters in Christ, the resurrection of our Lord and Savior Jesus Christ propels the Church to engage her world with Christ, with his love and his call. This is the Church's mission. This is our mission. Today we are called by Christ himself to make disciples of all nations, and to spread the good news of his salvation, and to bear witness to his resurrection from the dead. It is important to take note that this gospel to which we are witnesses is good news! The good news we are talking about is that we can experience the resurrection of Christ. This is fantastic news, and we cannot keep this to ourselves as if it were our secret. It must be preached to all nations, just as Christ Himself has instructed us to do.

In the gospel narratives of Christ's resurrection we see that the first apostles of the good news of Christ's resurrection were the women who came to anoint his body; who instead witnessed the empty tomb and the risen Lord himself. Their example of taking this good news back to the fearful disciples is in direct contrast with the guards who chose to lie about Christ even though they experienced the earthquake and the stone rolling away. A similar example of this sort of witness on the part of a woman can be seen at Cana of Galilee, when Mary, the Mother of Christ, says to the servants, "Whatsoever he saith unto you, do it."[10]

Mary said these words after she had informed Christ that the wine that was served at the wedding feast had been finished. Jesus responded to his mother by saying, "Woman, what have I to do with thee? Mine hour is not yet come."[11] This shows us that Christ is full of respect for his mother. The word, "woman," is a title of respect and distinction. In addressing his mother thus Jesus gives womanhood great dignity. Christ's answer to his mother shows that he is not refusing her request nor embarrassing her, but reminding her that the time for public disclosure had not yet arrived. We see here, sisters and brothers, that despite Christ's reply, his mother still expects him to act. Today, Mary, the Mother of God, is requesting us to pay attention to what her son is telling us. We need to listen to Christ, as he is the only source of our salvation. He died for us on the Cross and was raised for our sakes. Brothers and sisters in Christ, our Lord is sending us to the world to preach the good news, and the one thing that is required of us is that you and I do whatever he tells us. We must go, full of energy and

10 Jn. 2:5.
11 Jn. 2:4

wisdom, and without fear. And we must go to all four corners of the world and everywhere spread the Word of God.

In the Orthodox Church, the particular setting of the wedding at Cana is of great significance because here we have an example of Mary's gift of intercession. Our Church believes that Mary, the Mother of God, continually speaks to her son on our behalf. And what does the mother ask of us today but to do whatever Christ is telling us: to go and proclaim the gospel of her son to the world? We have no option but to take heed of what the most blessed woman is telling us today.

Mary is assuring us that if we listen and do what Christ requires of us, then we will be blessed, and in the long run will attain God's kingdom. It is that simple. Christ has a wonderful plan. He is calling us, commissioning us to be the means by which the world hears the good news. He is sending us to be his witnesses to the ends of the earth. And because he also wants us to be victors when we go forth in his Name with his gospel. Because he knows that we will fight with the evil one, he has therefore promised us that if we truly believe in him, then wonders and signs will always accompany us when we are out there spreading the good news. We see this in the Gospel of Mark when it says, "So then after the Lord had spoken unto them, he was received up into heaven, and sat on the right hand of God. And they went forth, and preached everywhere, the Lord working with them, and confirming the word with signs following. Amen."[12]

Beloved in Christ, these words gave the apostles the fundamental assurance that he would always be with them through the presence and help of the Holy Spirit, and that their good deeds would be accompanied by signs. These signs and deeds of power were meant to confirm Christ's presence among them. This same promise is given to us today, if we respond to his call to work as his missionaries. It is one of the best promises that Christ has granted us in this Great Commission.

Jesus Christ is calling you and me to complete the mission he gave to his disciples, a mission to all nations and all groups of people. Just as Christ has reached us and loved us, so we are to reflect his love and reach out sensitively and in love to the men, women, and children of each culture, not merely to people who are like us and close by. As long as there are people who have never heard the Name of Jesus, we disobey the Great Commission by refusing to cross the boundaries and preach to them the good news of Christ. Despite the explicitness of Christ's command, perhaps most of us use the "lack of a call" to missions as an excuse. Yet, it may be that the

12 Mark 16:19, 20.

Lord of the harvest has been calling us all along to join in his harvest field, through the need of the world, but we are not willing to hear. If Christ has already called his disciples to go, then none of us can use as an excuse the claim that he has not called us personally to mission work. Every single one of us is called. Discerning our call and then doing it is what is before us to do, not to come up with excuses.

"Teaching them to observe all things whatsoever I have commanded you: and, lo, I am with you always, even unto the end of the world. Amen."[13] Jesus Christ closes his address to the apostles with the above promise when they are undertaking their missionary duties. He will be with them until the end of the age. This particular text probably specifies the end of age because at that time the Son of Man would return in his kingdom and hence be prepared for the judgment. If today's Christians have lost a sense of Christ and purpose among us, it may be because we have lost sight of the mission our Lord has given us. If today we are willing to be his disciples, then we must prepare the way for our Lord's second coming and his kingdom just as John the Baptist did for his first coming. If, brothers and sisters, we truly long for our Lord's return, our mission is laid out before us. This is what we are to be busy doing until he comes.

"Fear not, little flock; for it is your Father's good pleasure to give you the kingdom."[14] Brothers and sisters in Christ, here we see the Lord concluding his exhortation. Our Savior turns more directly to the application of "little flock" to his address to the disciples as an image of easily frightened sheep, which need the tender care of a shepherd. Christ is quite deliberate in comparing believers to these fragile creatures rather than to lions or bears. The Father is the Shepherd and he promises to give everything associated with the Kingdom to his sheep. We may be fragile creatures, but God promises to take care for us and make us strong. My dear brothers and sisters, what Christ is telling us is that our mission here on earth will not be easy, as we will encounter persecution and rejection. Christ's promise to us is that we should not be scared, because whatever risk comes, we will trust in him; whatever ostracism or isolation, we should be assured that God will care for us. Kingdom blessings will be provided for us. But, beloved in Christ, notice that this is not a promise of abundant material blessings, but of sufficient provision to do what God really desires. Amen.

13 Matt. 28:20.
14 Luke 12:32.

CHRISTMAS ENCYCLICAL

December 25, 2010

Dearly beloved Spiritual Children in Christ, I pass to you my seasonal greetings and blessings in the Name of the Father, and of the Son, and of the Holy Spirit.

The time has come, dear brothers and sisters, for us to celebrate the birth of Christ in Bethlehem. We are full of jubilation and excitement, because this child that was born of the Holy Virgin Mary is the Savior of the world. He is going to be our Lord and Savior, our redeemer, our only hope, that is if we choose to welcome him in our hearts, in our lives, and in everything that we do. Today, God has humbled himself in order to save mankind and to redeem man from the bondages of sin; he has become man so that man might be like God. He has been incarnated to renew humanity's status, and this is the main reason for our happiness, our delight, and the best assurance we get from our Creator. He has come not only to wash away our iniquities, but in so doing, to justify us in the eyes of God. If this is the case, how are we as Christians supposed to treat sin? And what is there between our deeds and the law in relation to our justification? The following words from the book of Romans will assist us in seeking answers to those questions: "Therefore by the deeds of the law there shall no flesh be justified in his sight: for by the Law is the knowledge of sin."[15]

Beloved of God, if our salvation is by obedience to the Law, it would

15 Rom. 3:20

require our perfect obedience. If we offend in a single point we become guilty of the whole. Therefore, by law-keeping alone, we cannot be justified. To be justified means to have our past sin forgiven and to have righteousness imputed to us. What Saint Paul is saying to us is that there is no way anyone can receive forgiveness of past sins by obeying the Law. Present obedience does not do anything to wash away past sins. Of course there must be some other manner for sinners to receive forgiveness of past sins, if they are to have hope of entering God's kingdom. Salvation cannot be obtained by simply repenting and deciding to obey God's law. Merely keeping the Law will not justify anyone. Being justified, my dear brothers and sisters, means having our sins forgiven and coming into a right relationship with God.

Christ has been born today, and we are ready to receive our salvation through his sacrifice. But what does this mean to us? We are justified through faith in Christ's sacrifice. He is the payment for all our sins, thus freeing us from sin's penalty, and at the same time, God imputes Christ's righteousness to us. The righteousness that enabled him to be a perfect sacrifice is accounted as if it is ours. This enables us to have access into the presence of our Holy God. However it is important to mention that, this does not do away with the Law; it establishes and puts it in its rightful place our understanding of what God is accomplishing in our lives.

Brothers and sisters in the Lord, if Christ has paid the penalty for our sins, then we ought to put all our faith in him. Saint Paul says the work of law begins with the action of man, yet faith begins with God's action. He adds that every work of faith is the action of both God and man. Both faith and action find their source and fulfillment in Christ, and we experience them through our union in Christ, brought about in baptism. It is the Holy Spirit who gives us power for our ongoing life of righteousness in Christ, the life of blessings. When we walk in righteousness, we express our son-ship. Through union with Jesus Christ, we automatically become children of God. The source of our son-ship is God the Father and not humanity; from a divine promise, not human deeds; from faith and not from works. It is God who gave the Law to protect first the Israelites and then all humanity, until all humanity could receive the divine son-ship, when our union with the Son of God became possible. The purpose of our son-ship, my dear brothers and sisters, is for us to become like God and enter into his kingdom.

My beloved spiritual children in Christ let us rejoice in the Lord, for our Savior has been born, and we have been adopted into divine son-ship. Let us sing songs of praise, for we are no longer under the demands of the Old Testament Law, for Christ has fulfilled the Law. Let us be thankful to God, for through his never-ending mercy, we are brought into a new covenant relationship with him. How loving is our God that we believers are granted entrance into his kingdom by grace. Through his mercy we are justified. We are justified by faith and empowered by God for good works and deeds of righteousness that bring glory to him. Amen.

+ ARCHBISHOP MAKARIOS

HOMILY
on the Sunday of Orthodoxy

March 13, 2011

In the Name of the Father, and of the Son, and of the Holy Spirit.

MY DEAR CHILDREN in Christ, do you marvel at the beauty of our Church and the rich teachings that surround it from the tradition passed on to us from the apostles of Christ? Brethren, it is fascinating and very exciting to be in such a building surrounded by beautiful icons that depict so many saints, some of whom we recognize by a single stare, and others we may not know. The icons, which you will find at every Orthodox Church in the world, are of significant historical value to us gathered here. Every Orthodox Church member venerates these precious holy icons.

It is important to note that everything in the Orthodox Church has a purpose and a meaning in God's revelation to man. In the year AD 843, the iconoclast controversy, which had raged on and off since the year AD 726, was finally laid to rest, and icons and their veneration were restored on the first Sunday of Great Lent. Ever since, this Sunday has been commemorated as the "Triumph of Orthodoxy." That is why we are gathered here to pay tribute on this great day.

Brothers and sisters in Christ, we are proud of our icons, because the Seventh Ecumenical Council dealt predominantly with the controversy regarding icons and their place in Orthodox worship. The council passed a doctrine stating that icons should be venerated but not worshiped. The decree added an important clause that stands to this very day:

> We, therefore, following the royal pathway and the divinely inspired authority of our Holy Fathers and the traditions of the Catholic Church (for, as we all know, the Holy Spirit indwells her), define with all certitude and accuracy that just as the figure of the precious and life-giving Cross, so also the venerable and holy images, as well in painting and mosaic as of other fit materials, should be set forth in the holy churches of God.... For the honor which is paid to the image passes on to that which the image represents, and he who reveres the image reveres in it the subject represented. For thus the teaching of our holy fathers, that is the tradition of the Catholic Church, which from one end of the earth to the other hath received the Gospel, is strengthened.[16]

Our Church's teaching about icons, evidenced at the Seventh Ecumenical Council, is shown in the following extract we sung today in our liturgy:

> The prophets, inspired by Thy Spirit, O Lord, foretold that Thou, whom nothing can contain or grasp, and who has shone forth in eternity before the morning star from the immaterial and bodiless womb of the Father, was to become a child, taking flesh from the Virgin, being joined by men and seen by those on earth. At the prayers of these Thy prophets, in Thy compassion count us worthy of Thy light, for we sing the praises of Thine ineffable and Holy Resurrection.[17]

My dear brethren, today is an historical day because it reflects the great significance that icons possess for us Orthodox Christians. They are not optional devotional extras, but an important part of our Orthodox faith and worship. They are held to be a necessary element of our Christian faith in the incarnation of the Word of God, the second person of the trinity, in Jesus Christ. They have a sacramental character, making present to us the person or event depicted in them. This is the main reason that the interiors

16 "The Decree of the Holy, Great, Ecumenical Synod, the Second of Nice," in *The Nicene and Post Nicene Fathers*, vol. XIV, eds. Philip Schaff and Henry Wace (Christian Literature Publishing, 1890), 550.

17 First Stichera at Great Vespers of the Sunday of Orthodoxy, *The Lenten Triodion*. (South Canaan, PA: St. Tikhon's Monastery Press, 1978), 299.

of Orthodox churches are often covered with icons painted on walls and domed roofs, and there is always an icon screen—or *iconostasis*—separating the sanctuary from the nave, often with several rows of icons.

My encouragement to you today is a reminder that no Orthodox home is complete without an icon corner, where you ought to conduct the family prayers. We normally venerate icons by burning lamps and candles in front of them, by the use of incense and by kissing them. However, there is a clear doctrinal distinction between the veneration paid to icons and the worship due to God. In the former, love and respect is paid to the person represented in the icon. This distinction safeguards the veneration of icons from any charge of idolatry.

According to Saint John of Damascus, anyone who tries to destroy icons, "is the enemy of Christ, the Holy Mother of God and the saints, and is the defender of the Devil and his demons."[18] This is because the theology behind icons is closely tied to the theology of the Incarnation of Jesus, so that attacks on icons typically have the effect of undermining or attacking the Incarnation of Jesus himself, as elucidated in the Ecumenical Councils. Saint John proves to us that the use of holy icons in our Church is permissible. He further explains the use of the terms "worship" of God and "veneration" of holy icons. He concludes that veneration of the holy icons is an act of respect toward the prototype depicted on matter, while on the other hand, worship belongs to God alone. He finalizes by saying, "I do not worship the matter; I worship the Creator of the matter who became for me matter and in matter dwelt and through matter worked my salvation."[19]

The Orthodox teaching regarding veneration of icons is that the praise and veneration shown to the icon passes over to the archetype. Thus, to kiss an icon of Christ, in the Orthodox Church's view, is to show love toward Christ.

Jesus himself—not mere wood and paint—make up the physical substance of the icon. The Seventh Ecumenical Council expressly forbids worship of the icon as somehow entirely separate from its prototype. This is standard teaching in our Church. Saint Basil argues that, "I honor and kiss the features of their images, inasmuch as they have been handed down from the holy apostles, and are not forbidden, but are in all our churches."[20]

18 *St John Damascene on Holy Images,* trans. Mary Allies (London: Thomas Baker) 67.

19 *St John Damascene on Holy Images,* 16.

20 St. Basil, Letter 360 in *The Nicene and Post Nicene Fathers,* vol. VIII, Second Series, 326.

Many of the church fathers observe that the prohibitions in the Old Testament are not absolute. They concede that the Ten Commandments clearly prohibit the use of idols, but note that the same Lord and God instructed Moses to make a serpent. "And it came to pass, that every one that is bitten, when he looketh upon it, shall live."[21] Another important lesson we get from the Bible, which proves that icons should be venerated in our churches, is from the King and Prophet Solomon, when he made the sea and the basin, and the twelve oxen under the sea. Between the projections were lions and oxen and cherubs. These images of cherubs were not to be worshiped, but were used mainly to remind the children of Israel, that place was holy and that they should be holy, too.

Brothers and sisters in Christ, we should be proud of having all these beautiful icons around us and respect them, as they are rightly important for us in our daily worship. Apart from assisting us in worship, some very beautiful and important lessons emerge from them daily. The benefits we receive from them are quite immense. The saints are represented with wonderful skills and colors and when we look at them, they stimulate in us the desire to imitate them. They are to us vessels and channels of divine grace. Let us therefore, brethren, adorn our churches, homes, and work places with the holy icons, so that we can always be full of divine thoughts. At the sight of them, we are reminded to be close to God and worship him always and forever. Amen.

21 Num. 21:8.

HOMILY
for Holy Friday

Saints Anargyroi[22] Cathedral,
Nairobi, Kenya,
April 22, 2011

In the Name of the Father, and of the Son, and of the Holy Spirit.

BRETHREN IN CHRIST, before Jesus our Lord and Savior came into this world, the law prevented man from committing moral sins, and his conscience was always awakened to the feeling of guilt and the need for a savior or a redeemer. During this time, man performed ritual purification and sacrifices to gain redemption from his creator. This was done on appointed days, when all people gathered together to beg for divine mercy.

Then came a period of judges, who gave people a hope of the coming of the messiah. They longed for a king more like David, and this was supported by the promise given to King David through the Prophet Nathan. Most Prophets prophesied the coming of the messiah and the Day of Salvation. They described him as being like a shepherd guarding all nations and becoming the light of the nations as well as salvation of Israel. They added that the messiah would offer his life to redeem all mankind; through his wounds, we would all be healed, and through his passion and death the

22 Saints Anargyroi: from the Greek Άγιοι Ανάργυροι, refers to the holy unmercenaries Sts. Cosmos & Damian.

nations would return to God. All this was summed up by Paul's proclamation when he said:

> But before faith came, we were kept under the law, shut up unto the faith which should afterwards be revealed. Wherefore the law was our schoolmaster to bring us unto Christ, that we might be justified by faith. But after that faith is come, we are no longer under a schoolmaster.[23]

Brothers and sisters in Christ, before all time, God had prepared our reconciliation through the sacrifice of Christ, whom he would offer on the Cross, as a high priest. It was up to God, who had been insulted by man's fall, to determine how divine justice and holiness would be satisfied and thereby fallen man would be reconciled with the infinite Lord under the guilt of his conscience. Unable to set himself free, sinful man made God's grace essential for obtaining the knowledge of, and means for, reconciliation with God. This reconciliation is achieved and secured only through Jesus Christ our Lord and Savior. Our Savior had to be put on the Cross in order to save mankind. He fulfilled the priesthood on the Cross by presenting himself to God the Father for the salvation of the human race. As the holy apostles said, "[Christ] gave himself as a ransom for all,"[24] and "Christ also hath loved us, and hath given himself for us an offering and a sacrifice to God for a sweet smelling savor."[25]

Today, my dear brethren, God is demonstrating his own love toward us, in that when we were still sinners, Christ died for us. On the Cross, our Lord completed the mediation between God and man as stated by the same apostle who wrote, "that he might reconcile them both unto God in one body by the Cross, having slain the enmity thereby."[26]

The atonement of sin was required for us because sin had entered the world. This atonement could only be achieved through the sacrifice. Consequently, it was necessary that an ultimate sacrifice be offered for sin: the Lamb who carried the sin of the entire world, as witnessed by Saint John the Baptist, who exclaimed, "Behold the Lamb of God, which taketh away the sin of the world."[27] This is the reason we are gathered here today, brothers and sisters; to witness this great sacrifice of Christ, who accepted being

23 Gal. 3:23–25.
24 1 Tim. 2:6
25 Eph. 5:2.
26 Eph. 2:16.
27 Jn. 1:29.

put on the Cross for the sake of our sins. This sacrifice is one of the greatest to be witnessed in all of our human lives. His great love for us cannot be compared to any other love. If Christ passed through all these sufferings on the Cross, then what have we done for him to show our appreciation? What have we done to show him that his crucifixion is important for our salvation? These are among the questions we ought to ask ourselves today.

Brethren, through Christ's sacrifice on the Cross, he convinced and informed us humans that we have peace with God. And that this exchange that was offered by our Lord and Savior Jesus Christ, no other man could make because he gave it in exchange for his soul. For this reason, we ought to follow his goodness as a way of proving to him that we value his crucifixion. Saint Ignatius of Antioch urges us all to, "Be thou more diligent than thou art. Mark the seasons. Await Him that is above every season, the Eternal, the Invisible, who became visible for our sake, the Impalpable, the Impassible, who suffered for our sake, who endured in all ways for our sake."[28]

"[Christ] his own self bare our sins in his own body on the tree, that we, being dead to sins, should live unto righteousness: by whose stripes ye were healed."[29] From this verse, we see that Christ took the sins we committed onto himself to pay the price for *us.* Not only does this verse teach us about the substitute that Christ was for us, but it also teaches us that he was the atonement; meaning he satisfied the payment due for our sinfulness.[30] We can only pay the price of sins on our own by being punished and placed in hell for eternity. But God's son Jesus Christ came to earth to pay the price for our sins. Because he did this for us, we now have the opportunity to not only have our sins forgiven, but to spend eternity with him. In order to do this, we must place our faith in what Christ did on the Cross. We cannot save ourselves; we need a substitution to take place. The death of Christ is our substitute, our atonement. Jesus said, "The Son of man must suffer many things, and be rejected of the elders and chief priests and scribes, and be slain, and be raised the third day. And he said to them all, 'If any man

28 "Letter of Ignatius to Polycarp," *The Apostolic Father,* eds. J.B. Lightfoot and J.R. Harmer (New York: Macmillan & Co., 1890), 3.

29 1 Peter 2:24.

30 Note: Christ's substitutionary atonement is but one aspect of the Orthodox Church's vision of the economy of salvation. The 11th century archbishop, Anselm of Canterbury, constructed a view of salvation that isolated the atonement to the exclusion of all else. This one-dimensional approach was later adopted by many of the Protestant reformers. Archbishop Makarios exhibits a broader vision, noting elsewhere the importance of the Incarnation and the believer's participation in the life of God (see pages 14, 22, 34, etc.).

will come after me, let him deny himself, and take up his cross daily, and follow me.'"[31]

Dearly beloved, Christ assumed his sufferings and resurrection and our relationship with them. He assumed our suffering, our pain, and our death out of love for us, to abolish death and make all things new. By death he overcame the power of sin and by obedience overcame sin itself. He suffered and died to show us how to endure suffering and to give meaning to our own suffering and death. He accepted the Cross so that we might be able to bear our cross. He fulfilled the Law and was obedient to his Father to the point of death, showing what obedience is all about. Today Christ reveals to us that God is our loving Father, who suffers all things for the sake of our salvation.

If Christ portrayed all these for our sake, then we ought to always follow his precepts. What he actually requires from us is to deny ourselves, take up our crosses daily, and follow him. This might not be an easy task because it entails keeping a constant closeness with God by doing what is right in his eyes. Christ was not put on the Cross to abolish suffering in this world. He accepted suffering so that he might accompany us in our daily suffering, being like us in everything but sin. He takes on suffering so that he might show us how to hope in the midst of suffering; that it might not lead to despair. Despair—the loss of hope—is in essence the fear of death, and thus, the root of sin. So, brethren, it is good to take up our crosses with courage and follow Christ, because in him there is hope; there is victory and peace in knowing that if we follow him, we shall conquer death and be with him in everlasting life. May God bless you all.

31 Luke 9:22–23.

PASCHAL ENCYCLICAL

April 24, 2011

Christ is risen!

> Blessed be the God and Father of our Lord Jesus Christ, which according to his abundant mercy hath begotten us again unto a lively hope by the resurrection of Jesus Christ from the dead.[32]

BELOVED OF CHRIST, he is risen indeed! It is another wonderful moment that we experience our spiritual life and rejoice in our salvation with Christ's resurrection. This is a time when our hope in Christ as our only Savior—one who was laid to death by being put on the Cross—is increased. Jesus Christ, the Son of God, who conquered death, so that all of us can be saved from the curse of sin. We are all freed from this curse and therefore we ought not dwell in sin anymore. Today, dear brethren, is a new dawn for the history of mankind, because not only death has been defeated, but also all our inclinations toward sin have been destroyed. We are no longer bound by the curse of sin. Our Savior Jesus Christ became sin for us and bore our sins in his body on the Cross; thus fulfilling the Law as portrayed by the Epistle of Paul to the Corinthians when he says, "For he hath made him to be sin for us, who knew no sin; that we might be made the righteousness of God in him."[33]

32 1 Peter 1:3.
33 2 Cor. 5:21.

Brothers and sisters in Christ, we may ask ourselves, "How was Christ made sin for us?" He, the incarnate Son of God, voluntarily assumed the consequences of our sins—corruption and death—without sinning himself. And he was submitted to unjust suffering because of the sinful passions of men and of angels. The meaning of these words for us today, as Orthodox Christians, is that our salvation is far more than the forgiveness of sin. It is actually a new life: our reconciliation to God, our becoming new creatures and participants in the very righteousness of God. Our salvation, brethren, is not just like a static legal pronouncement of a judge, but rather personal and relational—the dynamic, sacrificial love of a Father for his child: "Who his own self bare our sins in his own body on the tree, that we, being dead to sins, should live unto righteousness: by whose stripes ye were healed."[34]

The apostle Peter's advice is that Christ is our example of service and our response to mistreatment. Christ, as our Great Servant, is shown to be a suffering one, offering himself on our behalf, "by whose stripes ye were healed."[35] It is important to note, however, that no washing away of sins was necessary for Christ, who did not sin. It was done for those who do sin. Therefore, brethren, we should then live for him, who did not spare his own son, that in his body, he might crucify our passions. For Christ died for us, that we might live in the renewed body of the Church. By being hanged on a tree, Christ has saved us from the curse of sin, as the apostle Paul emphasizes by his writing to the Galatians, when he says, "Christ hath redeemed us from the curse of the law, being made a curse for us: for it is written, 'Cursed is every one that hangeth on a tree.'"[36]

My spiritual children in Christ, what a perfect and a wonderful love this is: Our Lord and Savior Jesus Christ accepting to be a curse in order to redeem us from the curse of the Law. He perfectly obeyed the Law and accepted its curse. Brothers and sisters in Christ, today we are happy because we are blessed through his suffering. We have been renewed in Christ, and at the same time, redeemed from the curse. Today, we participate in his perfect faith and obedience. This, brethren, is the meaning of our Pascha celebration today—our redemption through Christ's death and resurrection. Let us therefore rejoice; let us be happy because our redemption and Christ's victory calls for it. Let us express our joy by loving each other. Let

34 1 Peter 2:24.

35 1 Peter 2:24; Is. 53:5.

36 Gal. 3:13.

not selfishness be seen amongst ourselves, because this goes contrary to the ways of our savior. "And walk in love, just as Christ also hath loved us, and hath given himself for us an offering and a sacrifice to God for a sweet smelling savor."[37]

Since Christ gave himself for us as a sacrifice, then we ought to walk according to his teachings and follow all his precepts. This is what Saint Paul calls a "walk worthy of calling."[38] He defines this walk as a walk in love, a walk in light, a walk in wisdom. We should strive to walk a slow, steady pace. It's a daily effort, a marathon, not a sprint. Brethren, there should be in us a sharp contrast between the way of darkness and the way of light. Animosity and shouted words should be avoided. We should always judge what the world says is reasonable on the basis of what God says is true. The Resurrection of Christ is bringing a new meaning in our lives today. It ushers us into a life of new hope and energy to continue our missionary work here on earth. This same encouragement is what was spoken to the Church of Corinth, when she was battling doubts concerning the very central Christian doctrine of the bodily resurrection of Jesus Christ on the third day after his death. Paul wrote, "And if Christ be not risen, then is our preaching vain, and your faith is also vain."[39]

My dear Spiritual children in Christ, these words of Saint Paul make us raise some important questions: "What is Christianity without the Resurrection—both Christ's and ours?" His death would do us no good without his resurrection. "What would be the need of forgiveness if we remain dead?" These are the most important questions we ought to deeply ponder about this Pascha. It is evident that Christ's disciples were transformed by his resurrection, and they preached about it above all. We must emulate them and preach to our fellow men how his resurrection has transformed us into new beings. This is the same reason why we sing today, in all Orthodox churches around the world, that "Christ is risen from the dead, trampling death by death, and upon those in the tombs bestowing life!"

"That I may know him, and the power of his resurrection, and the fellowship of his sufferings, being made conformable unto his death; If by any means I might attain unto the resurrection of the dead."[40] These words are not from my mouth, but from the apostle Paul to the Church of Philippi.

37 Eph. 5:2.
38 I Thess. 4:1.
39 1 Cor. 15:14.
40 Phil. 3:10–11.

He reckons that true righteousness is the knowledge of Jesus Christ, *the pearl of great price,* and eternal life. A faith that obeys Christ is the very content and meaning of life. Faith is the relationship that gives us full participation in the life of Christ and in his resurrection. Faith includes our consent to the articles of belief in the Church, but it is also our openness to God's action in our lives.

Brothers and sisters in Christ, the meaning of our sufferings comes in sharing in Christ's suffering and death, becoming like him so that we can be with him in glory. Brethren, we must be engaged in the struggle of faith and have the zeal to press on toward the completion of our salvation, the prize of the upward call of God, the resurrection to eternal life. Let Christ's resurrection bring a new meaning to your lives today and forever. Amen!

Christ is risen!

+ ARCHBISHOP MAKARIOS

CHRISTMAS ENCYCLICAL

December 25, 2011

Beloved Clergy, Brothers and Sisters in Christ: Christ is born! Glorify him! *Kristo amezaliwa*! *Tumtukuze*!

> It was the good pleasure of the Father: the Word became flesh, and the Virgin bore God made man. A star spreads abroad the tidings: the Magi worship, the shepherds stand amazed, and the creation is filled with mighty joy.[41]

Beloved Spiritual Children and Co-Workers in the vineyard of the Lord,

When we remember Christmas, let us visualize the happenings of this glorious day two thousand years ago, when our Lord Jesus Christ deigned to be born from the Most Holy Theotokos and ever Virgin Mary in Bethlehem of Judea, all of creation gathered to offer him honor and worship. The earth offered a cave; the heavens, a star; the beasts, a manger; and the angels, a doxology. Following the star, the Magi came from the east to see him who is the Son of Righteousness, Christ our God. They worshiped him and offered him their precious gifts of gold, frankincense, and myrrh. The shepherds left their daily duties to come, witness, and reverence the King of Glory. These were gifts of different groups

41 Second stichera at Lauds, Matins of the Holy Nativity of Christ, *The Festal Menaion* (South Sanaan, PA: STM Press, 1998) 284.

and persons. What about us, my beloved spiritual children? What can we offer to our Lord, King and Savior, Jesus Christ?

This year has been quite a challenging one for our country and the globe at large. I can bear witness that many of the same challenges have tremendously affected us in different ways, mostly negatively. The difficult financial situation has left many jobless, with no ability to continue educating their children, or even sometimes to put food on their table, amongst other terrible situations. The war on the Al-Shabab has also had its own effects on various communities and persons of our society.[42] There are serious climatic changes that we are gradually experiencing, and which are causing various environmental challenges. We in the Third World cannot even cope with this. While we acknowledge the existence of all these challenges, among many others, that we are going through personally or as communities, they should not stop us from offering something to our Lord during this Nativity season.

"How excellent is thy loving-kindness, O God! Therefore the children of men put their trust under the shadow of thy wings."[43] It is upon us to wholeheartedly trust in our God, keeping in mind that "the knowledge of the holy is understanding,"[44] the holy here being we who have received him as Lord and Savior. God is capable of taking away all our tribulations and those of the times in which we live. Ours is only to trust in him.

It was not an easy task for the Lord to come into the world as a man and even die for us. It was out of his utmost love for mankind that he was born, and through his birth the world is reborn, nature is refashioned, and the division between man and God is abolished. The incarnation of the Word of God is the perfect expression of divine love and charity for the entire universe. This love of God is what we confess in the festivities of today, even amidst worldly troubles.

As Orthodox Christians, we must bear in mind the reasons behind Christ's coming into the world. Like Saint John, "I write to you, little children, because your sins are forgiven you for his Name's sake."[45] This is the reason for Christ coming into the world, to save us from sin and damnation. The removal of our sins paves way for our holiness. On this great feast of our Lord, we need to affirm our calling to be witnesses of holiness,

42 Al-Shabab became an Al-Qaeda affiliate in 2012 and has conducted terrorists attacks in Somalia and neighboring Kenya.

43 Ps. 36:7.

44 Prov. 9:10.

45 1 Jn. 2:12.

indeed to be bearers of his holiness. God created us to be holy as he is holy. He calls us to live holy lives, and the life of holiness has always been a part of his divine plan for our salvation. Let us therefore be mindful of how we live and act.

Unfortunately, the people of today run after and overwhelm themselves with worldly things. We should get rid of this behavior and concentrate on our spiritual lives. Yes, it is not easy to live in these times, but again just as Christ warns us, if we are to follow him, we must each one of us carry our cross, something that is not easy at all. Let us therefore be mindful of these things and bring to our incarnate God a pure heart instead of gold, flaming prayer instead of frankincense, and works of love and mercy instead of myrrh.

The one gift we can offer our Lord this Christmas is love. Love him by doing and living in accordance with his commandments. We love his Church by attending to our spiritual lives and receiving all necessary sacraments as much as we can, and by loving and praying for our neighbors—those who love us and those who hate us—as we love and pray for ourselves. And we love the Church by being there for all those who need us and also by implementing what we can manage spiritually, physically, and also by implementing what Saint James says of material help: that we should also give those things "which are needful to the body."[46]

My beloved clergy, brothers, and sisters in Christ, it is our responsibility to transform our country, our communities, and our families with this same love with which God loved us, a love that caused the Father to send his Only-begotten Son into the world to save us from our sins. Just like Christ transformed the world two thousand years ago by his incarnation, crucifixion, death, resurrection, ascension, and enthronement at the right hand of the Father; just like he transformed us during our baptism; just like he transforms us every time we confess our sins and receive the Holy Eucharist, he will continuously transform our world, country, and society, and will use us to do so if we make ourselves available to him in love. With this love, I humbly adjure and challenge all of you, my beloved children, to give of yourselves—even in the slightest way—for the transformation of others this Christmas.

In his service,
+ ARCHBISHOP MAKARIOS

46 James 2:16.

HOMILY
for the Sunday of the Cross

Saints Constantine & Helen Orthodox Church,
Kereri-Nandi,
March 18, 2012

TODAY, we venerate the Cross of Jesus Christ, the Cross that gave us power, life, and protection. Our Lord was crucified on that Cross for our salvation. He was humiliated, and he accepted this treatment even though he was the Son of God, for the sake of the salvation of all human races. We are like martyrs today, testifying the importance of that Cross because of the constant temptations bedeviling our lives daily.

Although this place is in a very remote part of Kenya, and we had challenges reaching it, and we thought of our journey as a difficult one for the sake of our faith, nevertheless, as true soldiers of the Lord Jesus, we were able to manage.

Brothers and sisters in Christ, Orthodoxy was planted in this area almost fifty years ago. The people here saw the true light, and through it they experienced salvation through the sacraments that sanctify us and make us full members of the One Holy Catholic and Apostolic Church. For your part, do not count yourselves isolated, but always remember that in our Orthodox faith our Church is universal. We embrace all people regardless of their tribe, race, color, or culture.

As we rejoice in the beauty of the Cross today, we should remember that we exist as a Church because of Jesus Christ. There is no time that we have ever been separated from his love and it is through the Holy Trinity that we are able to evangelize and to continue that wonderful mission of hope and resurrection to all our people.

Last Monday, I was invited to Mombasa to attend the funeral service of one of our Greek brothers, although I never knew him personally. The man had decided to marry one of our African sisters who was actually a Muslim. When I arrived to perform the service, the church was actually filled with men and women who were Muslim. It was my first time conducting a service consisting of a completely different congregation who adhered to a completely different faith. They were wondering who I was, and I decided to take the opportunity to give them a message of salvation and resurrection, the message of the life to come. I told them that they should actually rejoice in death for there is no death for Orthodox believers, but just rest awaiting them in the life to come. We actually believe that we are all created in God's image and likeness and that Muslims and Christians are not enemies, for each and every human being is a creation of God; thus, we should honor, love, and respect everyone. It is no one's business to judge the other, for the Mighty Judge will judge us all.

The message of Orthodoxy is all about forgiveness and the acceptance of each and every human being. This is a mystery of the Orthodox Faith, nowhere to be found but in the sacraments. What else do we need? With Jesus Christ, the Author of Baptism and Chrismation, we have received the gifts of the Holy Spirit, and have thereby become alive spiritually.

This is a day that I will remember, and I hope you will remember it, too. Let us continue praying for each other and remember that God is among us all, and if we love and respect each other, we will be able to experience Christ in our midst. May God bless you all.

PASCHAL ENCYCLICAL

April 15th, 2012

Beloved Clergy, Brothers and Sisters in Christ: Christ is risen! Truly he is risen! *Kristo amefufuka! Kweli, amefufuka!*

> That through death he might destroy him who had the power of death, that is, the devil; And deliver them who through fear of death were all their lifetime subject to bondage. For verily he took not on him the nature of angels; but he took on him the seed of Abraham.[47]

Christ's resurrection has given us two principal gifts, which I will share with you on this glorious day of the Resurrection in the year 2012. The first is the forgiveness of sin and a chance to reconcile and unite us with God, and the second is the freedom from the bondage of death.

But why is the physical resurrection so important to us when Christianity seems to dwell on the spiritual part of man? Man is made of two interdependent parts: body and soul. Separating the two means that man is no more. When Christ resurrected, he did so in both soul and body. That is why the two apostles who went to the tomb after his resurrection found just his clothes.[48] God originally created a physical and spiritual man, and put him in a physical world. For the fallen man to be saved, both components of man had to be saved. Christ's resurrection completes not only the

47 Heb. 2:14–15.

48 Jn. 20:6, 7.

salvation of man, but also the physical world in which man lives.

The triumph of life over death is realized in the only feast of the resurrection, the Feast of Pascha. By resurrection here, we should not only think of that of our Lord Jesus Christ, but ours also. The fact that we have a resurrection reminds us of one unavoidable and electrifying event: death. The Bible reminds us that we shall all die: "And as it is appointed unto men once to die, but after this the judgment."[49] But we need not fear death. It may come as a surprise to some, but as Orthodox Christians our fear of death has been overcome by the hope of the resurrection.

Humanity has tried in so many ways to overcome the slavery of sin and death, but it has not been able. Then, one like us, the incarnate Son of God, has opened and given us a way through his death and glorious resurrection to be set free from our own fear of death.

The triumphant Church meets once a year, on a day like today, to celebrate this indescribable joy of the resurrection. The assurance of being delivered from death and living forever that is given by the Church's message of the resurrection is what has kept the human race going.

As a Church, we should take the advantage of the Resurrection of our Lord. We can achieve this both with the help and power of the resurrected Christ, and through our faith in him. This resurrected Christ "is the new Adam who grows old no longer, but is the source from which the world is continually renewed."[50] If anyone wants to be part of this renewed life—also known as eternal life—that Christ gives, he needs to avoid the evil one. The devil rules in our lives through disuniting humanity from God and from each other. This he does by creating confusion amongst us, and in the midst of that we lose God and our fellow brethren. That is why enmity and hatred, amongst other vices of disunity, tend to pilot the lives of many in the world today. Losing God and the other means we are in isolation and therefore have become easy targets of the chief thief, the devil. Let us not forget this: "The thief cometh not, but for to steal, and to kill, and to destroy."[51] In that case, "Let us commend ourselves and one another and our whole life to Christ our God."[52]

The salvation that we have received is only possible in unity with the others, not in isolation. All Christians must strive to be in harmony, love,

49 Heb. 9:27.

50 Attributed to St. Gregory Palamas.

51 Jn. 10:10.

52 The Divine Liturgy of Saint John Chrysostom, *The Hieratikon*, vol II (South Canaan, PA: St. Tikhon's Monastery Press, 2017) 92.

and unity with each other, which builds into full communion—*koinonia*—with Christ. To be saved is to be pulled out of isolation, and in that case, to be united with the Creator and all of his creation. We must be rid of the world, her pleasures, her way of life, and her passions, because we are not of this world. "Love not the world, neither the things that are in the world. If any man love the world, the love of the Father is not in him. For all that is in the world … is not of the Father, but is of the world. And the world passeth away."[53] The world and her isolation will only lead us to separation from God and the others, a sure ticket to eternal damnation.

That is why I urge you to live a life of harmony, love, union, and of continuous forgiveness. This can only be achieved if we see the resurrected Christ in the other person. This is because Christ has put his face in the other in his endeavor to save all humanity. That means that, whatever we do to the least of humanity, we do it to Christ.[54] If we see the other as God, then we will always see our unworthiness and the need to repent before him, if not continuously, and thus seek union with the other and God. Being one with the other is in Orthodox spirituality being one with God. Thus the famous ascetic saying, "Have you seen your brother? Then you have seen God." Let us all work hard to be united with the resurrected Christ through union with each other, and our chance to inherit the eternal life he gives will become a reality to us. By doing this, we shall have "passed from death into life."[55]

"I have written unto you, young men, because ye are strong, and the word of God abideth in you, and ye have overcome the wicked one"[56] through accepting the message of the resurrected Christ. By proclaiming "Christ is risen!" and responding, "Truly, he is risen!" we affirm that Jesus Christ has destroyed the power of sin, and that of the death that has held humanity—that is, us—captive. Therefore, those who have received Christ as their Lord, God and Savior, have no need to fear death anymore, because they have been delivered from it and are now free. Let these words of joy brought by the resurrection of Christ abide in your hearts always, as we await "the resurrection of the dead and the life of the world to come" of which we shall all be a part.

With paternal blessings and much love,
+ ARCHBISHOP MAKARIOS

53 1 Jn. 2:15–17.

54 See Matt. 25:40.

55 Jn. 5:24.

56 1 Jn. 1:14.

PASCHAL ENCYCLICAL

May 5, 2013

Reverend Fathers, Brothers, and Sisters in Christ: *Kristos anesti!* Christ is risen! *Kristo amefufuka!*

"Rejoice in the Lord always: and again I say, rejoice."[57]

IT IS INCORRECT for Christians to rejoice only when things are going well for them and then when things go badly, to change drastically their faith and their view on God and the Church. Instead of praying, hoping for the best, and waiting for God's will to be done, some Christians opt to complain, give up, lose heart, and even reduce their energy in the journey of faith, if not even change their faith. In most cases we care much more about the material side of our lives than the spiritual part. That is why when our material lives are affected, many of us forget what part our spiritual lives play. When our lives are shaken, either financially, physically, mentally, or even spiritually, let us remember to expect fierce temptations from the devil. The evil one snatches many believers away from the Kingdom of God, ruining their spiritual endeavors. During difficulties and tragedies, we should stand most strongly and pray persistently to avoid being swept off by the devil, keeping in mind that it is at our weakest points that God makes us the strongest.[58]

Today, as we celebrate the feast of the resurrection, let us remember that God will never abandon us, just like he never abandoned sinful humanity

57 Phil. 4:4.

58 See 2 Cor. 12:10.

that disobeyed him. In his great mercy, God gave his Only-begotten Son to come and save the sinful world: Christ was born, grew, and ministered in a world sick with sin. Even though it is clear that sin and evil are opposed to the holiness in which God lives, this did not stop him from offering humanity much-needed salvation and reconciliation.

While in the midst of problems, let us remember that our God will never abandon us, no matter the magnitude of the problems we are facing. "Weeping may endure for a night, but joy cometh in the morning."[59] There is nothing without an end, and in most cases, where God is the spearhead of our lives, we have joy, success, and rewards coming at the end of it all. After the Passion and Crucifixion came the Resurrection; so with us, after a dry season comes the rain; after a stressful life comes a time to relax; after a stressful youth comes an old age full of wisdom. Even though we sometimes live in very distressing situations, and with extreme struggles, we should not give up on perseverance while waiting for God's hour, because once it comes, all our hurts will be gone, our tears wiped, our wounds cleaned, our hopes revived, and our pains and struggles replaced with joy.

> By Thy Cross, Thou didst destroy death! To the thief, Thou didst open Paradise! For the myrrh bearers, Thou didst change weeping into joy! And Thou didst command Thy disciples, O Christ God, to proclaim that Thou art risen, granting the world great mercy![60]

When Christ died, his apostles and disciples were wondering who would lead them henceforth. Some even decided to go back to their earlier lives. They were low in spirit, and did not foresee any chance for their comeback. What they did not know was that they would be gloomy for just a brief period of time, all of which ended with the third day Resurrection of Christ. The apostles and disciples were hiding and locking themselves inside with a lot of fear during this distressing period, but after their knowledge of the resurrection, and their reception of the Holy Spirit fifty days later, they even had the courage to stand before big crowds and proclaim the resurrected Christ, as did the apostle Peter in Acts, chapter two.

When we see much trouble in our lives, when in the midst of terrifying temptations, when in much pain, when not even able to discern where our next meal will come from, when not able to help our suffering brethren,

59 Ps. 30:5.

60 Resurrectional Troparia, Tone 7, *Common Book of Church Hymns: Great Vespers* (South Canaan, PA: STM Press, 2020) 216.

when we have no school fees to offer our children, when we can't even pay the hospital bills of our loved ones, when without a job, and with many other tribulations that we have no human ability to fix, let us keep our eyes fixed on the resurrected Christ. Just like Christ saved man from eternal damnation through being crucified on the cursed Cross, dying, and resurrecting on the third day; just like he gave life to those who had departed this life and were already in Hades; just like he resurrected the life of the only son of the widow of Nain; just like he healed the many sick who came to him after having tried all human cures to no avail; just like he delivered the three young men from the fire of the furnace, so should we expect the unexpected out of any complicated situation in which we find ourselves.

Even in the midst of our present financial crisis, I urge you to not waver but instead be faithful to our callings in Christ. When looking with the limited human eye and mind, our problems sometimes look impossible, "but with God all things are possible."[61] Our hope, our power, and more importantly, our faith should always be in the resurrected Christ, who will always deliver us from our tribulations.

> O Lord of hosts, be with us, for beside Thee, we have no other helper in adversity, O Lord of hosts, have mercy on us.[62]

With paternal love,
+ARCHBISHOP MAKARIOS

61 Matt. 19:26.

62 "O Lord of Hosts," Great Compline, *The Horologion*, 2nd ed. (Jordanville, NY: Holy Trinity Publications, 1997), 227.

PASCHAL ENCYCLICAL

April 20, 2014

My dear Children in Christ, Clergy and Laity, Orthodox Archbishopric of Kenya, Christ is risen! *Kristo amefufuka! Kristos anesti!*

Brothers and sisters in Christ, today is a great day that we celebrate yet another Holy Pascha. First and foremost, we give thanks to our Almighty God for enabling us to cross the fasting period successfully and reach our highest peak, which is the celebration of Pascha.

The Bible says that we are to love one another. As we celebrate the Holy Resurrection, let us remember our brothers and sisters from all religions and denominations who need our attention. This phrase sounds good, but can we do it? I have heard people, many times, say: "People are just irritating." Even people at church can be difficult to love. Sometimes during the Divine Liturgy we exchange a kiss of love, but we need to ask ourselves, "Is it really a kiss of love?" While other churches sing, "I'm so glad you're a part of the family of God," we look at the person beside us and sing, "I'm surprised you're part of the family of God." Why are we surprised? Simply because we lack love in our hearts. And this is why God asked Cain, "Where is Abel thy brother?" And Cain said, "I know not: Am I my brother's keeper?" And he said, "What hast thou done? The voice of thy brother's blood crieth unto me from the ground."[63] God also asks us today, "How about your brothers and sisters who have fallen asleep both

63 Genesis 4:9, 10.

spiritually and physically because of you?" May I remind you that God said, "Let us make man in our image, after our likeness."[64] Thus, "God created man in his own image, in the image of God created he him; male and female created he them."[65]

One of the hardest things in life is to be kind to those who have offended us. It seems to come naturally to respond with resentment, anger, and judgment toward those who treat us poorly. This is true in our personal relationships, in our families, at work or school, and it is also true when we think of how nations get along—or often do not get along. In the world as we know it, it is easy to do good to those who do good to us, but terribly hard to love our enemies. So we may wonder why the Lord gave us such a difficult teaching to follow. Be merciful even as your Father in heaven is merciful. Love your enemies. Do good to everyone; lend expecting nothing in return. Treat others as you wish to be treated. Christ himself tells us that this is the difficult path to the blessed life of the Kingdom of God. I know that we are tempted to say that this message somehow does not apply to us.

Although it is natural and usual to love those who love us and to do good to those who do good to us, to love our enemies is distasteful to our nature. One can say that it isn't in our power but is an attitude that can only be the fruit of grace, given by the Holy Spirit. Saint Silouan the Athonite writes, "The soul that has not known the Holy Spirit does not understand how one can love one's enemies, and does not accept it. When you love your enemies, know that a great divine grace is living in you."[66] Indeed loving people is difficult. Yet this is what the Bible commands: "For this is the message that ye have heard from the beginning, that we should love one another."[67] We spend time on what we deem important. For many of us these choices are valid: time with family and friends, work, prayer, serving the poor, fighting for rights, protesting wrongs. But as the Scripture reminds us, "Though I bestow all my goods to feed the poor, and though I give my body to be burned, and have not charity, it profiteth me nothing."[68]

This may sound irrelevant to our generation that depends on force—police departments, guns, swords, *pangas*, *rungus*, stones, etc.—to uphold

64 Gen. 1:26.
65 Gen. 1:27.
66 Arch. Sophrony, *Saint Silouan the Athonite*, (Crestwood, NY: SVS Press, 1991).
67 1 Jn. 3:11.
68 1 Cor. 13:3.

and fulfill the law. Yet Jesus's simple command requires greater strength than any of us naturally possess, more power than any man-made weapon. For if one loves his neighbor, he will not commit adultery with his neighbor's spouse. If he loves his coworker, he will not lie to him. And if he loves his neighbor he will not poison him or his child; he will not slander him. If he respects his neighbor, he will also respect his rights: right to worship, right of association, and freedom of speech. Love fulfills the Law, because if we truly love every person because he is a person, we will not desire to hurt, kill, or violate him or her, and thus we will never break the Law. God established love as the impetus for obedience.

When we demonstrate Christian love, it distinguishes believers from the rest of the world. Jesus goes on to say, "By this shall all men know that ye are my disciples, if ye have love one to another."[69] Notice Jesus did not say that people will know that you are my disciples if you wear Christian t-shirts. The love of enemies is completely bound to the love of God. We have seen that the principal foundation for the love of enemies is the love that God has shown to all his creation. Christ gave us a perfect example of such love throughout his earthly life. The love of God leads man to accomplish his will and to imitate him as much as possible, and so also to love his enemies.

To love one's enemies is also tightly bound to humility. All the difficulties we encounter in loving our enemies are linked with pride, from which flow the afflictions that follow upon insults: hatred, bad temper, spite, the desire for revenge, contempt for one's neighbor, and the refusal to forgive and to be reconciled. But even while pride excludes the love of enemies, love excludes pride. If we love our enemies, pride will have no place in our souls. It is the link between humility and love of enemies that proves the presence of grace and the authenticity of love. If we have compassion for all creatures and love of our enemies, and if at the same time we judge ourselves the worst of all people, this shows that the great grace of the Lord is in us.

Humility is the indispensable condition to receive and keep the grace that teaches us to love our enemies and gives us the strength to do so. The elder Silouan advises us that if we humiliate ourselves, then grace will teach us. Grace causes us to lose grace in order that we might learn humility.[70] The soul is then tormented by bad thoughts and does not understand that

69 Jn. 13:35.

70 See Arch Sophrony, *St. Silouan the Athonite.*

one must humiliate oneself and love one's enemies. For without that, one cannot please God. How do we demonstrate the distinctiveness of Christian love? Because virtue is moral action in practice, how can we practice the glorious virtue of love?

Let's not confuse Christian love with its modern counterfeits of lust, sentimentality, and gratification. Love is a wonderful, warm feeling, but it is not only a feeling. Love is primarily an active interest in the well-being of another person. Love acts for the benefit of others; love is the spirit in the heart that will never seek anything but the highest good of its fellow man. God loved us not because we had something to offer him, but rather because he had something to offer us. Love opens up its life to another person. It goes beyond sentimental feelings. It breaks down barriers. Love makes a statement and leaves a legacy. It does the unexpected, surprising, and stirring. It performs acts that steal the heart and leave an impression on the soul.

We need to realize how much of our lives we spend looking at tiny dots in our brothers' and sisters' lives. We oftentimes focus on the single fault of another and overlook the many worthwhile qualities of the person. We seldom count the many blessings we already have because we are too preoccupied with the many things we still want. Because we live in a fallen and imperfect world, not one of us is perfect and unblemished. We all have at least one dot, and most of us have many. But when we stop and think about it, even the sheet of paper with many dots on it has far larger areas that are clean and unmarked. Of course, it would be dishonest to ignore the dots or to pretend that they are not there. But would it not make life more pleasant if we attempted to see the whole of the picture that others hold up to us? We must stop allowing the tiny dots, the faults of others, to overshadow the many positive aspects of their personalities. Not only will this make others easier to love, it will help others to see the Resurrected Christ.

About forgiveness, we can learn from the example of an Armenian nurse who was captured by the Turks along with her brother. Her brother had been executed by a Turkish soldier before her eyes. She, however, somehow managed to escape and later became a nurse in a military hospital. One day she was stunned to find that the same man who had killed her brother had himself been captured and brought wounded to the hospital where she worked. Something within her cried out, "Avenge your brother." But an even stronger voice called for her to love. She listened to that voice and nursed the man back to health. When the recuperating soldier finally realized who she was, he asked her, "Why didn't you let me die, or better yet, why did you not kill me?" Her answer was, "I am a follower of him who said, "Love your enemies, do good to them which hate you.[71]"

Just as all of us have certain weaknesses, so too, we also have our particular strengths. God, in his providential and infinite wisdom, has gifted every human being for the good of the Church. He has given each of us, even the most humble, an equal opportunity to be of service to one another. In this way, we come to understand that we need each other. It doesn't matter from which church or religion or denomination anyone comes from; we were created with one purpose: to love one another and to be patient and understand one another's weakness. This is what Saint Paul meant when he wrote that we cannot do without the parts of the body that seem to be weaker.[72]

My beloved children in Christ, there is nothing wrong with thinking big and aspiring to do something important and lasting. But, as Christians, we need to be mindful that all of our goals and plans must be laid at the altar of God, and all of our aspirations must be motivated by a desire to do the will of the Lord. In this offering of obedience, we must count it an equal honor to start at the bottom, with little things, if that is his plan for us. We must be mindful that in God's service, promotions to greater usefulness are given to those who are faithful in little things, and who are willing to start with "peanuts." In the parable of the gold coins, the faithful servant is told by Jesus, "Well, thou good servant: because thou hast been faithful in a very little, have thou authority over ten cities."[73] It is a big thing to do something small, if you take care to do it well, and consecrate it to God.

No matter what century or country in which we live; no matter our age or marital status or occupation, we all struggle against the spiritual diseases that make it so hard to forgive, love, and serve those who have violated our pride by offending us. We have turned away collectively and individually from the truth that we are made for a common life in the image and likeness of God. We have forgotten that it is our very nature as persons to be united with one another in love, as are the members of the Holy Trinity.

My brothers and sisters in Christ, our calling is not simply to love friends or family members. Even terrorists and gangsters have them, for it

71 Luke 6:27.

72 See 1 Cor. 12:22.

73 Luke 19:17.

is easy for people to love those who love them even if they are so filled with hate against others that they think nothing of killing innocent people who get in their way. But what kind of love is that? It is a love not even worthy of the name because it is really nothing more than self-centered desire, nothing more than simply judging others in terms of whether or not they please us. If so, we will be kind to them. If not, we will find a way to destroy them. Have we ever looked in the mirror to find instances that hit closer to our lives? If our spouse, child, or best friend needs help, we usually do not even think twice about doing what we can.

But if it is someone whom we do not like, who has wronged us, or a stranger whose request is simply inconvenient, we make excuses. And sometimes we treat even our spouses, children, and friends in such poor ways. When we do so, we live according to the lie that whether people please us is what determines whether we relate to them as those who bear the image and likeness of God, or as nuisances not worthy of our attention.

How tragic, then, that we so often choose to reject this high calling and instead to live according to the same corrupt principles that continue to bring crime, war, and broken relationships of all kinds to the world. How sad that we so often prefer death to life, pain to joy, and the hollow victory of self-exaltation to the blessedness of growing in communion with one another and with the Lord himself. And if we as Christians live this way, what hope is there for a world where helping our friends and cursing our enemies is just business as usual?

Jesus Christ is certainly the hope of both the Church and the world. He is our hope because he brought a new way for human beings to relate to others and to God. He died and rose again for those who rejected him, who nailed him to a cross and thought that he was demon-possessed. He not only healed his own people, the Jews, but showed the same mercy to Gentiles, Samaritans, and even a Roman centurion—a foreign soldier who occupied his homeland. He was at times very frustrated with the disciples for their lack of faith; they largely abandoned him at his arrest and crucifixion, but Christ still appeared to them after his resurrection and blessed them as the leaders of the Church. Our Savior is the embodiment of mercy to everyone, for he came to save and transform the entire world, the whole creation, and especially every human being, for we are all created in the divine image and likeness with the glorious calling to share fully in his victory over sin and death, to ascend with him to the peace and joy of eternal life.

Even more amazing is the truth that we are able to participate in him, to be nourished by his Body and Blood, the medicine of immortality and holiness. And, yes, we really are able to become merciful as our Father in Heaven is merciful. By being filled and transformed by his grace, we may become living icons of the divine love and light even in our most difficult relationships.

So, despite our spiritual brokenness and imperfect relationships, let us put aside everything that stands in the way of opening ourselves by prayer, repentance, and faithful reception of our Lord's Body and Blood to the joy and reconciliation that are ours as the sons and daughters of God. As we celebrate this Holy Pascha, let us be strengthened in our ability to be kind even to the ungrateful and selfish, and to be merciful like our Father in Heaven. Let us make all our relationships visible signs of the great salvation that Jesus Christ has brought to the world, and thereby grow closer to him and to one another.

Christ is risen!

May the risen Christ be with you and guide you throughout your lives and bless you always. Amen.

+ ARCHBISHOP MAKARIOS

CHRISTMAS ENCYCLICAL

December 25, 2014

> Fear not: for, behold, I bring you good tidings of great joy, which shall be to all people.[74]

My beloved Children in Christ,

I GREET YOU with the love, joy, and glad tidings, fitting of this marvelous feast of the Nativity of our Lord and Savior Jesus Christ. Christmas is a time of joy, a time of sharing and giving, a time of peace and calm promised by the Prince of Peace, who today is born in Bethlehem.

I know that our lives are often filled with pain and suffering and a lack of basic necessities, like food and clean water. There are many of us who lack proper clothing. There are even some who are still suffering the harsh elements, protected only by the tattered tents and polythene shanties they have called home since the post-election violence of 2007 and 2008. Many who were also evicted from the Mau forest are still living in despair, having no place to call home. These circumstances take joy out of life. They make life an unpleasant ordeal. They leave people with no interest in living, afraid of the future.

But, in the Gospel of Luke, the Angel of God promises great joy to all people. Even the people I have just mentioned are promised this great joy.

74 Luke 2:10.

It is up to us, my beloved children of God, to make this joy a reality to those in dire distress.

We are called upon, in this joyous season, and indeed all other seasons in our lives, to impart a little joy into the lives of those in need. As I said, Christmas is a time of sharing. We are called upon to rise to the challenge, move out of our comfort zones, and share joy with those in need. To take our Christmas to the needy, the hungry, the naked and the suffering, is the true meaning of this joyous festival.

As I write this message of the Nativity of our Lord, my prayer and desire is that the newborn King of Peace will be at the center of your lives. With Christ Jesus as the focus, his message of hope will truly emanate from us, our actions, and even our intentions. As we take the joy of the Nativity to those in need, we are not only showing them the love they so much need, we are also imparting to them hope, which, to many of them, is a memory of days gone by.

Let us remind those who are suffering that they need not be afraid, "for there is born for us all a Savior", a Savior from our sufferings and distress, a Savior from all sin and filth of this life. Let us therefore joyfully cuddle the swaddled Baby in our hearts, and indeed with our actions. Let us have hope in the newborn Christ, hope for the forthcoming year, hope that our lives will change and be guided by his will, not our will.

Finally, brothers and sisters in Christ, I wish you all the joy and peace that the birth of the Messiah brings forth. As we depart from church for our homes and to the festivities, let us depart in peace. Let us carry forth that peace to our homes and to our neighbors. The festivities will pass, but peace should remain in our lives. The love and joy should remain even after the festivities. Only then can the message of the angels ring true to us, and to those around us.

I wish you a Merry Christmas and a joyous New Year, two thousand and fifteen. With much love in Jesus Christ, born in Bethlehem,

+ ARCHBISHOP MAKARIOS

HOMILY
for the Feast of the Dormition of the Theotokos

Church of Saints Anargyroi,
August 15, 2012

Beloved Brethren in Christ, I greet you all in the Name of the Father, and of the Son, and of the Holy Spirit. Amen.

Great is the Name of the Lord!

TODAY IS A VERY SPECIAL DAY for the life of each and every Orthodox Christian. Each one of us has a special life. Everyone has specific special programs in their lives. We all have our own agendas. For this we make sure to do everything in our capacity to ensure that our agenda comes to fulfillment. This does not mean that our lives are stress free; no, problems are always there. That is why this feast that we celebrate today is very important to us. It actually reminds us not only of the falling asleep of the Mother of God, but also the special role that the Theotokos plays in our lives: the role of intercession!

We always call upon her when we are in trouble. Whenever we find ourselves in a troubling situation, we always mention her name and ask for her intercession. In Greek we say "Panagia Mou," meaning, "O, Mother of God," and we always look upon her intercessory role as the Mother of our Savior Jesus Christ to intercede on our behalf for our salvation.

Great is the Name of the Lord, whose mercy and grace endures forever! Today we are also blessed to witness the Holy Spirit at work! By the Grace of God, the most devout servant of God, who was a deacon moments ago, is now vested with the grace of priesthood. It is a miracle and a great one. Today is a special day in the life of Father Cosmas as well as that of the Church. He will now serve the Holy of Holies, administering the mystical sacraments of the One Holy Catholic and Apostolic Church. It is a day that the father and his *presbytera*[75] have looked forward to for so long. It is also a lesson on the timing of God. His timing is always so special and perfectly precise. His timing is always the best.

It is, however, important for the father and the presbytera to note that this event will change their lives completely. The society will look upon both of you from a different perspective. You have now been elevated to the priesthood, but also humbled to a servant. You will be required to sacrifice yourselves for the Church and her ministry. Don't be afraid to sacrifice yourselves. I am sure that the Church will benefit greatly from your service. You have traveled all over Europe, studied in different institutions and even earned a doctorate from the University of Thessalonica. I am sure that your input will greatly benefit the Church.

Be always humble, as our Savior showed us with his own example. Follow in his footsteps and learn also from the fathers of the Church. I assure you that your service will be beneficial to you and to the Church. And may the Mother of God always watch over you.

I welcome all of you to celebrate this wonderful feast. I welcome all the dignitaries who are with us today, the High Commissioner of Cyprus and all the visitors. To all of you I say, feel at home!

May God bless you all, and may the Theotokos intercede for us! Amen.

75 From the Greek: πρεσβυτέρα. An honorary title given to a priest's wife and used interchangeably with *papadhia* and, in slavic churches, *matushka*.

HOMILY
at the Ordinations of Priest Kalinikos Kinuthia & Deacon Cosmas John Ngigi

Kamangu, Kenya,
August 5, 2012[76]

My beloved Children, Parishioners of Holy Transfiguration in Kamangu, I greet you in the Name of the Father, and of the Son, and of the Holy Spirit.

TODAY IS A VERY SPECIAL and significant day, not only for our two brothers who have joined the royal priesthood, but also for the whole parish, as we prepare for one of our Great Feasts—Holy Transfiguration—which is celebrated on August 6.

"And after six days Jesus taketh Peter, James, and John his brother, and bringeth them up into a high mountain apart. And was transfigured before them: and his face did shine as the sun, and his raiment was white as the light."[77] This was the event to which our Lord was referring when he said, "There be some standing here, which shall not taste of death, till they see the Son of man coming in his Kingdom."[78]

By his Transfiguration, the faith of the disciples was strengthened and prepared for our Lord's trial, his passion, and his death. Because of it they

76 The eve of the Feast of Holy Transfiguration.

77 Matt. 17:1, 2.

78 Matt. 16:28.

were able to see in it not mere human suffering, but the entirely voluntary Passion of the Son of God. The apostle Paul says:

> For we are laborers together with God: ye are God's husbandry, ye are God's building. According to the grace of God which is given unto me, as a wise master builder, I have laid the foundation, and another buildeth thereon. But let every man take heed how he buildeth thereupon. For any other foundation can no man lay than that is laid, which is Jesus Christ. Now if any man build upon this foundation gold, silver, precious stones, wood, hay, stubble; Every man's work shall be made manifest: for the day shall declare it, because it shall be revealed by fire; and the fire shall try every man's work of what sort it is. If any man's work abide which he hath built thereupon, he shall receive a reward. If any man's work shall be burned, he shall suffer loss; but he himself shall be saved; yet so as by fire.[79]

As members of one Body, each is responsible for the health of the whole Body, which is the Church of Christ. We have a duty to defend the life of the Church, its faith, doctrines, teachings, and practice. The Lord says, "If you bring your sacrifice to the temple and there remember that your brother has something against you, leave there your gift, and go first to be reconciled to him."[80] He is not telling us to be reconciled only when we know that we have offended someone, but also when a brother has no peace because of us, even if we are not to blame. God wants us to humble ourselves as much as we can before our brother, regardless of the apparent justice of the matter. Our brother's heart will then be moved by our humility and he will be able to draw near to God again. In this way we work with God for our brother's salvation.

In every person, there is a special seed of the good and unique. Just as a seed cannot grow and ripen without moisture and light, so does the soul of man remain barren until it is irrigated by the grace of God. Feeling the need for divine help from within himself, King David prayed to God, "My soul thirsts after you, as a thirsty land."[81] And all people who have a genuine thirst for righteousness realize that, without the help of God, without his guidance and support, spiritual life is totally impossible.

We pray that, through this transfiguration, which is our resurrection,

79 1 Cor. 3:9–15.
80 Matt. 5:24.
81 Ps. 143:6.

God will enable us to be transformed from our old habits—from our natural life—which have been always troublesome to our families, our spouses, to become useful members of the society, especially to our families. The grace of God will renew our soul: purifying our consciences, enlightening our minds, fortifying our faith, guiding our wills toward good, warming our hearts with love for God and love for our neighbors, directing us toward heaven, inspiring us with the desire to live according to spiritual priorities. The Lord's transfiguration purifies and sanctifies man's entire being, changing it into a special vessel.

In the book about the Blessed Elder George Karslides, the writer compares priests with the candle that has been lit and blessed on the candle stand.[82] When you were baptized, you became like a candle stick that is blessed on the candle stand. Let your life in this world shine like a candle. It applies to priests, papadhias, and all young and old. We receive the spiritual illumination, the grace of God that brings peace and joy in our souls, so that all earthly riches and all physical delights seem pitiful and insignificant in comparison to our spiritual lives.

The Holy Spirit descended on Peter, James, and John, and they became enriched with spiritual wisdom. Then, their inspired words began to attract not only simple people to the faith, but even the rich and wealthy.

The grace of our Lord will fill your hearts and words with wisdom that will penetrate the depths of your own hearts, disposing of your sinful nature and leading you to repentance and correction. Even the fainthearted will be led to diligence. From being timid, such as the apostles were during the Savior's life on earth, they became courageous and fearless after the descent of the Holy Spirit. The gifts of grace, received during Holy Baptism, will be renewed just as they were for the apostles of Jesus Christ. In fact, many sinful people—people of little faith and of exclusively worldly interests—upon receiving the Holy Spirit, became deeply religious, righteous, full of zeal, and fervent in their love for God and others.

> And all that believed were together, and had all things common; And sold their possessions and goods, and parted them to all men, as every man had need. And they, continuing daily with one accord in the temple, and breaking bread from house to house, did eat their meat with gladness and singleness of heart, praising God, and

82 Monk Moses, *The Blessed Elder George Karslides (1901–1959)* (Thessaloniki: Orthodox Kypseli Publications, 1998).

> having favor with all the people. And the Lord added to the Church daily such as should be saved.[83]

In other words, spiritual interests and a striving for that which is heavenly displaced all that was sinful and lowly in them. My beloved sons and daughters, priests and papadhias, spiritual life is impossible without aid from above. You must learn to endure suffering for the salvation of one another. Many young men and women are having problems simply because they have forgotten the Cross of Jesus Christ, which we must carry every day. Look at the Cross of Jesus and you will be saved, see Christ in your partner and you will be able to share in his or her suffering. The apostle Paul calls all Christian virtues "the fruit of the Spirit," saying, "But the fruit of the Spirit is love, joy, peace, long suffering, gentleness, goodness, faith, meekness, temperance."[84]

After the Transfiguration, your inner spiritual growth and perfection will take place unnoticed, just as the Lord explained in the parable of the invisibly growing seed. Of the mysterious action of the Holy Spirit upon a man's soul, the Savior said, "The Spirit blows where it wills, and you hear the sound thereof, but cannot tell from where it comes and where it goes. So it is with every one that is born of the Spirit."[85]

The Transfiguration is a prefiguring of our Lord's Resurrection and his second coming. It is the visual manifestation of God's kingdom on earth. This applies to the transformed state in which Christians shall appear at the end of the world, and in some measure, even before then. In the foreshadowing of future glory that is celebrated on the Feast of the Transfiguration, we are reminded, in the persons of Elijah and Moses, that after our temporary sorrows and deprivations with which this earthly life is filled, the glory of eternal blessedness will shine forth. In this, the righteous will participate. In appealing to the Holy Spirit, the All-bountiful One, we ask that we be cleansed of all sinful stains which arise within us from various passions, and which stick to us as a result of our contact with the world that is lying in iniquity. We ask him to stay within us and guide our lives toward the salvation of our souls. Moreover, as we pray to the Holy Spirit, we should humbly feel ourselves poor and unworthy, because God "resists the proud, but gives grace unto the humble."[86] Amen.

83 Acts 2:44–47.

84 Gal. 5:22–23.

85 Jn. 3:8.

86 James 4:6.

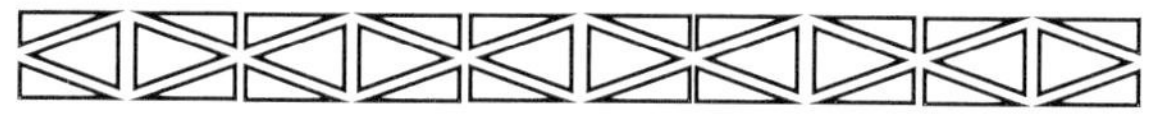

Political & Ecumenical Addresses

CHRISTMAS ENCYCLICAL

on the Fiftieth Year of the Independence of Kenya

December 25, 2013

Christ is born! Glorify him! Kristo amezaliwa! Tumtukuze!

As we celebrate the feast of Christmas this year, while celebrating fifty years since our independence as a nation, let us reflect on our past as a nation: how we struggled for independence; the role we, as the Orthodox Church, played in the liberation of this country; how we lost close and distant relatives, friends and neighbors; how our relations lost property and other precious items in the struggle; how our country was liberated from colonialism; and how the peace, love, and unity we enjoy today was attained.

Christmas is a feast realized after a long wait on the part of humanity. As the above passage—the first gospel—reminds us, Christ was foretold to come and liberate mankind soon after the fall of Adam and Eve. Man lived in the slavery of sin and death for thousands of years before Christ was incarnated. The preparation to receive the freedom from sin and death took years, taking us through the entire Old Testament era.

Just like our salvation, the liberation of this country took years of preparation, perseverance, dedication, and the effort of different individuals, some now alive and some departed from this life. Kenya was under the slavery of colonialism, and at that time life was not easy for anyone in

Kenya, be they rich or poor, young or old, literate or illiterate. To liberate this country from the colonial masters, most of our forefathers in the Orthodox Church gave their lives to help realize the goal of freedom.

> Bethlehem has opened Eden: come, and let us see! We have found joy in secret: come, and let us take possession of the paradise that is within the cave. There the unwatered Root has appeared, from which forgiveness flowers forth: there is found the undug Well, whence David longed to drink of old. There the Virgin has borne a Babe, and made the thirst of Adam and David to cease straightway. Therefore let us hasten to this place where now is born a young Child, the pre-eternal God.[1]

To remind those who know, and to enlighten those who don't, I will mention a few Orthodox leaders and their contributions to the independence of our country, Kenya.

Archbishop Makarios III of Cyprus & his encounter with Kenyan leaders

Born in Cyprus in 1913, the young Cypriot boy did not know he would end up as the Archbishop of Cyprus, as the one who would lead his fellow countrymen to fight for their independence from British rule, as well as becoming their first president. By God's grace and love, he grew to be a God-fearing and respected person in the church and society. It was his leadership skills and his love for his nation that drove his patriotism to such heights that the colonial government sent him out of his country to Seychelles in March 1956, considering him as a danger to their destructive mission.

One journalist in 1956, writing for the Sunday Post, had written on the connection between Mzee Jomo Kenyatta and Archbishop Makarios. For him, these two men of very different societies were very much alike in so many ways. Both were the leaders of the liberation movement in their countries, which were under the British colonial rule. They were both considered criminals and terrorists by the British government, while their countrymen considered them to be liberation leaders and cherished heroes. Although the opposition party in the House of Commons called both men moderate and asked the British government to stop harassing them, the

1 Ikos at Matins of the Nativity of Christ, *The Festal Menaion*, 278.

British government did not consider them as such, so it severely punished them both. One leader was sent to prison and the other into exile.

A year after his exile (c. 1957), Archbishop Makarios was released, and it was during his travel through Kenya that he got to meet the Orthodox Christians and distinguished freedom fighters within Nairobi and Central Kenya for one week. During his one-week visit in Kenya, Archbishop Makarios went to the prisons holding most of the freedom fighters, encouraging them and giving them hope. He even had meetings with different national leaders heading the liberation movement in Kenya. In one such meeting, the Archbishop met, among others, some of the eight newly elected Legislative Council (Legco) members, including the late Tom Mboya (Nairobi), Jaramogi Oginga Odinga (Nyanza North), and Lawrence Ogunda (Nyanza South), who had come to see him. His admirers knew of his feelings about the colonial rule, not only in his own country, Cyprus, but also beyond, and even more so in Kenya. On April 13, 1957, the Archbishop met representatives of the District African Congress of various areas including their president, Mr. C.M.G Argwings-Kodhek.

In his own words, Archbishop Makarios said to the press, "All I would like to say is that I met these gentlemen at their request. I would describe it as a courtesy call. They asked for information about Cyprus, and I answered their questions."

All these Kenyan leaders were meeting, for the first time, a foreign Orthodox ecclesiastical personality who was a prelate, a freedom fighter, a great activist for the rights of his people and an ethnarch (national leader). Amidst all these qualities, the Africans were much impressed by his humble personality, his dress, and physical appearance: the black beard, the black robes (cassock and *riassa*) and the black hat (*karimafia*). Addressing a press conference after the meeting, Mr. Mboya told the press that he and his colleagues were surprised that His Beatitude had been elected to the position of Archbishop and leader of his people in Cyprus.

Admiring the prophetic role the Church and her Archbishop played in the liberation process in Cyprus, Mboya indicated that if the Christian Church in Kenya practiced what it preached about the respect and dignity of man then it would help eliminate or minimize the problems facing Kenya. On the common objectives of their meeting, Mboya told the press that their meeting focused on freedom from domination and colonialism, and the security of an effective voice in the government. In all these topics, the African leaders had a lot to learn from the Archbishop's experiences and the Cypriot people's self-determination in their struggle for independence. After the meetings, the African leaders even wrote to the Archbishop to express their gratitude for his inspiration and advice, as well as to wish him the leadership of God in the cause of his country's liberation.

His Beatitude, in his usual polite and exceptional ways, spoke to them about his visions and ambitions for the achievement of the liberation of his home country, Cyprus. He told them how he had no fear of the British Empire, and assured these African leaders that although his island was very small, he would continue fighting the British until the day these colonial masters left his country. He emphasized to them the importance of not giving up their struggle, but instead encouraged them to continue until they also saw the colonial government leave their country. All of them were very impressed and became even more committed to finding more ways to fight the foreign administration in Kenya.

The best description of this meeting is given as a testimonial to us by someone who was then a boy of ten, the present politician Raila Amolo Odinga, who was listening to his father narrate enthusiastically his meeting with Archbishop Makarios, that same evening after his father's return home. All eyewitnesses, or their relatives mentioned that the spirit and determination of His Beatitude Archbishop Makarios in fighting the colonial government and winning against them, deeply guided the freedom fighters and leaders of Kenya, helping them to intensify their struggle against the British rule.

On the same week, while preaching at the cathedral of Saints Anargyroi—that is, the cathedral along the Valley Road—on Sunday April 14, 1957, Archbishop Makarios condemned colonialism and gave the Orthodox clergy and laity, as well as all other visiting dignitaries and colonial leaders, the hope to continue the struggle against the British government. His very strong and public message to the people of Kenya emphasized the virtue and the importance of gaining freedom. He emphatically condemned the pressure that the foreign administration was exercising on the people, emphasizing the need for the liberation of all nations suffering under the British colonial rule.

For His Beatitude, the Church had a very special part in the liberation of each nation. In his speech he expressed this by saying, "Freedom is a Christian ideal and that is why the Church is leading the struggle for freedom in Cyprus. God says that all men should be free and that is why the struggle for freedom will be triumphant." The Orthodox Christians (then known as "Karing'a") were among the most "notorious" Mau Mau fighters and anti-colonialists, and so passing the message to their comrades was easy. The news of this speech was thus quickly spread everywhere within and outside Kenya, to the extent that even those Mau Mau soldiers living in the dense forests of Central Kenya away from the British soldiers were encouraged greatly by this message of Archbishop Makarios, even while physically fighting for the liberation of Kenya.

The impact this speech made on the Kenyan people, and the intensity with which the freedom fighters started attacking the colonial government, made the British administration of the House of Commons in London order the immediate expulsion of Archbishop Makarios from Kenya. The British government, expressing its feelings on the Archbishop's stay in Kenya, mentioned that he was not a welcome guest in Kenya and that the government was embarrassed by his visit. They offered His Beatitude the choice of going anywhere else but Kenya and Cyprus. This speech was the first time during the emergency period that the people of Kenya received such an encouraging message from an Archbishop and ethnarch, a part of history written and sealed in unforgettable, golden words.

Archbishop Makarios III's continued presence in Kenya

Kenyan and Cypriot leaders since this time have become very good friends. The friendship between Archbishop Makarios and Mzee Jomo Kenyatta solidified this because it did not end even after the struggle for independence came to an end.[2] Archbishop Makarios visited Kenya several times, where he was received as a hero for his steadfast fight against the British in both Kenya and Cyprus. It was this friendship that made if possible for Archbishop Makarios to get a piece of land within the Dagoretti area to build an Orthodox seminary and technical school, provided by President Kenyatta. The land was easily obtained and offered to him with pleasure, a process that culminated with His Beatitude laying the foundation of the same on March 22, 1971.

On his two-day visit to Kenya in September 1972, Archbishop Makarios met President Kenyatta in the State Lodge of Nakuru on September 15, 1972. On this occasion, the President was with his Vice President, Mr. Daniel Arap Moi; Minister of Foreign Affairs, Dr. Njoroge Mungai; Mr. Jackson Angaine, the Minister for Lands and Housing; and the winners

2 Kenya gained independence from Great Britain on Dec. 12, 1963.

of the just completed Munich Olymic Games. President Kenyatta introduced Archbishop Makarios as a Cypriot leader who liberated his people from colonialism, and mentioned that he regarded him as a true freedom fighter just like the Kenyan Mau Mau freedom fighters. His Beatitude thanked the Kenyan leaders and citizens for always giving him a hearty welcome whenever he visited Kenya, making him feel very much at home. The Archbishop even promised to attend the 9th celebration since the independence of Kenya on December 12, 1972.

There was a negative attitude toward African culture planted by the colonial-led churches. The Orthodox Church, among other independent churches in Kenya, had struggled to eliminate the hostility of some Christians toward some or all African cultures. So, President Kenyatta, in his addresses on the occasion of laying the foundation stone of the All Africa Conference of Churches headquarters on December 2, 1975, called for the Africanization of Christianity, whereby Christianity would respect the African culture and the African Christians would practice their cultures as well as their religion without any conflicting teachings. For him, this was the only way to give authentic, relevant, and credible Christianity to the African continent, as had been witnessed in the first centuries of Christianity in North Africa. This stand was what the Orthodox Church in Kenya had struggled to attain amidst other needs.

After the repose of His Beatitude Makarios in July, 1974, His Excellency President Jomo Kenyatta, in his condolence letter, called Archbishop Makarios "a friend of Kenya," citing his passion in the struggle of both the freedom of the people and of religion in Cyprus and beyond.

Bishop George Arthur Gatung'u Gathuna

Bishop Gathuna was born in Waithaka in 1905, and was educated in Alliance High School alongside most of the fathers of this nation. He later went for teacher's training in Meru, before embarking on his teaching career. He became a very steadfast Mau Mau supporter and a national politician, as well as the father of Orthodoxy in Kenya.

It was during the colonial era that the Orthodox spirit came upon some Africans who wanted to be in a church that was led by Africans and that would give them freedom of worship as well as the freedom to live and practice those indigenous and traditional ways that did not affect their Christian faith. This spirit was much felt within Central Kenya and Nairobi, where the Mau Mau liberation spirit was also strongest. The strongest revolt that formed the Karing'a group was the 1929 declaration, authored by the Church of Scotland (the Presbyterian Church, today), whereby all their Christians were to sign a declaration against female circumcision and any association with the Mau Mau revolts. Some Christians at Thogoto (Kiambu) and Kambui (Murang'a) left the said colonial-led churches and formed their own. Their children were also chased out of the colonial-led schools, forcing the Africans to also form their own schools. They built their churches and schools on donated or bought lands.

When one of the Karing'a members, James Beauttah, met Archbishop Daniel William Alexander of the African Orthodox Church from South Africa in the port of Mombasa in 1931, on transit from visiting the Ugandan flock for the first time, he informed Kenyatta and the other freedom fighters, as well as the Karing'a group, about their success in meeting someone who could help resolve their religious problem. They eventually managed to bring in Archbishop Daniel William Alexander, who taught them his faith and ordained some of them on July 27, 1937. One among those ordained was Father George A.G. Gathuna, who had been encouraged to join the Orthodox Church by Mzee Jomo Kenyatta, *et al.*

Later on, when the Orthodox realized that the church they had joined was not an authentic Orthodox Church, they, together with their Ugandan counterparts, contacted the Paschan Orthodox Patriarchates through the help of Archimandrite Nicodemos Sarikas (1907–1941). Replies were received from the Patriarchate of Alexandria, especially important were those received from Patriarch Meletios Metaxakis (1926–1935) and the Metropolitan of Johannesburg, the latter dated February 28, 1934. The Patriarchate of Alexandria sent an envoy to Uganda in November, 1942. On November 10, 1942, the patriarchal emissary, Metropolitan Nicholas Abdallah of Axum, while on his way from Uganda, met Father Gathuna, who expressed the desire of the Karing'a Orthodox Church to join and be recognized by the Patriarchate of Alexandria. This would not only offer the Church of Kenya the authenticity they very much desired, but would also help ease the official registration of the Church in Kenya, formerly complicated by the colonial government and the incitement of the colonial-led Protestant churches.

While the fight against the white colonialists continued, the Mau Mau supporters and their families were treated with suspicion. The Karing'a school teachers were very organized, and at the same time fully supported the fight against colonialism. The Karing'a school children and their parents felt the same way. The leaders of the Karing'a Orthodox, led by Father George Gathuna, among others, were the ones who passed on the official communications of the Mau Mau to the people in towns and villages. They also financially supported the freedom fighters, giving them the encouragement to continue. It was for these reasons that the colonial government closed all the Karing'a schools and churches on October 20, 1952. While some Karing'a churches continued operating underground, not much was done with the schools.

On October 20, 1952, a state of emergency was declared in Kenya and most supporters of the Mau Mau were arrested, along with all leaders of independent churches and schools (including the Karing'a Orthodox), between October 1952 and October 1953. Among those arrested were Mzee Jomo Kenyatta, the founding father of the Nation of Kenya. His comrade Father George A.G. Gathuna, the father of the Orthodox Church in Kenya, was arrested at his home on June 1, 1953. They were all treated like criminals of war. Father George Gathuna was detained for eight and a half years, being held at Senya detention camp in Kajiado (1953–1955), then Lamu detention camp (1955–1958), and at Hola prison (1958–1961).

Before his imprisonment, Father Gathuna had around thirty thousand followers spread out over 310 congregations. While he was in detention, his flock was left without a leader. The Orthodox churches were set on fire by the police, the Karing'a schools were snatched by the colonial government, and, even worse, the Greek community in Nairobi disowned any association with them. The Archdiocese of East Africa tried sending some Ugandan clergy to come help take care of the flock in Kenya while Father Gathuna was in prison, but these clergymen were denied access to minister in central Kenya and Nairobi. All these problems led to the former adherents of the Orthodox Church and Mau Mau to give up on the Church and return to their former churches, or to newly join the colonial-led churches and schools. The Karing'a churches and schools were only reopened after independence, but unfortunately the schools were never returned to the Orthodox Church. Instead, they were henceforth turned into public and government-led schools.

Earlier, in June 1942, some people from Western Kenya had expressed their desire to join the Orthodox Church. Father Gathuna, after receiving them in July, 1946, initiated the parish of Saint Gerasimos (Ebuyangu) and four other churches. Father Gathuna visited the Western Kenyan churches annually and every time appointed several leaders and erected new parishes. It is from these parishes that Western Kenya, Nyanza, and Nandi areas received Orthodoxy, either directly from the Christians taught by Father Gathuna and his team, or later, when the Ugandan clergyman Father Obadiah Basajjakitalo and the Greek Archimandrite Father Chrysostomos Papasarantopoulos (active, 1959–1970) were sent to evangelize and take care of the Church while the spiritual father of Kenya, Father Gathuna, was in prison.

This is especially the case with most of the Nyanza area, as well as the Nandi area, where Serem was elected as the Center of Orthodoxy in the early 1960s. At this time, the first Metropolitan of East Africa, Metropolitan Nicholas (1958–1967) was able to come several times to Western Kenya through Uganda. After the Holy Archbishopric of Irinoupolis moved its headquarters from Uganda to Kenya, Father Basajjakitalo of Uganda, who was at the time working in Western Kenya in the absence of Father Gathuna, was invited to Nairobi by Archbishop Nicodemos. Here Father Basajjakitalo was to revive the Kagira church and the old seminary until the 1961 release of Father Gathuna, who took it from there.

After Kenya gained its independence in 1963, Father Gathuna went around where the Orthodox Christians had churches and initiated the rebuilding of those that were demolished. The attached schools had already been taken by the government, never to be returned. Some of the churches, especially those built next to the Karing'a schools, like Saint Paul (Kagira), acquired new lands away from their old establishments. Father Gathuna also registered the Orthodox Church under the new government as the "African Orthodox Church of Kenya," a dream realized after many years. He later traveled abroad to look for donors for various projects, and while in Kenya looked for many plots of land for building Orthodox churches, a responsibility which was not complicated for him, especially because he was a known clergyman, teacher, politician, and Mau Mau leader. Any door he knocked on was always opened, and so the Orthodox got many lands in Kenya.

> The sea monster spat forth Jonah as it had received him, like a babe from the womb: while the Word, having dwelt in the Virgin and taken flesh, came forth from her yet kept her uncorrupt. For being himself not subject to decay, He preserved His mother free from harm.[3]

3 Irmos of the Sixth Ode, Matins of the Nativity of Christ. *The Festal Menaion,* 276.

Concluding Remarks

This Christmas season, as we celebrate fifty years since the independence of this country, let us pray that God pardon the souls of all freedom fighters, living or dead, because it was through them that we have a country called Kenya, a country where we can practice our faith freely and with no more persecutions. Let us also not forget our forefathers, who gave their lives so that we could have our own. As we celebrate the Nativity of Christ let us joyfully sing and glorify God who became man for our salvation, and pray that we become defenders of our faith and country in all aspects of life. May Christ who is born in our hearts keep the spirit of peace, love, and unity in all of us.

With paternal blessings, love, and best of wishes for Christmas and the new year: two thousand and fourteen.

A WORD OF THANKSGIVING
for Vice President Kalonzo Musyoka

April 10, 2010

The Vice President, Honorable Kalonzo Musyoka, Honorable Ministers, Dignitaries, and the Wanainchi of Mwingi, I greet you most cordially in the Name of Christ.

I FEEL HONORED to be standing in front of you addressing this important gathering. I also feel honored to be associated with the Vice President, who is also the member of Parliament for Mwingi, Honorable Kalonzo Musyoka, who has been my good and close friend since 1992 when we started working together for the welfare of the people in this area. Today is a great day in honor of the Vice President's twenty-five years in politics. I can say that I am proud of his great achievement and his great zeal to represent the people of Mwingi. I cannot hide the fact that all these years I have admired his strong will, his perseverance, and mostly, his humility. His philanthropic deeds have moved the people of Mwingi repeatedly to re-elect him. It is a fact that the people of Mwingi cannot today hide their immeasurable joy for the admirable representation that he has offered them in terms of initiating projects that are helpful to the entire community.

We thank the Lord our Savior, who has brought us to this auspicious day to sing a hymn on this day of thanksgiving for His Excellency, the Vice President Kalonzo Musyoka. Our leaders today are gathered to commemorate this wonderful and great event that Christ's right hand has accomplished in our days. This reminds us that there is a Day of the Lord that will come upon everyone that is insolent and arrogant, a day of falling for all who are haughty and self-exalted. For Christ will shake all those who are mighty in their own eyes and will crush the proud and the insolent with power. Your Excellency, today indeed is a blessed day for you, because through your humility and perseverance you have been able to achieve a lot through a short period of time. Today I congratulate you for your achievements. We also praise God because a person who does not trust in him could not realize all of these achievements. You are a spiritual man—a man who honors and fears God, and that is why today, without fear, we can sing this prayer:

> Do you yourself, O All-Holy Master, accept our prayers of thanks-giving, for liberation and rebirth of our beloved Vice President, and hear us, who in faith fervently pray to you: give rest for the souls of those who nobly fought for our country, Kenya, and died in glory. Make us all worthy of freedom. Preserve in peace and concord every authority and power in the nation, and make them favorable and well-disposed toward the Church and all your people.

We should praise God, who holds together the universe in his power, and who, by his divine and mighty power, governs the world. He created from one blood all the nations of mankind that inhabit the face of the earth, and has assigned each its boundaries. God has conferred special blessings on our beloved country, Kenya, granting her people the knowledge of his truth, leading them to the light of true faith and raising up from their midst strong leaders, as we witness here today. On this particular day we are celebrating your achievements, we are honoring your hard work, and we are recognizing your dedication in serving the people of this region. And we all congratulate you and pray that God will give you many years.

Let me end my short speech by thanking His Excellency and all those who are present here. May Almighty God bless you all with his abundant love.

ADDRESS
at the Annual General Meeting of the Orthodox SACCO[4]

April 24, 2010

Distinguished Guests, Representatives from the Ministry of Cooperatives, and Orthodox SACCO members, I greet you most cordially in the Name of the Father, and of the Son, and of the Holy Spirit.

GLORY TO GOD in the highest for enabling us to assemble once again at the great annual general meeting of the Orthodox SACCO. It is indeed a wonderful time to reflect on the outstanding and most remarkable achievements that our SACCO has managed to bring about. I might not be wrong to say that the SACCO has really improved the lives of some of you who are present at this seating, and these achievements can be used as good evidence that this organization is living up to its vision, and is accomplishing its noble goals. You will all agree with me that there is always some happiness and comfort when important goals in one's life, or in a team, are achieved, or when mission is accomplished.

Today being a very important day, I would like to convey my heartfelt and most sincere gratitude to all those who have toiled so hard for this organization to be a success. Though this has not been an easy struggle, we as Christians, or Orthodox Church members, believe that with prayer everything is possible. We are a Church of miracles, and our constant

4 SACCO (Savings and Credit Cooperative Society) is a Kenyan economic co-operative.

inclination to the life of prayer has made us come to the realization that all goals that we set here on earth can only succeed through dedicating ourselves to prayer. We can only conclude and say that whatever achievements have been realized in this organization, it has been through the hand of God, with the blessing of our heavenly Father.

Brothers and sisters in Christ, most of the time when we talk about our success or achievements, we tend to turn a blind eye to the challenges or the hurdles that we encounter on the path to achieving our goals and aspirations. I know that it does not sound wise to dwell on these challenges, but it is important to look back and see where changes may need to be made in order to avoid repeating some mistakes that hinder success in any organization.

I find it necessary to base my address on elements of leadership, as acquiring good leadership is one of the common challenges that face organizations. Today's activities involve electing new leaders. The words, "leadership" and "management" bring a bit of confusion as to their meanings. However, it is important to note that leaders are not managers, for their functions are different, especially in this modern and developing world. In business spheres, some people exercise a mix of management and leadership, which are both vital to running a successful business or organization. I would say that leadership provides direction while management provides systems to enable any organization to achieve its goals. These are both important in steering an organization to greater heights.

While it is a fact that the top management can set direction in an organization, setting direction is different from setting goals, because setting goals is concrete and measurable while general direction is broader. It is important, therefore, that leaders set a direction with a vision, a mission, and operating principles that embody the organization's values. The characteristics of becoming a good leader are not that extensive. You don't have to be tall, well spoken, and good looking in order to be rated as a good leader; you don't have to have a special charisma in order to carry out a leadership role. The most important thing is to have clearly defined convictions, and to make sure that you see them through to reality. It is only when we understand our role as a guide and a servant—based on our most deeply-held truth—that we can graduate from managers to leaders.

Dear co-operators, it does not matter what the group you oversee is called: "the faithful," "church members," "associates," "co-workers," or "teammates," etc. What they are looking for is someone in whom they can place their trust—someone working for a greater good, both for them and for the organization. Brothers and sisters in Christ, when you see that there are people who are under you and they have placed complete trust in you, then you are definitely a leader. And if your organization or society is exhibiting the qualities of being productive, innovative, and with revenue achievement, then this is a clear indication that your organization is sufficient and giving itself back to the society. And, more importantly, the organization is attaining its goals. My advice today is that if you are chosen to be a leader, then be a sound leader who will ensure that everything is under control. Make sure you solve all problems that arise. Work with your team since they have put their trust in you and are helping you create a successful organization.

Today, it is important for us to understand that leadership requires a lot of sacrifice and hard work. Christ Jesus set a perfect example of what sacrifice and hard work means when leading people. He persevered through ridicule and opposition; he sacrificed himself in order to achieve his goal—salvation for all mankind. He also delivers to us a very good lesson, that in order for a leader to be effective, good people must surround him, just as Christ chose a team who could work well with him in spreading the Gospel of his Father.

Jesus Christ set a good example that we can emulate today so that we can be successful in leadership. In the light of the Word of God, a leader should be a person who does the right things. He should be a person who innovates and introduces new things that are creative and that benefit the whole organization. A leader is a person who places focus on people; who inspires trust and knows how to empower those that he leads. Through prayers and following the precepts of Christ, a leader should have courage in his convictions. He should be a person who is most concerned with issues of substance, and he should also be able to ask, "What?" and "Why?" Just as our Lord Jesus Christ gave instructions to the twelve apostles, a good leader should be able to initiate what is to be done. He should place his eye on the horizon and be able to figure out what is about to happen, or that which is apparent.

A good leader has vision. He should be farsighted, an entrepreneur, and adventuresome. A vision is a long-term picture of the preferred destiny of one's business, organization, church, or company. All good leaders should have a vision of the future toward which they are working. If one cannot see where he is going, then he is not likely to get there, because one cannot go to a place he has not seen. Vision gives leaders direction and prevents them from straying away. The book of Proverbs gives us an important lesson about vision when it says: "Where there is no vision people perish: but he that keepeth the law, happy is he."[5]

The Bible states that where there is no vision, the people are not hooked up to their objectives; they scatter in all sorts of directions. We see many churches and organizations—or even nations—that have no vision. They are bound to be side-tracked. Today I leave with you this: great leaders inspire great people and great organizations.

Finally, brethren in Christ, there was a great need for our Lord Jesus Christ to come in our time of need to rescue us from the curse of sin. It was the need of God to save humanity, to redeem us from our sinful nature and bring us back to glory. We needed Christ because we had already sinned against God.

Today, in secular business and other organizations, leaders place special emphasis on responding to people's needs. I urge the leaders of SACCO to do this. People will always run toward what meets their needs, and the organizations that meet the needs of the people are seen to be relevant to the community, attracting many people of good will. So, dear leaders, let us get our vision from God and not seek the opinion of man. Let us all seek the will of God, just as Jesus never sought the opinions of people or followed the crowd. Jesus always moved with, and trusted, his Father. Let us keep our trust in God and all other things shall fall into place. May Almighty God bless you all.

5 Proverbs 29:18.

ADDRESS
Concerning the Proposed National Constitution

Church of Saints Nicholas & Anastasios,
Riruta (Nairobi), Kenya,
July 17, 2010

Reverend Fathers, Civic Educators, distinguished Guests, Brothers and Sisters in Christ: I greet you all in the Name of the Father, and of the Son, and of the Holy Spirit. Amen.

WHAT GREAT NATION is there that has statutes and ordinances so righteous as this proposed constitution, which I set before you this day? Allow me, brethren, to start by mentioning one of biblical history's greatest prophets: Moses. He posed a question to the Children of Israel in Deuteronomy when he set before them the Law from the Lord their God. And, it is a question that every nation desires to ask regarding the law for its people—that is, how to come up with a law that promises righteous statutes and ordinances? This is the utmost desire of every lawmaker, in any given nation.

However, man continues to evolve in his technology, lifestyle, and even governance. This has required him to adjust and re-adjust the law governing his day-to-day life. As we gather here today, our beloved nation is trying to do just that: to adjust our existing law in a bid to better govern our day-to-day lives. Yet still, after all is said and done, this historic exercise should not detach itself from the law and counsel of God, from whom the ultimate law emanates. He clearly states through the prophet Isaiah that, "a law shall proceed from me, and I will make my judgment to rest for a light of the people."[6] It is absolutely clear from Holy Scripture that throughout the writings of the prophets, the Lord set forth the Law for his people to be a light for all the nations. The law in this context is for guidance and direction, but not to be used to lord it over the masses. This law was founded on values of righteousness, and was designed to cultivate peace and prosperity for his people. He desired that this law would illumine the rulers' paths.

Our Lord Jesus Christ in Matthew clearly states that he came to strengthen the Law, "Think not that I am come to destroy the Law, or the Prophets. I am not come to destroy, but to fulfill."[7] By this binding statement, without fear of contradiction, Christ Jesus declares his conviction for the importance of the Law. He emphasized that the Law and the Prophets are founded on selflessness, love, and equality. This could not be more clear than his own words, "Whatsoever ye would that men should do to you, do ye even so to them: for this is the Law and the Prophets."[8]

Selflessness, love, and equality are values that should emanate from the law of our people. This kind of law embraces the sanctity of life, equality of rights, and fair distribution of resources; it is blind to tribal boundaries, and it views all people as part of one, united nation. The good law paves a way for freedom of worship, respecting and treating as equal the different faiths and creeds found within the land. The apostles of Christ, following in his footsteps, emphasized the importance that the people's lives be founded on the Golden Rule of love. The Christian churches, being the largest unit of a nation, should be really prominent in charting the course for the laws of the land. Some issues, like the sanctity of life, land distribution, administration, and religious differences have been treated as contentious in our proposed document. Yet, all of us desire, just as the prophets, apostles, and Christ himself, that we usher in a document that is embraced by all, respected by all, and held in high esteem by all.

Concerning the life of the unborn, from the earliest days, the holy fathers were fully aware that human life begins at the exact moment of conception. The church fathers, Tertullian, Saint Basil, Gregory of Nyssa and others, along with very strict and uncompromising canons of the Church Councils, spoke strongly against abortion. Severe penalties were exacted

6 Is. 51:4.
7 Matt. 5:17.
8 Matt. 7: 12.

against those who even assisted in the killing of innocent human life. Our society, therefore, should not be a permissive one that views abortion as a "private matter of choice." We should not forget the stringent law of the Church, set to deter us from sin whose wages are clearly death.[9]

From the point of view of the church fathers, we should therefore not slay the child by abortions; hence, by refraining from destroying the life in the womb, we will embrace the fact that Christ, by reason of his immeasurable love, became what we are in order that he might make us what he is himself.

Reverend fathers, brothers and sisters in Christ, in our present situation, in order to have peace and reconciliation (not forgetting some very trying times our nation has gone through), we should really emphasize the importance of having and respecting laws from the civil authorities. As the Church, we have always known and respected this. We have always included in our prayers a petition for the president of the land, those in civil authority, and even the armed forces; all because we appreciate and respect the presence of law to govern and facilitate the smooth and peaceful existence of all.

"Peace I leave with you. My peace I give unto you."[10] Countless times does Christ exhort his disciples to have peace in their hearts. This is the peace we preach; we always preach peace. Where peace abides, rational thinking is forthcoming.

Reverend fathers, brothers and sisters, having lived in this beautiful nation for over thirty years now, never before have I felt more compelled to emphasize the importance of cultivating peace as I do now. Let us preach peace. A constitution is not like an election that can be recalled after five years. It is a standard that will guide our people for generations to come once it is passed into law. The constitution is not a document that we would wish to ratify with feelings of animosity, hatred, and tribalism.

Let us faithfully educate and advise our people with sincerity. Let us give them the freedom of choice—an informed choice. History will judge us harshly if we mislead the masses or stand aside and watch as they are misled. Remember, choose not for me, but rather help me make an informed choice. Let this be our guideline. May the peace of our Lord, which surpasses all understanding, be with us and guide us through this historic period in our nation.

9 See Rom. 6:23.

10 John 14:27.

ADDRESS
to an Inter-Denominational Gathering

October 29, 2011[11]

Most Reverend and beloved Clergy from all denominations here gathered, dignified Ambassadors and Consulars, beloved Brothers and Sisters, I greet you all with the peace of our Lord Jesus Christ!

TODAY WE ARE GATHERED here to pray for world peace, reconciliation, and co-existence. Being a representative of the Greek Orthodox Patriarchate of Alexandria and all Africa in the various inter-faith dialogues that are taking place, I have come to understand the great need and urgency to cultivate peaceful ties amongst the various creeds, cultures and communities of our mother earth. After all is said and done, we come to realize that we need each other.

This event was first held twenty-five years ago, setting the faiths of the world on a noble path of cultivating peace—the path on which we tread today. Our world has changed so much in the past twenty-five years. More than ever, we need to foster a deeper dialogue that leads to peace. Rather than only looking for a pathway to peace, we must ensure that peace is the pathway along which we all walk together.

Saint Francis's life eight hundred years ago was a strong example of peace and dialogue with all peoples. It is a life that continues to inspire

11 Address given on the Silver Jubilee of the Spirit of Assisi at a gathering hosted by the Roman Catholic Church of Bomas, Kenya.

people of all faiths and those who struggle with faith. We are called today to humble ourselves, to swallow our ego, to move out of our comfort zones and to be in the front lines of fostering world peace.

Let us remember the words of our Lord Jesus Christ, "Love one another; as I have loved you."[12] The words of Mother Teresa still challenge us today—that among them that need financial help, there is one who needs our love. Let us therefore hold fast to the cause that was set twenty-five years ago, and pray that our world will be a place of peace and harmony, hope and reconciliation, justice and respect. May God Bless us all.

12 Jn. 13:14.

FAREWELL MESSAGE
to the Outgoing Ambassador of Greece to Kenya

The Loundras' home,
Nairobi, Kenya,
December 20, 2011

I greet you most cordially, honorable Diplomats, Ambassadors, Consulars and distinguished Guests.

IT IS AN HONOR and a great joy that I have the opportunity to stand before you this evening and say a few words concerning His Excellency Dimitri, a man of true integrity, dignity, and purpose in whatever he sets out to do.

It is hard to believe that in a week's time, you will be retiring from service in the Ministry of Foreign Affairs. It is surely one of the most important dockets, since it deals with intricate and sometimes delicate balances in the interrelations of foreign governments. It therefore exerts unimaginable demands on the person serving in your capacity. For these, we applaud your immeasurable service to the nations of Greece and Kenya. Here, you were the voice, ears, and eyes of Greece, while at the same time bringing to Kenya the well-wishes of the people of Greece. We congratulate you for your long service full of selfless dedication and sacrifice. It goes without saying that a diplomat sacrifices the opportunity to stay at home among his or her own people, and instead accepts to take on life in a foreign land, making it home away from home, especially far people from his motherland. We commend the great effort you showed in your work in Kenya.

I cannot forget your great and cordial relationship with the Greek Orthodox Church in Kenya. You humbly graced all of our occasions, feasts, and celebrations. You truly have walked hand in hand with the Church in her growth during your service in Kenya. For all these memorable moments, our Pope and Patriarch of Alexandria and all Africa, His Beatitude Theodoros II, wishes that I honor you with the "Cross of Saint Mark" in recognition of your long service in the diplomatic sphere.

Today, I would also like to make a very special gesture of appreciation for your wife's work. I must say that Mrs. Christine Loundras's great love and affection for our philanthropic work has really touched our hearts. Your heart went out to the needy children in our Saint Clement Primary and Kindergarten, as well as the destitute orphans in our Nyeri Orphanage. We greatly appreciate your substantial contribution toward our philanthropic work. I also know, Mrs. Loundras, that you speak fluent Greek and actually feel that Cyprus is like your home. For this, allow me to humbly offer you a small Cypriot gift, in appreciation for your love and contribution toward many facets of philanthropy in Kenya.

It is true that immortality lives not in what we have done, but in the hearts of the people we have positively touched. Mr. and Mrs. Loundras, you came and touched our lives positively in your service among us. For these gifts and many more, we will always remember you and pray for you, wherever the grace of God may lead you.

I wish you joy and happiness in your retirement, and may God bless you abundantly. Amen.

SPEECH
at the Global Peace Initiative of Women

Gigiri, Kenya,
March 2, 2012

I greet all of you with the ancient greeting of peace: "Shalom!"

Allow me to read to you a statement recently made at the World Council of Churches:

> If all ears would hear the cries, no place would be truly silent. Many continue to reel from the impact of wars; ethnic and religious animosity, discrimination based on race and caste mar the facade of nations and leave ugly scars. Thousands are dead, displaced, homeless, refugees within their own homeland. Women and children often bear the brunt of conflicts: many women are abused, trafficked, killed; children are separated from their parents, orphaned, recruited as soldiers, abused. Citizens in some countries face violence by occupation, paramilitaries, guerrillas, criminal cartels or government forces. Citizens of many nations suffer governments obsessed with national security and armed might; yet these fail to bring real security, year after year. Thousands of children die each day from inadequate nutrition while those in power continue to make economic and political decisions that favor a relative few.[13]

WITH SUCH CHAOS existing in the world today, the subject of peace should not escape our lips and our activities. Peacemaking according to the Orthodox Church is not an optional commitment, but a requirement of the faith. This is what all humanity should

13 World Council of Churches (WCC), "Ecumenical Call to Just Peace," Geneva, Feb. 10, 2011.

work to achieve. The merging of faith and reason is one sure way to fend off war, and failure to accomplish this will cause the present world to misunderstand the religious approach. I will mention a few points that are essential for religious leaders and other stakeholders working with religious institutions.

The Church collaborating with others

Today the Church is called upon to dialogue with all concerned civic and religious groups. This means that the Church must realize that she cannot stand alone if amicable solutions are desired. Faith-based organizations have proved to have "more resources, more skilled personnel, a longer attention span, more experience, more dedication, and more success in fostering reconciliation than any government."[14] In many war-torn countries and towns, the social services and support groups and forums are religiously affiliated. Such would include hospitals, schools, social service centers, relief centers, and human rights programs, among others. In fact, religious institutions are deeply rooted in the local communities long before the conflicts arise. This is a position that is very helpful in peace-building initiatives. Religious bodies help to bring international awareness about the conflicts and violence within local communities. Having grassroots organizations allows for a warning of simmering conflicts to be broadcast to a wider sphere.

The religious bodies are communities of people, and thus they are in a position to reach, educate, inspire, and mobilize the masses. Most of the labor involved in religious institutions is actually free because the workers are also doing it for their community (themselves included), and for their faith. The religious leaders have moral credibility that political, governmental, media, and corporate leaders sometimes lack. In fact, over the past twenty-five years, almost half the Noble Peace Prize laureates have been religious leaders or religiously-inspired lay people. All these are ways that the Church and other religions can collaborate with other stakeholders in the field of peace.

"Only when grounded in God's peace can communities of faith be agents of reconciliation and peace with justice in homes, churches, and societies, as well as in political, social, and economic structures at the global level."[15] The Church that lives the peace it proclaims is what Jesus called a city set

14 Madeleine Albright, *The Mighty and the Almighty*, , Harper, 2006. 77.

15 WCC, "Ecumenical Call," Feb. 10, 2011.

on a hill for all to see.[16] Believers exercising the ministry of reconciliation entrusted to them by God in Christ point beyond the churches to what God is doing in the world.

Peace and human dignity

God, who is the peace of all, is reflected in the human person. He happens to be the owner of life, and therefore each human life is considered sacred. Each person not only "reflects God, but is the expression of God's creative work and the meaning of Christ's redemptive ministry."[17] In that case, then, "the pursuit of both justice and peace is designated to protect and promote the dignity of every" human person.[18]

Promotion of peace should lead to reducing war. Pope John Paul II declares that peace not merely the absence of war; "it involves mutual respect and confidence between peoples and nations."[19] Mutual disarmament and ratifications of treaties should be ongoing to prevent war. Nations defending others should avoid annihilation and know that while security is a right to all, it must be subject to divine law and limits defined by law. Educational programs on issues and effects of war should be ongoing toward prevention. True peace calls for reverence of life, which is God-given. Prayer, which leads to communion with God, will lead us to the peace given by God, while penance to eradicate sins and evil in our lives is paramount for communion with God. Prayer is itself incomplete without penance.

While geography, laws, ideologies, and other matters divide countries, the Church already possesses a unifying factor: Jesus Christ, who treasures each soul and body. Christ, "who hath made both one, and hath broken down the middle wall of partition between us."[20] Christians also believe and know that peace in its fullness will be achieved in the Kingdom of God. The Church is itself the Kingdom of God in history and should act as so. Therefore, churches should join hands and give their views to institutions dealing with peace: the political, cultural, economic, social, military, and legal sectors of life, among others.

Sin and conflict

Sin and hatred are obstacles to union with God. It was through sin that

16 Matt. 5:14.
17 "The Challenge of Peace," Catholic Bishops of the United States, May 3, 1983.
18 Ibid.
19 Pope John Paul II, "Homily on Holy Pentecost" (Liverpool, England), May 30, 1982.
20 Eph. 2:14.

man was disunited with God and thus lost the ultimate peace of God. The tension now lies in living in the *already, but not yet* Kingdom of God. The world we live in manifests the effects of the Fall, which brought wars that sometimes we cannot stop, just like we can't stop sin from existing until the next life begins. Although peace is possible but not assured, all Christians are called to work toward the new and coming peace, strengthening hope and faith. In the Kingdom of God, peace and justice will be fully realized, but all the same, both need to be worked for in this world.

> Wherever there is forgiveness, respect for human dignity, generosity, and care for the weak in the common life of humanity, we catch a glimpse—no matter how dim—of the gift of peace. It follows, therefore, that peace is lost when injustice, poverty, and disease—as well as armed conflict, violence, and war—inflict wounds on the bodies and souls of human beings, on society and on the earth.[21]

Prayer, the Orthodox liturgy, and peace

Anyone who has ever attended an Orthodox worship service will have noticed that the first supplication litany or petition, also known as "Ta Ephnika," or "The Great Litany of Peace," entails calling for peace. The first few lines call for "the heavenly peace, and salvation of our souls" and "for the peace of the whole world ... and for the union of all men." Then the Church goes on and prays for her country, the president, and all in civil authority; she prays for her parish and city; for every city and land, for temperate weather, abundance of the produce of the earth, and for peaceful times; she prays for travelers, for the sick, the suffering and those in captivity, and for their safekeeping. At the end the Litany, the Church asks God to spare us all from all afflictions, wrath, danger, and necessities.

Peace is God's gift to a broken but beloved world. We should strive to keep what Christ left for us when he said, "Peace I leave with you, my peace I give unto you."[22] This is the peace the Orthodox liturgy is talking about. Through the life and teachings, the death and resurrection of Jesus Christ, we perceive peace as both promise and present—a hope for the future and a gift for here and now.

All this shows that the Church is conscious of her surroundings, which are full of violence, pain, and sufferings. The Orthodox Church recognizes that the heavenly peace can also be experienced in this life; whether in

21 WCC, "Ecumenical Call," , Feb. 10, 2011.

22 Jn. 14:27.

public, civil, religious, or personal life. Peace in this set of supplications is guaranteed for those within and those outside the Church, whether they are present in the prayer meeting or absent. In this set of prayers, the biblical experience of love for the neighbor highly guides the Church in praying for the *other*. In the Orthodox tradition, there is no salvation without the *other*; the "other" here being every person, even those with whom you don't have a relationship either by religion, racial and ethnic ties, or by skin color. The emphasis is to pray for the entire creation of God, and more so all those created in the image and likeness of God. This fulfills the Lord's call for loving not only our neighbors but also our enemies.

> Ye have heard that it hath been said, Thou shalt love thy neighbor, and hate thine enemy. But I say unto you, Love your enemies, bless them that curse you, do good to them that hate you, and pray for them which spitefully use you, and persecute you: That ye may be the children of your Father which is in heaven.[23]

Women and peace

With the fact that women have organized this event, it would be unfair if I finished without mentioning something about women and peace. In most instances we think of women as victims of violence, and not necessarily as peace initiators and builders. God created man and woman equally and in his own image. Humanity was, from the beginning, a composition of both male and female. Women can participate in all avenues of bringing peace, just like their male counterparts.

Women are probably best equipped for meaningful peacemaking. This is because of their moral authority and their leadership role, which they practice within their homes and in their communities. Mothers are the first teachers of their children. They are thus the best in laying the foundation for lasting peace in the present and future life of their children. As informal educators they instill the proper discipline in their children by teaching them love for others, reconciliation and forgiveness, respect for others and the property of others, tolerance, a sense of justice, equity, and many other values. All these qualities are not only basic foundations for their lives, but are also necessary for establishing a sustainable peace. When children learn something from their parents they will trust in that

23 Matt. 5:43–45.

and even go ahead and teach their closest friends. If this kind of teaching continues, then an entire community could share the knowledge originally meant for one child.

Some of the most famous theologians and hierarchs of the Church were taught about the fundamental Christian life by women. Examples of women in this kind of role include Macrina the Elder, the grandmother of Saint Basil the Great and his brother Saint Gregory of Nyssa, as well as their sister Saint Macrina the Younger. Saint Gregory calls his sister a true philosopher and true theologian. The mothers of Saints John Chrysostom and Augustine were great facilitators of these men's faith in Christ and growth as Christians. In the scriptures we have Saint Priscilla who taught Apollo. "This woman took him, instructed him—that is, catechized him in the way of God, and made him a perfect teacher."[24] As educators, therefore, women should learn more in order to teach their families.

Women as ministry financiers

When Christ was on earth, his ministry included both men and women. The women who followed him, ministered to him and to his disciples by providing for them; a certain woman even anointed him before his burial.[25] After his burial, other women, whom we now call the "Myrrh Bearers," carried quite expensive oil, which they had bought for anointing Christ's body before they knew that he had risen from the dead.

The New Testament women who were involved in Christ's ministry helped to raise funds, working diligently to support his ministry. The evangelist Luke says that they "provided for [Christ] from their substance."[26] They followed Christ wherever he went to minister, even at the most crucial points in Christ's life, like the Crucifixion, as we see in Matthew: "And the many women, who followed Jesus from Galilee, ministering to him, were there looking on from afar,"[27] and furthermore, they even followed him at the tomb. They were in fact the first to know of the Resurrection of Christ.

In many instances, many local churches and most church projects have been started with the support and uplifting of women's associations or

24 Acts 18:24–28.
25 See Jn. 12:3.
26 Luke 8:1–3.
27 Matt. 27:55.

groups. Women, being the largest group among all churchgoers, have the best chances and opportunities to see what is lacking in their church communities. Again, as the main order keepers of homes, women have a better eye and chance to realize what is missing in their spiritual homes—that is, their parishes—and in the same way are more active in implementing whatever is missing. In today's practice, women are the greatest fundraisers of our Church. They are very effective in doing this, especially for peace-related issues.

Ministry to the afflicted

As a part of the Body of Christ, and as one person in union, when one is sick then the entire body, the entire humanity, is sick.[28] It is the work of the non-afflicted part of the Body of Christ to work with the ailing part and to see that the sick part of the Body of Christ gets well. All possible means of making the one sick join the ninety-nine healthy are used. The means used have to go by what the Church teaches because the aim is to go on living in the Church, but in a healthier spiritual, physical, and psychological manner. The Church does not watch only, but it walks with all who struggle in whatever difficulties they are going through. Women have been seen as the best in helping others due to their emotional characteristics; the fact that they are said to have soft and good hearts. I feel that the characteristics of women have not been fully utilized by peacemakers in the past, and that the time has come to engage our women in the task of peacemaking, for the sake of the Church and the world beyond.

I will close by asking that the peace of God be always with us all! Amen.

28 1 Cor. 12:26.

MESSAGE
of Congratulations to the Newly Elected President of Kenya[29]

April 9, 2013

Your Excellency,

On behalf of the Orthodox Church in Kenya and on my behalf, I extend my sincere congratulations to you on becoming the fourth president of the Republic of Kenya. I wish you continued success, God's guidance, and strength while working for the development, common good, and unity of the people of Kenya, an action you have already shown by inviting your political opponents and their supporters to work with you. I am confident that you will lead this country to a brighter future, and make Kenya a more valuable contributor to regional development, as well as the its development in the international arena.

I hope that, with you as president, the lost closeness, contact, and friendship between the government of Kenya and the Orthodox Church in Kenya will be restored. The Orthodox Church has been a valuable institution in the struggle against colonial rule and the development of this country after its independence. The relationship between the first president of Kenya, the late Mzee Jomo Kenyatta, and the first president of Cyprus, Archbishop Makarios III, was founded amidst their mutual struggle for their nations' independence. This bond strengthened the Church's and

29 His Excellency Uhuru Muigai Kenyatta.

the government's friendship further. I hope that you can help renew, extend, and continue this friendship, taking it to the next level.

May I again congratulate you in your new position as the duly elected President of the Republic of Kenya, wishing you every success in discharging the duties of your position. The Orthodox Church in Kenya pledges her continued support and highest considerations of you and all organs of your administration and government.

Sincerely, in the Lord's service.
+ ARCHBISHOP MAKARIOS

ADDRESS
on Orthodoxy in East Africa[30]

Saint Vlash Theological Academy,
Durres, Albania,
September 3, 2013

I greet you all in the Name of our Lord Jesus Christ!

ALLOW ME to first express my gratitude for having this opportunity to address you on a subject that is so dear to my heart, and one that has become part of my life in so many ways. As a church historian, a professor of theology in the African continent since 1981, and a hierarch in Africa since 1992, I have much to share with you, but due to the limited time we have, allow me to go through a brief outline of how the Orthodox Church was planted in East Africa and its current status. I speak especially of Kenya, which is where I serve, and which is the largest Archdiocese of the Greek Orthodox Patriarchate of Alexandria and all Africa.

> I am come a light into the world, that whosoever believeth in me should not abide in darkness.[31]

Orthodoxy is the expression of tradition and the teaching of Jesus Christ from the time of Pentecost, when tongues of the fire from the Holy Spirit

30 At a formal consultation of Evangelicals, Lutherans, and Orthodox.
31 Jn. 12:46.

were sent to the disciples. From Pentecost to today, Orthodoxy has adhered to the apostolic tradition.

The colonial government, the missionaries and the splinter groups

Orthodoxy in East Africa had a rather unique origin as it was not the result of missionary endeavors, nor was it originally inspired by an non-African introduction. East African Orthodoxy had two focal points: Uganda and central Kenya. In the 1930s, it was the attitude of the colonial government and the foreign missionaries (particularly from the colonial motherland: the United Kingdom) that forced the Africans to look for an alternative Christian denomination that would act differently upon their lives, and that had nothing to do with colonialism.

The colonial government did not hold enfranchisement as one of their goals, nor did it have the finances to assume the responsibilities of educating the Africans. Thus, they allowed the missionaries to have direct supervision over the education of the Africans. In the beginning, many Africans were not interested in the white man's education, especially because they thought the colonialists would eventually go back to their country and leave the local system to continue as it did before their arrival. As time went on, the Africans realized that the white man was there to stay, and that the western-style education gave better opportunities for employment as office workers, teachers, etc. And, with these jobs came better living standards.

Due to their misconceptions of the African culture, the missionaries held that Christianity must be linked with a cultural transference, an attitude that led ultimately to confrontation, especially among the Kikuyu of central Kenya. The matter of female circumcision, which erupted in 1929, was the straw that broke the camel's back. The Protestant Church Missionary Society (CMS) and the Presbyterian Church of Scotland (PCS) expanded their war against this cultural practice. This led to increasing pressure by the missionaries, with the consent of the colonial regime, for the Kikuyu to give up the practice, which was thought by the missionaries to be primitive. But, this interference was strongly opposed by the Africans. For this reason, the Kikuyu boycotted the mission churches in large numbers.

During this time, schools were church-sponsored. Once the Kikuyu had abandoned the mission churches, they had no schools. Thus, they set up their own schools by their own efforts. There were two groups doing this: the Independents and the Karing'a Association. The Kikuyu community firmly supported their schools, and they soon gained numbers not only in the area of Kikuyu and Nairobi, but also in the interior, rural areas. The established missions were much opposed to the schools and tried to pressure the government to close them. However, the demand for schools and the overwhelming need for more preserved the independent schools.

The formation of the African Orthodox Church

The word "karing'a" in Kikuyu means orthodox or pure, and the members of this group wanted to maintain their cultural traditions, identity, and beliefs. They also wanted Christianity in its purest form. Although the organization of the Karing'a schools provided for the educational needs of their children, they were without a church affiliation. Between 1935 and 1937 the independent KISA (Kikuyu Independent School Association) and the Karing'a KKEA (Kikuyu Karing'a Education Association) were coming closer in their efforts to feed their people academically, as well as spiritually. The local organizations had heard of Bishop Daniel William Alexander, a hierarch from South Africa. They raised funds and arranged for the bishop to come to Kenya and provide instruction of a religious nature to members of both organizations with the desire to establish an indigenous church based on a legitimate origin, and which would also be African led.

Bishop Daniel Alexander was the leader of the African Orthodox Church in South Africa.[32] This church was independent of any white-dominated church organization. It had association with the American African Orthodox Church. Bishop Alexander spent sixteen months in the Kikuyu areas of central Kenya, operating from a base in Murang'a. He baptized, lectured, and provided specific religious training to young men who had been put forward by both the Independent and the Karing'a Associations. Two men from Kiambu and Nyeri were ordained priests. These became the first priests of the African Orthodox Church of Kenya. The others, from Embu and Murang'a, were ordained as deacons, but they chose not to follow orthodoxy, but instead eventually established the African

32 Consecrated bishop in 1927 by Bishop George McGuire, founder of the African Orthodox Church, Bishop Daniel died in May, 1970. See "The African Orthodox Church: An Analysis of its First Decade," *Church History*, vol 58, no. 4 (Cambridge Univ. Press, Dec. 1989).

Independent Pentecostal Church. During the 1930s, Bishop Alexander had also ordained two priests in Uganda. They, too, had rejected the foreign dominated churches—in their case, the Anglican Church.

But how was Bishop Daniel Alexander connected with the orthodoxy of apostolic tradition? After World War I, in the United States of America, there was a strong demonstration of black independence and cultural nationalism. Out of this demand for recognition of black rights, blacks of West Indian origin formed the African Orthodox Church (AOC). This church was closely related to the Universal Negro Improvement Association (UNIA). The African Orthodox Church was comprised mainly of black Anglicans who were disaffected by the white dominance of their religious lives. The church made use of UNIA's official information service, "The Negro World," to send out its message of the creation of a black church based on apostolic traditions.

In 1892, a group of black Methodists who were against apartheid and racism in South Africa had split from the Methodist Church to form the Ethiopian Church, a group that later split into several groups in their search for episcopal links. Daniel William Alexander, a former Anglican clergyman belonging to the splinter Ethiopian Church, was the one who, in 1924, petitioned the AOC to open its doors in South Africa. Eventually, Alexander became the first African-based bishop in the African Orthodox Church.

George Alexander McGuire, who came from the British West Indies, headed the African Orthodox Church in America. He had been baptized an Anglican, educated by Moravians, and became a pastor of that sect at Saint Croix in the Virgin Islands. McGuire later immigrated to the United States and worked for some time with the African Methodist Episcopal Church. From there, he moved to the Protestant Episcopal Church and became archdeacon for the blacks who worked in the Diocese of Arkansas. This position was the highest to which a black could aspire at this time.

However, McGuire broke away from the Protestant Episcopal Church in New York and became deeply involved with the Black Nationalist movement being instituted by UNIA. He became the organization's Chaplain General in 1920, and within one year established the AOC. This was a period of black disillusionment and disenchantment with their existing status, and with the enactment of discriminatory laws. Such laws were much the case in the South, but in the northern cities the discrimination was often worse. It was a time when the idea of separate development of the races was being aired. The mainline churches, such as the Anglican Church, wanted to bring the faith to the blacks, but did not want to be seen as advocates of political and social equality.

McGuire, motivated by his elevation as the Chaplain General of the UNIA movement, conceived the idea of a universal black church that would unite blacks of all denominations. The leader of UNIA opposed this concept of a universal black church with denominational affiliation. McGuire resigned from UNIA and set up the African Orthodox Church, having himself declared its bishop by a local synod.

One wonders about the motivation in the selection of orthodoxy as the aspired goal. The answer is that the Orthodox Church was never associated with racism, colonialism, or religious imperialism, and it had not involved itself in universal missionary activity. Further, in America, the Orthodox people were not associated with the social establishment, as they were, for the most part, new immigrants, who often faced the same discrimination as the blacks. Further, the Orthodox Church existed in Egypt, Ethiopia, India, and the Middle East, and in the eyes of the AOC, they were kindred souls. Previous encounters with the Roman Catholic and the Anglican churches had brought rejection. Neither denomination wanted to recognize, or include the AOC in its communion. There were agreeable discussions with the Russian Orthodox Church, although the Russian Orthodox hierarchy wanted to reduce the AOC to mission status.

Finally, McGuire made contact with a bishop of a schismatic catholic church known as the Old Catholic Church, and from them he received consecration. This group's bishop, Bishop Rene Vilatte, had received his consecration from one of the Oriental Orthodox churches. His title was Mar Timotheos, Old Catholic Archbishop of North America and First Primate of the American Catholic Church. He was one of the occasional individuals who had valid episcopal orders, but was never recognized by any of the established churches. Bishop Rene Vilatte was born in Paris, and was educated by Roman Catholics. For many years, he facilitated discussions between Roman Catholics and Protestants before migrating to Canada, and later to the United States. He had missionary zeal, and eventually was ordained a priest in the Old Catholic Church by the Bishop of Bern, Switzerland: Edward Hezrog. Bishop Rene returned to the United States, where he continued to work, but he met many difficulties, particularly in achieving the episcopacy. Since he could not induce either the legitimate

Roman Catholic Church to consecrate him as a bishop, nor the hierarch of the Russian Orthodox Church, he looked far and wide for an alternative.

In 1920, some Roman Catholics in Southern India headed by a Goan priest, Antonio Francisco Xavier Alvarez, broke with Rome. Father Antonio sought consecration from the Syro-Jacobite Church of Malabar. This is an Oriental Orthodox Church under the jurisdiction of Patriarch Ignatius Peter III of Antioch, who did, indeed, give his blessing for this consecration. In turn, Rene Vilatte made his request to Bishop Alvarez to elevate him to the episcopate. Alvarez agreed and Vilatte went to Ceylon to be consecrated bishop. Vilatte pledged his church and himself to the authority of the Patriarch of Antioch, and in return was made the archbishop of the Old Catholic Church of America and granted the rights and privileges of a metropolitan.

Rene Vilatte, as bishop made more than twenty subsequent consecrations of new bishops in new churches. These consecrations became doubtful because they were made outside the authority of the Church, a fact that promoted the Syro-Jacobite Church officially in 1938 to withdraw recognition of the seceded churches. Further, Vilatte was accused of not upholding the canons, nor did he remain within the jurisdiction of the Church of Antioch. This rejection of Rene Vilatte and his churches did not have much impact on the African Orthodox Church in the United States, but it did have serious implications for the churches in Uganda and Kenya.

The link with the Greek Orthodox Patriarchate of Alexandria

Fr. Nicodemos Sarikas, a Greek priest belonging to the Patriarchate of Alexandria, was the one who connected the East Africans to the Patriarchate of Alexandria; through him, the Church of Uganda was the first to know that it was not canonically Orthodox. Fr. Nicodemos had worked in South Africa and then resided in Moshi, Tanzania. Hence, the church in Uganda immediately entered into correspondence with Meletios Metaxakis, the Greek Patriarch of Alexandria and all Africa. His Beatitude, Patriarch Meletios, was sympathetic and able to guide the Ugandans well. In 1946, His Beatitude Christophoros II, Patriarch of Alexandria, accepted the Ugandan Orthodox Christians into his flock. In 1959, a diocese was created for East Africa and a bishop given the title of Irinoupolis, in honor of Dar es Salaam. This bishop resided in Uganda and looked after both the Africans and the Greek planters, who had come to Africa after the dispersion of Smyrna.

The Church of Uganda, which had links with the Church of Kenya, informed those within that the AOC lacked authentic apostolicity. The Ugandan Church thereafter helped them through the process of uniting with the Patriarchate of Alexandria and all Africa. The Kenyan Church, thirsty to be connected with an apostolic Church that had no doubts, was pleased to be connected at last to one that had her headquarters in Africa.

The situation in Kenya was very difficult in this period. By October, 1952, both the KKEA and KISA were charged with subversion, and their schools were closed. It was widely thought that they were connected directly with the Mau Mau, who sought independence from Great Britain. The government offered to reopen the schools, but only under direct government supervision, or under the missions. A few of the schools of KISA re-opened, but all of the Karing'a schools remained closed. The AOC was forced to keep a low profile. For ten years, Karing'a Orthodox Christians were not allowed to participate in public worship, yet their faith sustained them until the state of emergency was lifted.

After Kenya gained its independence in 1963, President Jomo Kenyatta lifted the ban on the AOC. The Kikuyu Orthodox, under the leadership of Father Arthur G. Gathuna, opted to revive the Orthodox Faith in Kenya. Further links were made with the Orthodox Church in Western Kenya, which had initially received the Faith from Uganda.

The Orthodox Patriarchal Ecclesiastical School: Makarios III Archbishop of Cyprus

Among the many developments since independence, none can be more significant than the construction of the Orthodox Patriarchal Seminary in Nairobi. From the day of its opening and its functioning as a seminary, Orthodoxy in East Africa has grown by leaps and bounds, all within the framework of true Orthodoxy under the Patriarchate of Alexandria and All Africa. The Orthodox Patriarchal Seminary was the brainchild of Archbishop Makarios III, hierarch of the Orthodox Church of Cyprus and President of the Republic of Cyprus. In April, 1957, His Beatitude made a visit to Nairobi and celebrated the Divine Liturgy in the Cathedral of Saints Anargyroi on Valley Road. Later, as president of Cyprus, he made a state visit to Kenya as guest of the late Jomo Kenyatta, president of the

Republic of Kenya and his personal friend. It was during this visit in 1970, that he saw the heart of the African Orthodox Church.

As a hierarch, His Beatitude made a pastoral visit to Kenya in March, 1971 and performed mass baptisms in Nairobi and Nyeri. After visiting the poorly structured local seminary at Kagira in Nairobi that was led by Father George Gathuna, His Beatitude sympathized with the situation and saw the need for a seminary to meet the clerical needs, not only of the Kenyan Church, but of the entire Church of East Africa. He was also highly impressed by the favorable attitude of the government of Kenya toward his ideas, including that of the late President Kenyatta.

On March 22, 1971, Archbishop Makarios laid the foundation stone of the Orthodox Patriarchal Seminary at Riruta with the blessing of His Beatitude Nicholas, Pope and Patriarch of Alexandria and All Africa. In his address on that auspicious day, Archbishop Makarios said:

> "To help our African brotherhood, and with the blessings of Almighty God, we create here a center from which new apostles of Christ will spread the word of the Lord in this part of the world and administer the comforting joy of the Gospel in the hearts of our beloved African brothers."

He pointed out that the seminary went beyond its religious purpose in that it was a symbol and expressed link of friendship between the peoples of Kenya and Cyprus.

The ensuing political crisis that befell Cyprus in 1974 delayed the opening of the seminary until 1981. But right before that, one incidental and God-planned meeting made things go very fast:

While I was walking in the corridors of Apostoliki Diakonia in October of 1981, I met the then Bishop of Androusa, Dr. Anastasios Yannoulatos, who was also the General Director of Apostoliki Diakonia, and the newly elected Acting Archbishop (*locum tenens*) of the Holy Archbishopric of Irinoupolis (*i.e.* East Africa). Bishop Anastasios knew about my previous endeavors and connections with the seminary in Kenya and invited me to join him in his new Archdiocese for the same reasons, which I accepted. I thought I was to going stay in Kenya for about three months and then go back home. But, I have ever since been in Kenya, a place that has become my home and where I have been witnessing the spreading of the gospel of our Lord Jesus Christ in the heart of Africa.

The seminary has been in operation since 1981, initially training catechists and priests of the Archbishopric of Irinoupolis, which is comprised of Kenya, Uganda, and Tanzania. In 1993, it was made the Patriarchal Ecclesiastical School for all prospective clergy and theologians of the Patriarchate of Alexandria and All Africa. The seminary presently houses between forty-five and one hundred students, annually, and these come from different parts of the African continent. They are all offered a fully sponsored education, including room and board, school fees, travel, all stationeries, and other personal and academic necessities. Some graduates of this seminary have gone abroad to study and, upon their return, have become members of the teaching and administrative staff of this same seminary. Some perform these tasks in their respective diocese.

Orthodoxy in East Africa today and her ministry

Today, in East Africa, there are five Orthodox bishops: two in Tanzania—for Dar es Salaam and Mwanza—one in Uganda, one in Burundi, one Rwanda, and one in Kenya (the one addressing you). Three of these hierarchs are of East African origin. At present, there are three hundred Orthodox priests in Kenya, forty-five in Uganda, seventy-five in Tanzania, and five in both Burundi and Rwanda. All of these clergymen are Africans, almost all of them being graduates of the noted Patriarchal Seminary in Nairobi.

The Church of Kenya has, in her missionary endeavors, initiated different projects in her efforts to sustain her Christians and those surrounding them with both spiritual and tangible help. At present, some of these projects include: three tertiary colleges, over forty preschools, fifty primary schools, thirty secondary schools, fifteen clinics, at least three official orphanages, over twenty borehole projects, over thirty feeding programs for orphans and disadvantaged children, various clothing and food distribution projects, and finally a scholarship program that helps to raise school fees for all levels of education for disadvantaged children, youth, and parents who want to attend school or pursue further education. Other projects include building permanent churches where only semi-permanent ones existed, or where only a community of believers existed without even a roof, and other new and various upcoming projects. There are many ongoing national and local programs concerning Sunday school children, the youth, and gatherings for women and men.

Translations of the Orthodox divine services in local languages of the people are being done in many of the languages of East Africa and beyond. At present, over 100 new translations and re-edited editions have been completed since the Patriarchal Seminary started the translation project. These are either printed by friends abroad or done locally in Kenya. The rest of the East African dioceses have almost the same projects in different formats, only slightly fewer than those in Kenya.

As can be noted from the stated projects, most pertain to education, because education remains the only way to fully install African leaders as the original formation plan of the AOC of Kenya had intended. This is the main reason why the Orthodox Church in East Africa has fewer than five missionaries from outside Africa, while the rest are largely East Africans.

In the Archdiocese of Kenya, I am the only member of the clergy who was not born in Africa. However, having stayed in Kenya for over three decades, which is more time than I have stayed in my own country, I have also earned the title of being an East African.

To say Orthodoxy in East Africa is perfect or free of problems would be untrue. The Church, which is truly the African Orthodox Church, is struggling to find ways and means to support herself and to build upon the foundations of the original work of the apostle Mark, Evangelist of Africa. The Church has benefited from aid from Greece, Cyprus, Finland, and the Greek Orthodox Jurisdiction in America in the form of financial and human resources. At the moment, when some of these major donor countries are facing critical financial crises, things have not been easy for the East African Church. Plans to try to initiate local funding are underway, but this may take time before anything substantial comes out of it. All in all, we pray and hope that orthodoxy in East Africa comes to a point of maturity when it will be able to plan and implement self-sustaining growth and strength.

May God bless the Orthodox Church of Africa and all her leaders as they continue evangelizing in the lands of East Africa.

ON THE LEGACY OF
Archbishop Makarios III of Cyprus on His One Hundredth Birthday[33]

Nairobi, Kenya
October 15, 2013

To quote Mzee Jomo Kenyatta, first President of the Republic of Kenya:

> It is with profound shock and great sadness that I have learned of the tragic, untimely death of Archbishop Makarios.[34] President Makarios' life-long struggle for the true political independence of Cyprus, social and religious justice for all people, and his personal devotion to the service of humankind were admired by the many friends who will remember him for a long time. The noble ideals and universal principles for which Archbishop Makarios lived should remain a guiding-light for the entire world. In his passing away, Kenya has indeed lost an irreplaceable friend.

It was August 3, 1977 when the Archbishop and President of Cyprus Makarios died. His close friend, Mzee Jomo Kenyatta, who admired and respected him, made the above-mentioned statement. The story of the two builders of nations is briefly outlined below.

33 Paper presented on the 32nd opening ceremony of the Archbishop Makarios III Orthodox Patriarchal Ecclesiastical School.

34 Statement made on August 3, 1977 by First President of the Republic of Kenya, Mzee Jomo Kenyatta.

Building a nation—building a church

In Cyprus, as well as in Kenya, and perhaps universally too, the name of Makarios will always be associated with the end of the era of colonialism. Cyprus held a very important place in the history of colonial rule due to the fact that the leader of the struggle for the independence of the island was Archbishop Makarios, who was at the same time the head of the Orthodox Church of Cyprus and the *Ethnarch*, the leader of the nation. Kenya, during the same time, was also under colonial rule and the people or fighters, known as Mau Mau, were also trying to liberate Kenya from the British administration. Their leader was Mzee Jomo Kenyatta, a fervent nationalist and sincere fighter.

I believe that it was during the time of his exile that Archbishop Makarios understood the need for establishing missionary work in Kenya. When he was freed from the Seychelles Islands, he spent one week in Nairobi on his way to Athens. It was then that he met for the first time the Kenyan people and made public statements for freedom and justice to those under British administration. Archbishop Makarios and his entourage stayed at the Norfolk Hotel, Nairobi. On Sunday, April 14, 1957, he celebrated the Divine Liturgy in the Cathedral of Saints Anargyroi, Valley Road, in Nairobi. Thus, he became the first Orthodox bishop ever to officiate in that church. That day will remain a memorable ecclesiastical event in Kenya.

It was after the independence of both Kenya and Cyprus that Archbishop Makarios returned. In January, 1970, President Jomo Kenyatta invited Archbishop Makarios to pay an official visit to Kenya. As the guest of President Jomo Kenyatta, the Archbishop was received with much warmth and was welcomed not only as a friend of Kenya, but also as a hero and a national leader. It was during this visit that he came to know of the existence of the African Orthodox Church, because when he arrived at the airport, some priests of the African Orthodox Church were waiting to welcome him. With much joy, Archbishop Makarios felt the need to join this group in spreading the Orthodox faith in Kenya amidst the newly-found peace and freedom after independence, virtues that were part of his deepest wishes and desires. When the Archbishop visited what Father George Gathuna and his group were using for a seminary, a structure that could only be equated to a chicken house in Cyprus, he immediately made up his mind regarding his first contribution for the Kenyan Church.

Africans follow the Orthodox Faith

When the Archbishop had left Kenya, on his way back to Cyprus he stopped in Athens and made the following statement:

> What especially moved me was the fact that in the Paschan region of Africa there are thousands of Africans who follow the Orthodox faith. I sincerely believe that Greece can contribute greatly to the Christianizing of hundreds of thousands of Africans, and through Orthodoxy, the Greek spirit will shed light through the immense African continent.

This statement brought the attention of many in thinking about the Orthodox Church in East Africa. The Archbishop did not stop his desire there, but soon communicated with the Patriarchate of Alexandria about his interest in cooperating with the East Africans in the spread of the Gospel, as the whole of the African continent was under the jurisdiction of Alexandria.

When all the formalities were ready, Archbishop Makarios paid a private but pastoral visit to Kenya (March 19–22, 1971). The *Sunday Nation* reported:

> The Cypriot leader, who arrived here on Friday on a three-day private visit, has every reason—as he said in Embakasi—to feel comparatively at home in Kenya... the Archbishop said he was happy to be in Kenya briefly, secure in the belief that the Orthodox community were winning because Kenya's Uhuru struggle was entering its most crucial phase. Most of the local "Karing'a" (who were also known as Independent and Orthodox) denominational leaders and educators, among them some of the ordained priests now playing host to President Makarios, were in detention. President Makarios' visit should be able to disabuse those who in their calculated ignorance misinterpret African-Christian-Orthodoxy as 'paganism.'[35]

35 Henry Gathigira, "Makarios quite right to feel at home," *Sunday Nation*, March 21, 1971.

An offering to the African youth

Before leaving Cyprus, Archbishop Makarios made the following statement:

> The purpose of my visit to Kenya is of purely religious nature and importance. I am going to Nairobi, where today I shall lay the foundation stone of a seminary to be built by the Cyprus Archbishopric. The seminary will greatly contribute, I believe, to the promotion of missionary work in East Africa. The seminary will cater to African youth, who, once educated in the Orthodox religion, will subsequently serve as priests and missionaries on the African continent.
>
> I realized the possibilities of developing missionary work in Africa a year ago, during my state visit to the East African countries. I have since had the idea that the establishment of a well-organized seminary would be a significant contribution to this end. The idea has been readily adopted by His Beatitude, Patriarch Nicholas of Alexandria, under whose jurisdiction comes the Orthodox Church all over Africa. The realization of this idea has also been encouraged by the fact that the Kenyan government has made available a suitable site for the construction of the seminary and particularly by the very favorable attitude of President Jomo Kenyatta toward the project.
>
> The existence of a very wide field for Christians in Africa is also evidenced by the fact that Africans have been joining the Orthodox Church in large numbers. During my three-day stay in Kenya, I shall conduct mass christenings of some five thousand natives in two towns. It can be said that there has been no similar event since the christianization of the Slavs. And I am certain that many thousands of Africans may adopt Orthodoxy. I am glad that the Church of Cyprus has been given the divine blessing and privilege to be able to contribute to the development of missionary work in African countries.

As a modest and unassuming man, Archbishop Makarios III, full of charm and kindness, inspired many among the Africans and elsewhere, and linked his life with the missionary work in Africa in such a strong way that the locals consider him to be apart of the African Nation. He did indeed manifest all his charisma and used it to increase the Orthodox faith in Africa as a duty of his ecclesiastical mission to the world.

A mass baptism

On two occasions, during his visit to Kenya, he performed mass baptisms of more than five thousand people, mostly of the Kikuyu tribe. The two ceremonies took place, one at Waithaka and the other at Nyeri. After the performance of those baptisms, it was reported in the African press that there had been requests by members of the Orthodox Church all over the country for Archbishop Makarios to baptize them. It was reported:

> His Beatitude, the President of the Republic of Cyprus, Archbishop Makarios, yesterday conducted mass christenings of one thousand Africans, men and women of all ages, in an atmosphere of devout concentration at a suburb of Nairobi .... All members of His Beatitude's entourage acted as godfathers to one or more children, most of them chose to be named Makarios. His Beatitude gave a silver cross to each and every one baptized.

A theological seminary and a technical school

On March 22, 1971, Archbishop Makarios laid the foundation stone of the Orthodox seminary in Riruta, outside Nairobi. At the end of the ceremony, he gave the following address:

> Your Excellencies, dear Brothers, Ladies and Gentlemen,
>
> When, a year ago, I visited this country, at the kind invitation of my friend President Jomo Kenyatta, I had the opportunity to meet many African Orthodox Christians and also Orthodox Christians in other countries of East Africa, with whom I discussed their religious problems. These meetings and discussions have led me to the idea of establishing a theological seminary in Nairobi, which would serve the religious needs of the Orthodox Church in East Africa. And today, with the blessing of God, I place the foundation stone of the seminary of this beautiful site, which was so generously made available for this purpose by the government of Kenya. Our action today in founding this seminary is to help our African brothers in their search for the ways of God in Christian virtue and brotherhood. With the blessings of the almighty God we create here a

center from which new apostles of Christ will spread the word of the Lord in this part of the world and administer the comforting joy of the Gospel in the hearts of our beloved African brothers.

This seminary, beyond the religious purpose that it will serve, will constitute a symbol and an expression of a permanent link of friendship and brotherhood between the people of Kenya and the people of Cyprus. The foundation of this seminary constitutes yet another cornerstone in the consolidation of the existing friendly relations between our two countries, relations that have been founded by the belief in common ideas and common struggles.

I am deeply grateful to President Kenyatta and the government of Kenya for the generous gesture in making available this splendid terrain, thus making my idea of establishing this seminary a reality. I also wish to express my warm thanks to the Minister of Foreign Affairs of Kenya, Dr. (Njoroge) Mungai, for his valuable contribution to this project, and to all those who have helped in various ways.

Parallel to the seminary, I have plans for the establishment of a technical school for Kenyan boys and girls. I believe that such an institution will contribute in a small way to the efforts of the great leader of Kenya, Mzee Jomo Kenyatta, to develop the technical and industrial possibilities of this wonderful country. We in Cyprus are following with great interest the untiring efforts of the government of Kenya and especially of its inspired leader, to make this country prosperous and happy. A great deal has already been achieved in many fields since Kenya has gained its freedom.

And now, with the blessings of God, I place this foundation stone of the Orthodox Christian seminary with the wish to have the joy of inaugurating it in the near future.

THE ACT OF THE FOUNDATION

To the Glory of God the Father, the Son, and the Holy Spirit. The President of the Republic of Kenya, being His Excellency Mzee Jomo Kenyatta; the Patriarch of Alexandria and all Africa, being His Beatitude Nicholas VI; and the Bishop in the Holy Archbishopric of Irinoupolis, being His Eminence, Metropolitan Nicodemus, today, Monday the 22nd of March, the year of our Lord, one thousand nine hundred and seventy-one, in a holy ceremony and by the hand of His Beatitude the Archbishop of Cyprus and President of

> the Republic of Cyprus, Makarios III, the foundation stone was laid of this theological seminary in Nairobi which is built at the expense of the Holy Archbishopric of Cyprus.[36]

The same morning, the President of Kenya had met Archbishop Makarios and said that the Archbishop's name was like a passport throughout Kenya, whose people considered His Beatitude as a symbol of struggle and a fighter for world freedom. President Kenyatta also expressed great joy for the spreading of Christianity in Kenya by Archbishop Makarios and said that he himself was a Christian.

Common struggle for freedom

Early in the morning of March 23, Archbishop Makarios, on his arrival at Nicosia International Airport, made the following statement:

> My short visit to Kenya has been for me a religious experience that I shall always recall with emotion. Thousands of Africans of every age; families and individuals, have adopted the Christian Orthodox religion through baptism. Within two days, I conducted mass christenings of more than five thousand persons. And the numerous arrivals to the christening would continue for days, if it were possible to prolong my staying the country.
>
> The mass christenings conducted constitute an event that will occupy a position in our church history and, especially, in the history of foreign missionary work by the Orthodox Church. A black Orthodox church is being built and expanded at this moment in the Paschan part of the African continent, and the flock of this church will, in the future, number millions of Africans. I am glad that among the godfathers of this African Church are members of the Church of Cyprus.
>
> My visit to Kenya was of a religious nature and had no official character from the political point of view. However, there were many friendly manifestations toward Cyprus, both by the Kenyan government and the people. Yesterday morning, I had a meeting of common interest in a cordial atmosphere. The laying of the foundation stone of the seminary was attended by the Minister of Foreign

36 Address given March 22, 1971 by His Beatitude, the Archbishop of Cyprus and President of the Republic of Cyprus, Makarios III.

> Affairs of Kenya, Mr. (Njoroge) Mungai, who in an address to the gathering referred to as Cyprus's and Kenya's liberation struggles and stressed the friendly bonds between the two countries.[37]

Seminary completed a month before the "coup d'etat"

The construction of the seminary was completed in June, 1974, a month before the *coup d'etat* against Archbishop Makarios. Archbishop Makarios spent about five months in exile, during which he was trying to find a peaceful solution of the Cyprus problem. When he returned to Cyprus in December 1974, the island was in great distress, owing to the two invasions by Turkey. The archbishop did everything he could, using all his qualities and gifts, to improve the conditions of the two hundred thousand refugees displaced by the Turkish occupation. Due to these circumstances, the seminary was not in a position to open, but when the general situation started to improve he decided to start preparing the school.

Archbishop Makarios's next visit to Kenya was in August, 1976, when he had an opportunity to see the buildings of the seminary as well as of the technical school completed. During his stay in Nairobi, between August 10–26, 1976, Archbishop Makarios attended a Divine Liturgy that was celebrated at the Holy Trinity church in Muguga (Central Kenya). The following is a sermon that he gave on that occasion:

> Once again I am visiting your country. My ties with Kenya go back to the days of my exile to the Seychelles, 20 years ago. At that time Kenya was a British colony and the Kenyans, under the leadership of Jomo Kenyatta, were struggling for freedom and independence. When I was released from the Seychelles, and on my way back I came to Nairobi where I stayed for a week. Jomo Kenyatta, with some other leaders, were then in prison. During my short stay, I visited camps where many freedom fighters were detained. I also met many leading personalities, from whom I learned certain details of the then prevailing situation. A few years later, your struggle for freedom was crowned with success, and Kenya got its independence, and so did my country, Cyprus.

37 Address given March 23, 1971by His Beatitude, the Archbishop of Cyprus and President of the Republic of Cyprus, Makarios III.

Kenya is now under the leadership of the great leader, Jomo Kenyatta, who is making significant strides toward development and progress. Cyprus and Kenya, since their independence, have developed and maintained very friendly relations and have cooperation in many fields.

During my official visit here, at the kind invitation of President Kenyatta, I conceived the idea of establishing a Orthodox Christian seminary to meet the needs of the African faithful. With the permission of the government and the blessings of Patriarch Nicholas of Alexandria, under whose spiritual jurisdiction comes the diocese of Irinoupolis and the entire Orthodox Church in Africa, I founded the seminary in Nairobi. I planned this short stay here on my way back from the Colombo Conference to exchange views with your Metropolitan, the Most Reverend Frumentios, and to make arrangements for the opening of the seminary that was completed three years ago. I hope that by next January the seminary will function and will receive students from Kenya and East Africa generally. The students will be prepared for priesthood. I shall have the pleasure of being with you again at the official opening of the seminary.

Taking this opportunity, I wish to convey to you and to all Kenyans heartfelt greetings from the people of Cyprus and the expression of our appreciation for the stand of the Government and the people of Kenya on the Cyprus problem. President Kenyatta proved a trusted friend of Cyprus at critical moments. As you know, Turkey has invaded my country and a great part of Cyprus is now under Turkish occupation. Turkey violated the independence and territorial integrity of my country, and the people of Cyprus are striving once again for freedom. In our struggle, we have the support and solidarity of all freedom-loving countries, and Kenya is among the first. Despite the many difficulties, we do not lose hope that we will be able to restore our territorial integrity. We are determined not to submit to brutal force. Justice may be trampled upon temporarily but, in the end, it will prevail. God is just and will see that justice is done.

Once again, my dear brothers and sisters in Christ, I express my thanks for the warm welcome and the manifestations of your love for me and for my country. I bestow upon you the blessings of the

Church of Cyprus. May the grace of God be always with you and may the Spirit inspire and guide you in your life.[38]

Much hope rests in the Makarios III Patriarchal Seminary for the future needs of the rapidly growing East African Orthodox missions. Future historians will assess Makarios's great role in establishing a good relationship with Africa and especially Kenya, when he baptized thousands into the Orthodox faith and founded the theological seminary. His remarkable work for the African people, and his contribution to the expansion of orthodoxy, were much appreciated by the African people as well as by the leaders of the other Orthodox churches.

Its full significance, the full meaning of his life and work for Africa, and the renewal of Christian vision, is something we do not yet see, but that we may come to see if we are faithful to the vision that he himself saw and followed. He dreamed about Africa being full of the light of orthodoxy through his love for all human beings. Nothing is lost of what has been, but all is transfused with new light in the completeness of the picture in the heavenly glory.

During his lifetime, the most contradictory views have been expressed concerning his personality and conduct, yet he was a classic example of the times-serving prelate. He was a superb diplomat, who had an exceptional flair for appropriate conduct; he was a staunch defender of orthodoxy and a wise leader, who helped the Church to maintain its organization. His behavior often looked opportunist, but he was able to carry on his shoulders the heavy weight of responsibility for the conduct of ecclesiastical and political affairs during the most tragic and perplexing period of Cypriot history. His interest in expanding orthodoxy in Africa is well known, and one can only hope that the good work he invested in this field will continue and bear fruit. His soul will forever rejoice with the progress and expansion of the Church all over Africa.

Today, as we remember the one hundredth anniversary his birth, let us remember his ministry in Africa and how the same have impacted each one of our lives, as we continue burning the light that he left for all of Africa: our beloved school that is named after him: The Makarios III, Archbishop of Cyprus, Orthodox Patriarchal Ecclesiastical School.

May his memory be eternal!

38 Address given between August 10 and 26, 1976 by His Beatitude, the Archbishop of Cyprus and President of the Republic of Cyprus, Makarios III.

Addresses to Youth & Kenyan Mothers' Union

ADDRESS
at Mothers' Union Seminar[1]

Church of Saint Sophia,
Gikambura, Kenya
April 22–25, 2010

Beloved Presbyters, Deacons, invited Guests, and Members of the Mothers' Union: I greet you most cordially in the Name of the Father, and of the Son, and of the Holy Spirit.

BEFORE ALL ELSE, I would like to express my deep appreciation to the organizers and above all the members of the Mothers' Union for planning and hosting this significant event. It is indeed a great honor to say to you that the Church desires, on her part, to contribute to the upholding of the dignity, role, and rights of women, not only through the specific support of the beloved patriarchate, but also by speaking directly to the heart and mind of every woman. The Church takes to heart and is concerned about the situations and problems that face women in general, and seeks to promote the cause of women in the Church and in today's world.

I have a deep feeling that I would like to express directly to every woman here, and I want to reflect on the problems and prospects of what it

1 Mothers' Union was founded in England by Mary Sumner in 1876 as a means to bring together women of different social classes in order to support mothers in their efforts to raise their children in the Christian faith. The Mothers' Union in Kenya was established in 1918 and now boasts more than 450,000 members.

means to be a woman in our time. I would like to consider the important issue of dignity and rights of women as seen in the light of the Word of God. I do believe it is important for the Orthodox Church to give thanks to the Holy Trinity for the mystery of a woman and for every woman; for all that constitutes the eternal measure of her feminine dignity, and for the great works of God, which, throughout all human history, have been accomplished in and through her. These words of thanks that go to our Lord and Savior Jesus Christ are for his mysterious plan regarding the call of women in the mission of his Church, and for what women represent in the life of humanity.

Beloved sisters in Christ, allow me to express my humble gratitude to all the women who are present at this gathering. I especially thank all the women here who are mothers, as you have carried human beings within yourselves in a unique experience of joy and pain, and later, through the help of God, you nurture children into adulthood. I also thank all of you here who are wives, because you chose to join your future with that of your husbands in a blessed relationship, and to the love of God. Thanks to all the women present here that are working and are active in significant spheres of our society, in areas of work such as the social, economic, cultural, and political realms of our world. Your contributions have helped in the establishment of important economic and political structures, which are vital in our day-to-day lives.

I cannot forget to thank all the women here who have chosen to live their lives in chastity, for they have decided to follow in the footsteps of the Mother of God, and this has enabled them experience a spousal relationship to God. Lastly, let me thank every woman present here for the important fact of being a woman, because you have contributed to the world's understanding and made all human relations to have faith in each other. I recognize the presence of every woman here as very important, as you represent many other members of the Church in the respective parishes from which you come.

Today, though we celebrate the achievements of women, we must not forget to reflect on the setbacks that have been experienced in achieving their success. We cannot forget the fact that women's dignity has often been ignored and their voices misinterpreted or silenced. And, to add to this, women have often been pushed to the margins of society and their positions at times reduced to being slaves. All of these setbacks have been obstacles for them, and thus, have often led to spiritual poverty.

The Church is being called to reverse these negative notions and set women free from any kind of exploitation and domination. This freedom should be in reference to the Gospel of our Lord and Savior Jesus Christ, and it reflects his attitude. Christ treated women with openness, dignity, acceptance, and tenderness, and by doing so he honored the dignity that women have always possessed according to God's plan and love. Being the Church of Christ, and being the unchanged Church that upholds the teaching of Christ, we must try to find ways to further respect women and their identity. This can be accomplished only by considering every aspect of a woman's life, starting with the recognition of her dignity according to the Law of God, acknowledged not just in the Scriptures but also in the hearts of all human beings.

My dear sisters in Christ, the book of Genesis speaks of creation in a language that can be understood easily: "God created man in his own image, in the image of God created he him; male and female created he them."[2]

This passage states that man, in the first place, is regarded highly as compared to the rest of creation. It follows that, "Adam gave names to all cattle, and to the fowl of the air, and to every beast of the field; but for Adam there was not found an help meet for him."[3] "And the Lord God said, 'It is not good that the man should be alone; I will make a help meet for him.'"[4]

So God creates a woman who becomes the man's partner. This particular help is not one-sided, but mutual. Here we see that the woman complements the man, just as a man complements a woman. Therefore, they are complimentary, not only from the physical and physiological points of view, but also ontologically. God then commanded that the two of them should fill the earth through procreation. In this sexual relationship we see the unity of the two, which is the divine plan of God, and that enriches and confers responsibility. Women are important beings on the face of the earth, and all the progress of humanity is attributed to their contributions, as we are able to experience here today in this historical gathering. And hence, we can say that when God unified man and woman, it was not only for the sake of procreation, but also for the creation of history itself.

At times, it is discouraging to note that many women of today tend to lose hope. But today, I render my heartfelt appeal to every one of you—especially our government and other social institutions—to make every

2 Gen. 1:27.
3 Ibid.
4 Gen. 2:18.

effort to ensure that women regain their full dignity and role, and of course I cannot fail to recognize all women of good will who have devoted their lives to defending the dignity of womanhood by fighting for their basic, social, economic and political rights, striving hard to show their courageousness, even when circumstances are not in their favor. It is my prayer and hope that when women devote themselves to working in the Church, they remember and see Mary, the Mother of God as the highest expression of their femininity, and who called herself the handmaid of God.[5] She accepted the call to be a mother by putting herself at God's service and at the service of others. This was, and is, a service of love. We who are present here need to understand our authority, and each of us our fundamental vocation: that we are all chosen and created in the image of our Lord, and we are all called to be adopted sons and daughters of Christ.

My dear sisters in Christ, your service—when rendered in freedom, reciprocity, and love—expresses the true nature of mankind. Mary, the Mother of God brings to you the very essence of the offices you hold in the Mothers' Union and the services you render to the Orthodox Church. I urge all of you to actively participate in the role of building the Church, which is first and foremost the people of God, and secondly, a holy structure. In the Church we share in this task, each one of us in his or her specific way, in the priestly, prophetic, and royal mission of Christ. The prophetic mission can be emphasized by the fact that it was given to men and women, a good example being that of the Samaritan woman and her dialogue with Christ at Jacob's well. Martha and Mary are other examples that can be cited in the Bible. To Martha, who was the active one, Jesus reveals the Paschal mystery: "I am the resurrection and life: he that believeth in me, though he were dead, yet shall he live: And whosoever believeth in me shall never die."[6]

The active role and participation of women is much talked about in the passion narrative. So I call upon all women and mothers present here to have courage and take an active role in their calling as members of the Mothers' Union.

Finally, I would like to convey my deepest appreciation to those who are involved in organizing this seminar, which has been very useful. My special thanks goes to all the women here who are actively involved in various areas of education extending well beyond the family: nurseries, and

5 See Luke 1:38.

6 Jn. 11:25, 26.

schools, universities, social service agencies, parishes, various associations and movements within our church. We know that whenever women are called for in education, they are always on the front lines in serving others generously, and especially in serving those who are weak and defenseless.

May the Blessed Virgin look upon you all with special affection, the beloved sons and daughters on this occasion of today's gathering of the Mothers' Union. May she especially inspire in our hearts a burning desire for holiness.

With paternal love, I wish you God's blessings.

ADDRESS
at the National Gathering of the Mothers' Union of Kenya

Naivasha, Kenya,
August 26, 2010

To my dear Spiritual Children in Christ: I greet you most cordially in the Name of the Father, and of the Son, and of the Holy Spirit.

We have come a long way, through the grace and mercies of God, in order to realize what we are witnessing here today. We have observed the Mothers' Union grow every day, becoming a strong and important group, which propagates and safeguards our faith through its daily missionary activities. It has been able to recruit new members, both young and old. It has been able to pull together women of all walks of life and combine their resources for the common good of assisting the Church in spreading the good news of Christ. The formation of the Mothers' Union is our way of proving to the world that we respect and recognize the role of women in the Church, just as Christ allowed his mother in his missionary activities. I take this opportunity to thank all those mothers who are members of this noble group, and encourage them to continue with their wonderful activities, which are very important to our church. So I welcome all of you to this gathering, and give you my blessings and support in all your activities.

Brothers and sisters in Christ, my word of encouragement to you today comes from the Epistle of Philippians 2:5–11, which says:

> Let this mind be in you, which was also in Christ Jesus: Who, being in the form of God, thought it not robbery to be equal with God: But made himself of no reputation, and took upon him the form of a servant, and was made in the likeness of men: And being found in fashion as a man, he humbled himself, and became obedient unto death, even the death of the Cross. Wherefore God also hath highly exalted him, and given him a Name which is above every name: That at that Name of Jesus every knee should bow, of things in heaven, and things in earth, and things under the earth.

Paul's challenge to the Church of Philippi is one of the most well-known and moving passages in all his writings. These words are known as the Kenosis Hymn, from the Greek word *ekenosen*, which means, "he emptied." The Kenosis Hymn is generally recognized by scholars to be an early Christian hymn and an affirmation of faith, quoted secondarily by Paul. The apostle's relationship with the Church of Philippi had been warm and cordial. Although he had been put in prison on his first visit there, the Church of Philippi was the first church to be founded in Europe. The initial success was fondly recalled by the apostle Paul. The church continued to support Paul's missionary activities.

The Kenosis Hymn in this context gives expression to Paul's call for a worthy fulfillment of our Christian obligation of love and servanthood. Today, when we read these verses, we see that they focus on the activity of exalting Christ; hence, we see the movement of Jesus Christ within the hymn. Christ appears on a level of equality with God. Then, by his choice, he lays aside his equality and takes the role of a servant. And, finally, he is exalted again to a status equal with God. Brothers and sisters in Christ, Paul uses himself and his circumstances to illustrate to us the proper exercise of the role of a servant exemplified by Christ. He uses these words to set our minds on the humility and selflessness that he, like Christ, introduced to the Church of Philippi. The apostle Paul uses the words of the Kenosis Hymn to refer to his own selfless commitment, which he invites us to share. The strongest message for our gathering here today according to the apostle, is the call to lay aside all rights of personal privilege, to submit in the spirit of servanthood to the needs of each other. This is the heart of this passage and our message today.

From Paul's side, we see one who is a faithful servant following the servant Christ. From the Philippians' side, we see those who are called to exhibit the same servanthood as followers of Christ, just as we today are called to be servants of Christ in whatever capacity, whether in the Mothers' Union or any other offices we hold in our Church. My dear sisters and brothers, to see Christ as a servant is to perceive what being in Christ entails. To fulfill one's obligation as a citizen of the heavenly Kingdom means to empty oneself as Christ did, and to take on the role of a servant. We must commit ourselves, not only to share in his grace, but also to share in his suffering. We must be willing to be poured out in the service of others, to have a mindset and lifestyle that is different from the values of the world. We must exhibit true humility and have the understanding that to be in Christ means to be a servant, because Christ came to the world not only as Lord, but also as a servant.

The Kenosis Hymn represents to us an ethical example, a superb illustration of what it really means to be a Christian. Unity comes in serving God as we are witnessing here today. It means serving God through serving each other.

My spiritual children in Christ, the solution to the problems of our daily relationships and lives is in an attitude of humble commitment to each other. A spiritual self-sacrifice is an expression to others of the love exemplified in Christ. Love that was "obedient unto death, even the death of the Cross."[7] My dear brothers and sisters, today's passage reveals to us who are gathered here, that there is no room for triumphalism. There is no room for a victory that does not first know the fellowship of Christ on behalf of others. Today, brothers and sisters in Christ, we find that hope which is seen in the last part of the kenosis hymn.

God eventually exalts Christ. The Lord's humility becomes glory. Paul's word becomes evidence of Christ's exaltation when he says that God will transform the body of our humble state into the body of glory. We should all emulate Christ, whose path to glory led to the emptying of himself through the servanthood that led to his crucifixion. We also cannot forget Paul's path to glory that led him to be imprisoned through his humility. Sisters and brothers, this verse also introduces us to joy—real joy that is associated with servanthood, and that sings even in the face of death itself.

Finally my brothers and sisters in Christ, what you are doing here is noble. And the Church needs the unity of mind and the purpose to which

7 Phil. 2:8.

Paul is also calling the Philippians. Our Church needs a unity built on servanthood, a servanthood that has been illustrated by the emptied Christ and the poured-out Paul. Beloved, I urge you all to help the Church see herself in a new light: less a proclaimer and defender of divine truth, and more a servant of everybody around her. We, as the Church, should be like a foot-washer who expresses his love by humble service. We need to see ourselves in terms of obligations to the community, of those in Christ, of whom we claim to be a part. My dear children in Christ, we should live a life of commitment to servanthood, a life poured out in the service of others, totally emptied of self. We must make service to others a perfect love in action. This is our primary responsibility. An attitude of Christ-like humility does not demand rights or protect its own interest; it seeks out opportunities to serve.

I leave you all with my paternal blessings.

ADDRESS
at a Youth Seminar

Kapsanjon, Western Kenya,
September 4, 2010

Reverend Fathers and Deacons, the Faithful and the Youth gathered here today: I greet you all in the Name of the Father, and of the Son, and of the Holy Spirit.

TODAY I AM DELIGHTED to be with you, the faithful, and the members of the youth. I am also thankful to all of you for taking this noble initiative of organizing this gathering to help educate and encourage our youth. I don't hesitate to remind you that youth groups play a very important role in our Church, and therefore it is important for the Church to organize these important gatherings in order to enlighten the youth on various issues that are very challenging for them. It is in this spirit that I have always encouraged the parishes to plan for regular gatherings or seminars to help the youth better face their challenges. This is important because most of these seminars act as an eye-opener for most of the youth who normally wander in spiritual blindness. The teachings not only help restore spiritual sight but also give the youth guidelines on how to handle their impressionable lives in this world full of challenges.

My spiritual children, it is important to learn, and to follow what is right, to have good virtues, which lift up men and women to heaven as Saint Paul puts it when he concludes, "For if these things be in you, and abound, they make you that ye shall never be barren nor unfruitful in the knowledge of our Lord Jesus Christ. But he that lacketh these things is blind, and cannot see afar off, and hath forgotten that he was purged from his old sins."[8]

We are all God's creatures, composed of body and spirit; consequently, we have both physical and spiritual sight. When we don't possess physical sight, then it means we are not able to see the light of the sun, the beauty of the world, our loved ones, or even ourselves. But the worst disability of all is the lack of spiritual eyes, which we are normally given in order to think about God and the mysteries of the spiritual world. Spiritual sight is a gift of God, and one who does not possess it is blind in his soul. Most of us who suffer from this blindness know truly that through living a righteous life we may win eternal life, yet we still live in sin, and forget penance and cleaning of our souls in the sacrament of the Eucharist. We become blind and still affirm that we believe and confess Jesus, but in our deeds we reject him.

Saint John the Divine teaches:

> God is light and in him is no darkness at all. If we say that we have fellowship with him, and walk in darkness, we lie, and do not the truth: But if we walk in the light, as he is in the light, we have fellowship with one another, and the blood of Jesus Christ his Son cleanseth us from all sin.[9]

Brothers and sisters in Christ, we should often disturb ourselves by asking what we must do in order to rid ourselves of this pernicious blindness. According to the teachings of our Church, spiritual sight does not necessarily mean seeing visions, or appearances of angels and saints. Whoever among us thinks that spiritual sight means this is in danger of falling into sin. We must remember that our enemy often takes the appearance of an angel of light in order to destroy our souls.

At times, we do not recognize our spiritual blindness, and we assume that everything is okay. So how can we be rid of this blindness? The first step is for us to be aware that we are living in darkness, and then learn to hate sin with all our hearts. The second step is reading and listening to the Word of God, as this will help us to disperse the darkness, to open our

8 2 Peter 1:8, 9.

9 1 Jn. 1:5–7.

spiritual eyes and to expose our selfishness and the vices of our souls so that grace can shine in us and motivate us to fulfill Christ's teachings.

My dear sisters and brothers, the true spiritual sight, according to the fathers of the Church, consists in the ability to perceive one's sins and to recognize Christ our Savior. My fellow Christians, the way to perceive our weaknesses and spiritual poverty is to turn for help to our Savior Jesus Christ. If we want to live a sinless life, we must follow Christ—the Light of the World—who came into the world so that everyone who believes in him will not live in darkness. The Lord is assuring us that, "He that followeth me shall ... have the light of life."[10] Brothers and sisters, in order for us to follow Christ in his meekness and humility, and to endure the sufferings of the Cross, hate the darkness of sin and go away from it. For us to draw nearer to Christ and be illumined by him, we must be like the Lord in everything. We must be holy in our lives as Saint Paul puts it: "Follow peace with all men, and holiness, without which no man shall see the Lord."[11] We may see this as an impossible thing, especially in this world of difficult challenges, but Paul's advice is enough if we stand firmly on the saving path of cleansing our souls; if we diligently observe the Word of God, zealously fulfilling his commandments and struggling against sin, then we shall come to know there are such things as spiritual poverty and blindness, and to try to avoid them.

Finally my dear spiritual children, sins and vices always tend to destroy our prayers, and therefore we must strive hard to turn to our Savior Jesus Christ and say, "Lord Jesus Christ, Son of God, have mercy on me. Open my eyes, Christ God, and let me not someday sleep in death." It is only after we have acquired this state of awareness that the Lord will heal us. This ardent, tearful prayer will draw down on us mercy of our merciful God and he—the Physician of our bodies and souls—will heal us, illumine us with the light of knowledge, and grant us the ability to see him.

I leave you my paternal blessings.

10 Jn. 8:12.

11 Heb. 12:14.

ADDRESS
at a Mothers' Union Gathering

Rironi, Kenya,
September 26, 2010

Revered Fathers, Deacons and Leaders of the Mothers' Union, and all Faithful in Christ: I greet you in the holy Name of our Lord and Savior Jesus Christ.

> God is love; and he that dwelleth in love dwelleth in God, and God in him.[12]

BROTHERS AND SISTERS IN CHRIST, these words from 1 John express with remarkable clarity the heart of the Christian faith, that is, the image of God and the resulting image of mankind and his destiny. Today, we are Christians, not because of an ethical choice, or by means of some lofty idea, but because of an encounter with an event, an encounter with a Person who gives our lives a new meaning and a decisive direction. God's love for us is fundamental and it raises important questions about who God is and who we are. The answer to these important questions lies in Jesus Christ uniting this love for God, and the commandment to love our God, with the commandment to love our neighbor found in the book of Leviticus: "Thou shalt love thy neighbor as thyself."[13] Women and men of Christ, since God first loved us, love is no longer a mere command; it's a

12 1 Jn. 4:16.
13 Lev. 19:18.

response to his gift of love by which God has drawn near to us. Today this is my main focus: God is love.

My dear sisters and brothers, the love of God and love of neighbor reflected in the verse above are both foundational to how we live our lives as Christians in this world. The parable of the Good Samaritan offers two particularly important clarifications.[14] Until this time, the concept of a neighbor was understood as referring essentially to one's countrymen and to foreigners who had settled in the land of Israel. In other words, to the closely-knit community of a single country of people. Brothers and sisters in Christ, with the parable, this limit has been abolished. Anyone who needs our help is our neighbor. The Orthodox Church has a duty to interpret this as a new relationship between near and far with regard to the actual daily life of her members. Our call today is likened to that of Christ. Our Lord always identified himself with those in need, with the hungry, the thirsty, the stranger, the naked, the sick and those in prison: "Inasmuch as ye have done it unto one of the least of these my brethren, ye have done it unto me."[15] This is the challenge you are given today as women of God, that the love of God and love of neighbor are inseparable. In the least of those people around us, who cross our paths every day, we find Jesus Christ himself, and in Jesus we find God.

My dear sisters in Christ, today I pose to you two important questions: How do we love God even though we can't see him? And, can love be commanded? It is true that even among us here today no one has seen God as he is. And while it seems as if God is totally invisible to us and hidden from us, he is not completely inaccessible. It is important to know that God has taken the initiative with you and me, and that God loved us first and continues to do so. We, too, can respond with love. God does not demand of us a feeling that we ourselves are incapable of producing. God loves us. He makes us see and experience his love, and since he has loved us first, our own love can grow as a response within us.

God has made himself visible. In Jesus we see the Father. He is also visible in the love story of the Bible. He comes to us; he seeks to win our hearts, all the way to the last supper, to the piercing of his heart on the Cross, to his appearances after his Resurrection, and to the mighty great deeds by which he guided the Twelve and the new Church along its path. Even today the Lord is here present within us. He comes to us ever new. In the

14 See Luke 10:25–37.

15 Matt. 25:40.

women gathering here he is also present, because your gathering reflects his presence. We experience him through our reading, and more so in the Eucharist, in our liturgical services, in our daily prayers, and in the living community of believers. We daily experience the love of God. We perceive his presence and we finally learn to recognize that presence in our daily lives.

Today, Christ is showing us in the Bible that loving one's neighbor is possible. The Bible presents to us the truth that in God, and with God, we should and can love even the person whom we do not like or even know. This can surely happen though the help of God. It can only be achieved when we learn to look at this other person from the perspective of Jesus Christ. Seeing with the eyes of Christ, we can give to others much more than their outward necessities; we can give them the look of love, which they need. In this we see the great connection between the love of God and the love of neighbor.

My sisters in Christ, if we have no contact whatsoever with God in our lives, then we cannot see the other as anything more than the "other," because we will be incapable of seeing in this person the image of God. It is through our readiness to face our neighbor and show her love, that later makes us win God's favor. It is only through serving our neighbors that our eyes can be opened to what God does for us and how much he loves us. Love of God and love of neighbor work together and can never be separated. They form one single and strong commandment. Love grows through love. Love is divine because it originates in God and later unites us with God. Through this unifying process it makes us "we," and gives us a new identity that transcends our divisions and makes us one, until in the end—God is "all in all."[16]

We are all gathered here for this special meeting in unity because of the love of God and the love of our fellow sisters and brothers. We are all here for the common good, for your sakes, and for the sake of your neighbors, and for the Orthodox Church as a whole. Love of neighbor grounded in the love of God is first and foremost the responsibility of each individual member of the faithful, but it is also the responsibility of the entire Church. As a community, the Church must practice love. Love needs to be organized if it's to be expressed and experienced at the community level. In the Acts of the apostles, Saint Luke provides a description of the Church, whose characteristics included its dedication to the teaching

16 See 1 Cor. 15:28.

of the apostles, "communion" (*koinonia*), the breaking of the bread, and prayer. The point of communion consists in the fact that believers hold things in common and that among them there is no longer any distinction between rich and poor.

So, sisters and brothers in Christ, in conclusion, I would like to say that the Church is God's family on earth. In this family, no one ought to go without the necessities of life. And the love of a neighbor extends beyond the boundaries of our Holy Church. Let the parable of the Good Samaritan be the standard that leads us to demonstrate the love of Christ to the needy and indeed everyone we encounter "by chance." The advice we ought to heed today from Saint Paul's Epistle to the Galatians is, "As we have therefore opportunity, let us do good unto all men, especially unto them who are of the household of faith."[17]

Finally sisters and brothers, I take this opportunity to thank all the organizers of this gathering, the patrons, and all reverend Fathers present with us here today.

May God bless you all.

17 Gal. 6:10.

LECTURE TO THE YOUTH
on the Divine Liturgy

Holy Transfiguration Orthodox Church,
Kamangu, Kenya,
August 5, 2011

Beloved Children in Christ: I greet you most cordially in the Name of our Lord and Savior Jesus Christ.

I THANK ALMIGHTY GOD for his grace and mercy, and also for giving me this chance to be with you on this occasion. First of all, allow me to begin by quoting some very essential words concerning prayers:

> As you enter the church, lighting your candle and reverencing the icons—pray! As you are called to participate in the litanies—pray! As you join in the hymns—pray! As you think of the meaning of the symbolic acts—pray! As you read the inaudible parts—pray! As you recite the Creed—pray! As you approach the chalice for the Holy Communion—pray! Instruct yourself as you go to the church each Sunday to "pray the Liturgy." Prayer, no matter how offered, is essential to the participation in the Divine Liturgy. There are so many different ways for you to "pray the Liturgy" that no Sunday has ever to be the same as any other. Each Divine Liturgy can have fresh, new and inspiring content for you. If you truly "pray the Liturgy" you

will never be bored, never feel unrefreshed, and never lose the vitality, excitement, and vigor of the living Liturgy.

My spiritual children in Christ, prayer is very fundamental to our Christian lives. Our Lord and Savior Jesus Christ himself prayed and taught men how to pray. If we do not commit ourselves to prayers, then we automatically cease being followers of Christ. In our Church all our prayers are trinitarian, we pray in the Holy Spirit through Jesus Christ the Son of God and in his Name to God the Father. We usually call God "our Father" because Jesus has taught us and allowed us to do so. The reason why we call God "our Father" is because we are made sons of God by the Holy Spirit.[18] When we are in the church we address our prayers to Christ and the Holy Spirit, the Divine Persons, who are one with God and exist eternally in perfect unity with him, sharing his divine being and will. We also commemorate the saints, but not in the same way as we pray to the Persons of the Holy Trinity.

We remember the saints in our prayers as our intercessors, helpers, and fellow members of the Church Triumphant. The first saint that we commemorate is Mary the Theotokos, the Queen of the Heaven, the leader among our saintly intercessors before God. We also ask the angels, through prayers, to plead our cause before God.

Brethren in Christ, I know very well that we Christians face a lot of challenges, trials, and tribulations. But the people affected en mass by these predicaments turn out to be the youth, because they want to be without help—independent—and they tend to deal with their own problems without even seeking counsel from their elders. It is amid this crisis that the youth should understand that they have taken the wrong turn, and ought to run back to the Church, and see for themselves the blessings that result from constant dialogue with God through prayers. It is important to know how to pray, and the types of prayers we have within our Orthodox Church. The rationale of the prayers is to have communion with God, and to be made capable of accomplishing his will. We pray to enable ourselves to know God and to do his commandments. Unless a person is willing to change himself, and conform himself to Christ in fulfillment of his commandments, then he has no reason or purpose to pray. Our saints have warned us that it is eventually dangerous to pray to God without the intention of responding and moving along the path on which the prayer

18 Rom. 8:14.

will take us. It is significant for the youth today to know that a prayer is not merely the repeating of words, and saying of the prayer is not the same as praying. It should be done secretly, briefly, and regularly without many words, with total trust in God that he hears our prayer and with our willingness to do what God wants.

Our Church follows the Old Testament practice of having a formal prayer that is according to the hours of the day. We are encouraged to pray regularly in the morning, evening, and even at other times to have a brief prayer, which can be repeated all through the day, and under any and all circumstances. Many of us use the Jesus Prayer to do this. When we attend church, we do not go there to say our private prayers. But we bring ourselves and our concerns to the church, in order to unite them to the prayer of the Church, to the eternal prayer of Christ, the Mother of God, the saints, and brothers and sisters of our own particular church community. In the church, we pray with others, and we are expected to pray all together as one body in the unity of one mind, one heart, and one soul. Each one of us must put his own self—with his personal uniqueness—into the common prayer of Christ with his own Body. We go to church not to merely pray, but to be together, to meditate on the meaning of the faith together, and to have a union and communion together with God. This is especially true of the Divine Liturgy, which is the center of my lecture today: "The Youth and the Divine Liturgy."

Beloved of Christ, the Divine Liturgy is the most central celebration of the Orthodox Church's liturgical cycle, yet it is too often taken for granted by most of us, and especially the youth, with an approach of resignation, and not with anticipation. With this in mind, we often come across many people in the Church, and particularly the youth, being faced with this challenging question: "What should one expect from the Divine Liturgy?" Today I find it wise to restructure this query and ask, "What does the Divine Liturgy expect from the youth?" To respond to this question, I would say that one does not come to church to be a spectator; one comes to be an active participant. This answer leads us back to the definition of the Divine Liturgy. The common action of Orthodox Christians officially gathered constitutes the Orthodox Church. It is an action of the Church assembled by God in order to be together in one community to worship, to pray, to sing, to hear God's Word, to be instructed in God's commandments, to offer itself with thanksgiving to Christ to God, the Father, and to have a living experience of God's eternal Kingdom through the communion of the same Christ, who is present in his people by the Holy Spirit.

The challenge that is facing us regarding the youth is that they have failed to embrace the liturgical services that we have in our Church. They have refused to do something for the sake of the Divine Liturgy. My plea today is that the youth change their mentality regarding our liturgical services, and that they instead embrace it, knowing that the Divine Liturgy is a sacramental manifestation of the essence of the Church, the Church being the community of God in heaven and on earth. They should know that the Liturgy is a unique revelation of the Church as the mystical Body and Blood of Christ.

At times, the youth may find the Liturgy a bit boring and may wish that it were over so that they can find time to go home, to eat, to watch a football game, or go to a movie. Some of the youth often find themselves too concerned with the length of the Liturgy instead of being fully involved in it. Most of them are worried about losing their free time instead of sharing God's word, and being a vital part of their family. When they feel this way, they attend the Liturgy without proper commitment and reverence. They lose their concentration and sense of purpose. Then, they easily slip into temptation and forgo the prayerful attitude by focusing their attention on negative, rather than positive things, such as: "the choir is dragging," or "the reader is too slow," or "the sermon is too boring," etc.

Having discovered all these problems with the youth, we need to make them understand a few important things about our Divine Liturgy. They ought to understand that the Divine Liturgy is the central mystical action of the whole Church. The Divine Liturgy should be understood as one that is always resurrectional in spirit, and that it is always the manifestation of the risen Christ to his people. It is always an outpouring of the life-creating Spirit. The youth should understand, too, that the Liturgy has always been, and still is, the communion with God, the Father and that it should not be to them boring, mournful, or penitential. It should never be to them the expression of darkness and death in this world, but always an expression and experience of eternal life of the Kingdom of the blessed Trinity. The youth should be prepared and participate fully in this service, because if they are not properly prepared to participate, then how can it have any meaning to them?

I throw this challenge back to you today: If you are not prepared to "live the Liturgy," how can it become a changing point in your lives? "It is impossible for the believer to be saved, to receive the remission of sins and be admitted to the Kingdom of Heaven, unless in fear, faith, and love he receives Communion of the pure mysteries of the Body and Blood of Jesus." These words from Saint Nilus give us the purpose of celebrating the Divine Liturgy. We can now be able to see that the purpose of participation in the celebration of the Divine Liturgy is important for the preparation of receiving Holy Communion. The most important thing that you should know as the youth is that when you prepare yourselves properly for the Divine Liturgy you can get more out of the services. However, you must have "psyched" yourselves up spiritually in order to fully grasp the meaning of the liturgical services. When the youth enter the church with the proper state of mind, they are more capable of understanding the reason for being there. The service is then able to speak to them.

As I had mentioned earlier, there are two different kinds of prayer in the Church: private and public. Private prayers are carried out by most of us at home. Public or corporate prayer is that which is carried out when we are gathered together as a Church, the mystical Body of Christ. Both prayers are necessary for proper celebration of the Divine Liturgy. Our private prayers, which should begin at home before we even enter the church, should include daily morning and evening prayers. As the youth grow and mature in their daily prayers, they will be building their spiritual lives on a firm foundation. They will then be able to embark on their preparation for corporate worship. In public prayer, it is important for the youth to have a text of the service available to follow along. It is important for each and every member of the Church to carry a Bible so that he can follow the scripture readings. As a minimum, everyone should read the epistle and the gospel reading for the day before attending church. This will help him be familiar with the texts and, as a result, he will be able to follow and understand the explanation of the Word of God which will be given in the sermon.

The celebration of the Divine Liturgy is the celebration of the Eucharist, or the Holy Communion. The youth therefore should be encouraged to be ready and willing to receive Holy Communion. Not receiving the Holy Communion makes the attendance of the Liturgy futile, and one is not able to get as much out of the service as one should. The youth, therefore, should always be willing to partake of the Eucharist, and at the same time prepare themselves through the sacrament of Penance. They should then prepare themselves again by having private prayers as a foundation to the public prayers. The advice of the fathers of the Church is that attending the Divine Liturgy and receiving Holy Communion is the most important aspect of our spiritual lives. The youth today have failed to appreciate the beauty and the theology that they can share every time they enter into corporate worship of the Liturgy and other services of the Church. They tend to forget that they can prepare themselves to do spiritual battle in a world that rejects the very notion of holiness and goodness. They prepare through the Divine Liturgy and the Holy Sacraments.

Finally, my beloved children in Christ, the authority of the Divine Liturgy in our souls is deep. We celebrate it visibly and openly in the sight of the entire world, yet it is hidden. If we could only follow each act reverently and attentively, obedient to the bidding of the deacon, then our souls would be attuned to lofty things. We would find it possible to fulfill the commandments of Christ, the yoke of Christ would be easy, and his burden light for us. And, on leaving the church where we were present at the divine feast of love, we would look on all men as brethren.

Therefore, I urge you—the youth, tomorrow's future church leaders, and everyone who desires to advance and become better—to be present as frequently as possible at the Divine Liturgy, carefully following every word. The Liturgy imperceptibly forms and develops a man. If our society holds together, if we as people do not breathe complete irreconcilable hatred for one another, the reason lies hidden in the Divine Liturgy, which constantly reminds man of holy, heavenly love toward his brother. Great and incalculable may be the influence of the Divine Liturgy if we will only be present, listen, participate, and finally resolve to put what we hear into practice in our lives.

Lastly, I take this opportunity to thank all those in attendance both the young and the old, and especially the organizers who made this gathering to be such a success. May God bless you all.

ADDRESS
at a Youth Gathering for HIV *and* AIDS *Awareness*[19]

April 22, 2012

I greet you beloved Children in Christ with the love of the risen Christ: *Kristo amefufuka!*

IT GIVES ME IMMENSE JOY to be here with you today, not only for the inauguration of this auspicious and special seminar on HIV/AIDS, but also in knowing that all of you are here gathered and dedicated to sacrifice an entire week for the same. The love that you have shown proves your commitment and desire for an HIV-free society.

The commitment and love you have demonstrated compliments the vision and mission of our Church in the fight against this pandemic. The Orthodox Church in Kenya has for many years been on the forefront in the fight against this calamity, together with the Christian denominations. I remember that I was actually one of the three Christian leaders that signed the agreement to establish "Churches United Against HIV/AIDS" (CUAHA). At the same time, in collaboration with the Finnish Orthodox Church, we have always striven to bring this challenge to the youth, who are the leaders of today and tomorrow. Recently, we established the Department of Religious Education and Catechism. One of the priorities

19 This gathering was jointly organized by the Orthodox Church of Kenya and the Orthodox Church of Finland.

of this department of our church was to review, redefine, and expand our HIV/AIDS policy, to ensure a wider, all-inclusive approach in our commitment to fight the HIV/AIDS pandemic.

We are very grateful to the Finnish Orthodox Church, through whose sponsorship we are gathered here today. We feel the sting of this disease as individuals and as a Church. We are all part of God's wonderful creation, and we view all human beings as made in the image and likeness of God. We are therefore tasked with affirming the creation and the nurturing of inner and spiritual peace for the infected and the affected. It is only by attaining this inner spiritual peace that we can be sure of social peace. This is very possible especially in our African culture, since everyone is in a constant relationship with the other. We have a holistic perspective on interdependence, an inseparable web of relationships guided by a communitarian ethic, in which "to be" is to be in a relationship with others, the rest of the creation, and with God the Creator of all there is. It is this that defines African life. This is the atmosphere of peace in our daily communities.

Only such a community approach can de-stigmatize the pandemic and actually promote inner peace and eventual social peace. I say this because the one thing that makes HIV stand out is the stigma attached to it. It is easier for a patient to manage terminal cancer because no stigma is attached to it. However, living with a disease that is stigmatized makes it harder to cope. You are always ridiculed by society. You are judged and your sense of belonging becomes an issue in your daily life. You are judged as promiscuous, as having been sexually reckless. But it is a reckless society that makes its members harbor such attitudes. For in the same society, anyone can be affected by any other terminal disease and not be thus stigmatized.

Human beings are created by God to enjoy all the beautiful gifts of creation. The greatest of these gifts is life itself. Each one of us should marvel and and be grateful to God for the gift of life. But when we allow stigma to cloud our judgment, we actually end up judging and condemning our own selves. Each one of us is an icon of God; we see the face of God each time we look at our brothers and sisters. I am beholding the face of God in all of you, as I look at you now. I cannot segregate you by color, tribe, academic performance, fairness of skin, physical appearance, or even health status, because this will go against every value that we as Christians hold.

Our Church stands by its principle of marriage—that is, that marriage consists of one husband for one wife and vice versa. On top of this, it cultivates the virtue of faithfulness. Each couple is encouraged to be faithful to one another. A couple that trashes the value of faithfulness will only stand to hurt each other, and the children as well. The youth, leaders of today and tomorrow, on whose shoulders the progress and growth of our humanity rests, are not spared this pandemic; actually the highest risk faces them.

To this group, it should be explained clearly that the Church is committed to maintaining abstinence as the only holy and acceptable Christian way against infection. Many activists also campaign for the supply and use of condoms. Be it known that we as a Church respect their views, but we also have to uphold the purity and sanctity of sexual relations as God's gift to mankind for procreation. Even with the campaigns on condoms, the majority of the youth are still falling prey to low levels of maturity combined with high levels of testosterone. This boosts aggression and willingness to take risks. In the event of an absence of a condom, therefore, they are left open to the risk of infection, and the pandemic claims another victim.

The challenge is huge for us as church leaders. The clergy and laity alike are burdened with the duty of helping the Church know its status. With this I am guided by the words of Saint Paul that, in a body when one member suffers, the whole body suffers. And since therefore we are all members of the Body of Christ, we need to declare the Church HIV positive, for we all suffer the pain of our members who are languishing under the pandemic. Once we see ourselves as such, we will collectively, as one body, one Church, one society, and as one nation under God, be able to pursue our healing.

A fundamental role of church leaders is to inspire hope in those who have been reduced to a state of hopelessness. Our basis for hope as church leaders is centered on the fact that under the guidance of our compassionate God, HIV is no longer an automatic death sentence; this is what healing is all about. We have to follow in God's compassion and become a healing Church, not only physically but spiritually and socially, too. We have to join in God's healing mission and cure our people from stigmatization and exclusion. This will eventually change the attitude of the Church and encourage the people to know their own HIV status. Only after knowing her own status can the Church seek healing.

Once we in the Church are healed, we will become the angels that trouble the waters to release healing for the people. Once healed, we, the Church, will take the state to task to improve healthcare. Once healed, the Church will trouble the pharmaceutical industries to release healing for the afflicted masses. Once healed, the Church will find its compassion and will minister and wait on all without discrimination. The Church will finally attain to what it is supposed to be: a supportive, welcoming, truth-oriented, and God-fearing community.

I once again thank you for your love and dedication in educating yourselves on this pandemic, and I wish you God's favor in your endeavors to educate, care for, and reach out to both the infected and the affected. May God bless you.

SPEECH
at a Youth Day Rally

Saint Peter Orthodox Church,
Kanjeru, Kenya,
June 10, 2012

Serve the Lord with gladness: come before his presence with singing[20]

THE WORD, "SERVE," has many definitions. Such would include "work done for others," and a second one, "friendly help." Our understanding usually includes such definitions, and many more. When one talks about serving the Church, the first thing that comes to mind is usually ministerial priesthood. Ministerial priesthood involves a total dedication to serving Christ in the Church. This form of priesthood is not the only way to serve the Church, because different people have different talents, charismata, and capabilities. While just a few can or are chosen to become ministerial priests, all baptized Orthodox Christians have the royal priesthood in them. Apart from serving as a clergyman, there are many other roles within the Church that a Christian community cannot do without. Such would include members of the Parish Council, readers, chanters, janitors, catechists, altar servers, Sunday school teachers, youth directors, choirmasters, and specific church group leaders, to name a few.

20 Ps. 100:2.

The harvest truly is plenteous, but the laborers are few[21]

The Church has a lot of work that needs to be done, and in most cases all Christians are welcome to help in whatever ways they can manage. Services, like cleaning the church, dusting the pews, cutting grass, singing, ushering, helping care for the sick and old, are among the services that, in most cases, require several people. Churches may not always be in a position to pay for such services, and thus any and all volunteers are always welcomed. Another way to serve God is by praying for others. Prayer is the greatest gift and service we can offer anyone in this world. As the largest group in most churches, the youth should learn how to pray not only for the Church worldwide, but also for our communities and our country. Putting in mind that we should always sanctify all services rendered to others "by the Word of God and prayer."[22]

Serving the Lord in the Church is doing all that we can manage, no matter how little or insignificant our input is or may seem. God accepts and blesses us not because of how much we do, but how willing we are when offering ourselves.

It does not matter what others have to say about you or your work in the Church. What you are able to offer to God is all that you should care about, because, by the end of the day, you are serving the Lord and not any human being. Just like the psalmist reminds us, let us "serve the Lord with joy and gladness," which is the second thing that we should do when serving in the Church. Joy in serving comes when we are fully aware of our talents and therefore offering that which we do best, meaning we will offer ourselves to the very limit of our very best.

Even though sometimes the work that needs to be done within the Church is similar to any other in the secular life, working in the Church is unique in its own way. This is because we are all called to be prayerful when working in the Church. Even the very simple and powerful Jesus Prayer is enough when working in the Church. The prayer on our lips renews everything that we do within the Church, making our service better than any similar work done without prayer. Being in the presence of the Lord through prayer brings out a special sense of joy within us. A joyful worker will always be the most fruitful of all, and thus yield much for the Church.

Serving the Church, like in our earlier examples, is not only serving

21 Matt. 9:37.

22 1 Tim. 4:5.

within the boundaries of our parishes. Our service to God should be instilled in all that we do, no matter where we are. Hospitality to others, aiding the sick, the poor, the imprisoned, the hungry, and the naked—according to the Gospel of Matthew[23]—will not only help us serve God, but also help our chances of entering the Kingdom of God. When we serve others we serve God, because of how we were created, in the image and likeness of God.[24]

As the youth, you have the most potential to serve God through serving others, especially those who do not have the capacity to help themselves. Examples of helping the sick and the aged are helping on their farms, taking care of their animals, cleaning their houses, doing their laundry, shopping on their behalf, visiting them, and even just being there for them. When doing all these, let's keep in mind the fact that when we serve others we are serving God Himself, and there is a reward for that.

> Now there are diversities of gifts, but the same Spirit. And there are differences of administrations, but the same Lord. And there are diversities of operations, but it is the same God which worketh all in all. But the manifestation of the Spirit is given to every man to profit withal.[25]

We all have talents, and no one is without one. Our diversity of gifts and talents should help us build the body of Christ better. The strengths and the gifts given to one of us should help compensate for the weaknesses of the other. Some of these talents may not exactly fit in serving God, but we should fine-tune them to fit in doing so. Although we take service for God on a day-to-day basis, we should not forget that serving God lasts throughout a lifetime. Some gifts are short-term and others long-term. It is up to us to decipher and use our talents as they come, because God has reasons for giving them to us and not to others.

When called to serve God in any way, remember to do it prayerfully, with all your effort, with joy and with gladness. Even if the task may seem little or insignificant, remember that without it, the Church cannot be. Like the Swahili saying, "*Haba na haba hujaza kibaba*" ("Little by little fills the tin"), your continuous service to the Church, even though it seems little, is very important. Otherwise, the services you think are great and

23 Matt. 25:31–46.

24 See Gen. 1:26.

25 1 Cor. 12:4–7.

significant in the Church will not be complete. No matter what you call your little services to the Church, these complete the services of everyone else. Our services to the Church joined together make up the sum total of services offered by the Body of Christ.

The youth are usually the largest group in any country and any church, a fact that is not different from the Orthodox Church in Kenya. It is for this reason that I want you to keep in mind that without your input and services to the Church, we as a Church cannot be what God is calling us to be. I know that most of you are serving the Church in different capacities, but I want to call upon you all to join hands in serving God and his Church with more vigor and enthusiasm than before. Work "while it is day: the night cometh, when no man can work."[26] Now that you are young and energetic, please serve God earnestly. There will come a time when you will not be able to do so in the way that you can now. Remember also: do not concentrate only on those services that can be done within the church compound, but also serve outside the church, because we are Christians, both inside and outside of the church compound.

Give your services to God through serving those who are of our Faith and those who are not. Always keep in mind that our services to God do not end in the church, but rather we should carry on our duties as Christians even outside the church. I want to one day hear and be invited by our youth who are cleaning the streets, serving the aged and afflicted, visiting the sick at homes or in hospitals, farming for those who are incapable, offering rallies sensitizing the community on the effects of drugs and alcohol, planting trees, and other such services to God outside the church compound.

Above all let us "serve the Lord with joy and gladness."

26 Jn. 9:4.

MESSAGE
to the Kalonzo Musyoka Foundation on Drug and Substance Abuse

August 18, 2012

Distinguished Guests, Ladies, and Gentlemen:

I AM MOST HONORED and humbled to stand before you today and speak on such a gigantic issue, upon which many seated here today are more worthy to speak. I address you not simply as fellow guests today but as parents, grandparents, and as concerned leaders of our nation. It is holiday time for most Kenyan children, and while drug and substance abuse cuts across all generations, it's especially damaging to the young people on whom our future depends. So, I thank you and sincerely congratulate you for this important program that you are holding here today.

Kenya has accomplished so much in these last several years, whether it's been rebuilding our economy or serving the cause of freedom for its citizens. What we've been able to achieve has been done with us working together as a nation united. However, day in and day out we continue to face the problem of drug and substance abuse, which calls for an even stronger response and unity among us. Drugs are menacing our society. This is a problem as old as humanity itself. They're threatening our values and undercutting our institutions. They're killing our children and undermining our future.

The negative impact of alcohol, drug, and substance abuse cannot be underestimated. The fight against this menace is a clear priority as it not only impacts quality service delivery but also undermines public confidence in the public servants and individuals in the leadership realm.

Drug abuse is the use of illicit drugs or the abuse of prescription or over-the-counter medications for purposes other than those for which they are indicated, or in a manner or in quantities other than directed. Alcohol is one of the most abused substances in Kenya. It has been observed that many Kenyans of all ages are taken captive by alcohol and drugs, and that it is no longer only a teenage problem. Research has now shown that the prevalence of alcohol and drug abuse among adults in Kenya is expanding rapidly, to the destruction of the society. We are witnesses to shame of schools closing down due to lack of new students simply because people are so drunk they are not able to reproduce. Kenyans cannot afford to ignore, or be quiet about it anymore.

And drug abuse is not a so-called "victimless crime." Everyone's safety is at stake when drugs and excessive alcohol are used by people on the highways, or by those transporting our citizens, or operating industrial equipment. Drug abuse costs you and your fellow Kenyans a lot every year.

We have always thought of school time a special period: a time when we bundle our children off to school, to the warmth of an environment in which they can fulfill promise and hope in restless minds. But, so much has happened over these last few years, so much to shake the foundations of all that we know and all that we believe in. Now there is a drug and substance abuse epidemic in this country, and no one is safe from it—not you, not me, and certainly not our children, because this epidemic has their names written on it. Many of you may be thinking: "Well, drugs don't concern me." But the drug problem *does* concern you. It concerns us all because of the way it tears at our lives, and because it is aimed at destroying the brightness and life of the sons and daughters of our great nation.

For over thirty years, I've been traveling across the country—preaching, teaching, learning and listening. And one of the most hopeful signs I've seen is the building of an essential, new awareness of how terrible and threatening drug and substance abuse is to our society. I have witnessed families broken down by this substance abuse monster. Children with otherwise bright futures are turned into hopeless village hoodlums and murderous gangsters. I have seen the tragic neglect of families by parents who have fallen victims to the unforgiving wave of alcohol abuse. Little children grow up and turn into village, estate, and street gangsters—the very same who hijack your car while you drive home from a charity function. The very children you saw growing up turn to ruthless rapists in our own backyard. Now you can see why drug abuse concerns every one of us—the entire Kenyan family.

Drugs steal so much. They take and take, until finally every time a drug goes into a child, something else is forced out: love and hope; and trust and confidence. Drugs take away the dream from every child's heart and replace it with a nightmare, and it's time we in Kenya stand up and renew those dreams. Each of us has to put our principles and consciences on the line, whether in social settings or in the workplace, to set forth solid standards and stick to them. There's no moral middle ground. Indifference is not an option. We need, and we have to create, an outspoken intolerance for drug use. For the sake of our children, I implore each of you to be unyielding and inflexible in your opposition to drugs.

Our young people are helping us to lead the way. In the recent past, we have witnessed initiatives by the youth aimed at creating awareness in fellow youth regarding the dangers of drug and substance abuse. The recent slogan that has really spoken to our hearts, "Drugs drag you down" is a true expression of the repercussions of this vice. Well, the youth's participation and courage in saying "no" needs our encouragement. We can help by using every opportunity to force the issue of not using drugs even to the point of making others uncomfortable, even if it means making ourselves unpopular.

Our job is never easy because drug criminals are ingenious. They work every day to plot a new and better way to steal our children's lives. For every door that we close, they open a new door to death. They prosper on our unwillingness to act. So, we must be smarter and stronger and tougher than they are. It's up to us to change attitudes and just simply dry up their markets.

Let us work toward a drug-free workplace at all levels of government and in the private sector. Only then can we be sure to work toward drug-free schools. Finally, we have to ensure that the public is protected and that treatment is available to substance abusers and the chemically dependent.

And finally, to young people, those present here today and those to whom this message will reach. I have a very personal message for you: There's a big, wonderful world out there for you. It belongs to you. It's exciting, stimulating, and rewarding. Don't cheat yourselves out of this promise. Our country needs you, but it needs you to be clear-eyed and clear-minded. You have always heard people in rehab saying that when you are on drugs, everything appears in shades of black and gray, and after treatment one is able to see colors again.

So, to my young friends out there: Life can be great, but not when you can't see it. So, open your eyes to life, see it in the vivid colors that God gave us as a precious gift to his children, enjoy life to the fullest, and make it count. Say "yes" to your life. And when it comes to drugs and alcohol just say "no." You are made in the image of God, and no one ever has the right to destroy your dreams and shatter your life.

I challenge all stakeholders in the fight against drug and substance abuse in Kenya, you who labor in your efforts to protect the young lives of our nation, you who believe in a drug free Kenya, to make a final commitment to not tolerate drugs by anyone, anytime, in anyplace.

I wish to congratulate Mheshimiwa Kalonzo Musyoka, the Patron of the Kalonzo Musyoka Foundation, for his continued support of the youth. I will also continue to support and encourage all progress of the Kalonzo Musyoka Foundation, as I have always done since its inception, especially in educating the young people here in Kenya, and also in Cyprus.

May God bless you all; God bless our Foundation, and may God bless Kenya.

MESSAGE
at the Kerwa Youth Seminar

August 18, 2012

Reverend Fathers and Presbyteras, Youth Leaders, beloved Children in Christ, receive my greetings of love in the spirit of the Triune God. May the grace and peace and mercy of our Father the Creator, the Son, our Savior and the Holy Spirit, the Life-giver, be upon you.

> Let no man despise your youth; but be thou an example of the believers, in word, in conversation, in charity, in spirit, in faith, in purity.[27]

Based on the extent to which the spirit has penetrated the function of the soul, there are different kinds of lives we can choose. We can choose one that is intellectual and physical. This life ignores the spirit and gives priority to intellectual pursuits based on the physical world. It has its own worldview, behaviors, and relationships and is quite different than a life that is spiritual and intellectual. In the spiritual and intellectual life, the spiritual dominates the physical. Saint Paul encourages his spiritual son to be an example of a spiritual being, one whose character is above reproach, and therefore leaves no room for anyone to despise his youth. This is the spirit of Orthodox life; the kind of life I encourage you today to cultivate.

27 I Tim. 4:12.

> When the spiritual reigns supreme in someone, then although this is his exclusive character and attitude, he does not err. This is because, in the first place, spirituality is the norm of human life, and so as a result, being spiritual, he is a real person, whereas the intellectual or carnal man is not a real person. Secondly, no matter how spiritual someone is, he cannot help but give the intellectual and heart their rightful place; he maintains just a little of them, in subordination to the spirit.[28]

According to natural purpose, man must live in the spirit, subordinate everything to the spirit, be penetrated by the spirit in all that is of the soul, and even more so in all that is physical—and beyond these, and in the outward things, too, that is, family and social life.

This is the challenge we face in our spiritual growth and development. We must learn how to integrate spirit, to lift ourselves up to where spirit has the top priority in our way of life. This requires much effort. This is why Christ came and established his Church with its sacraments and all its traditions and ascetic practices. When we surrender ourselves to Christ and his Church and to her teachings, we grow, allowing spirit to live within us and to take top priority. We can then lead what would be called a spiritual and virtuous life.

"For bodily exercise profiteth little: but godliness is profitable unto all things, having promise of the life that now is, and of that which is to come."[29] Beloved spiritual children, these words from Saint Paul to Timothy encourage us to train our spiritual lives over and above our physical lives. Paul dwells on the promise of eternal life as the vision toward which our spiritual life is aimed. To attain *theosis* is the ultimate goal of each and every Orthodox Christian.

I also plead with the youth leaders to work toward unity of all youth groups in Kiambu and its bishoprics. I understand there is a parallel youth program today in another part of Kiambu. I applaud your efforts in working out these diverse and special training programs for our youth. Life in the 21st century is vibrant and always moving. But above all else, cultivate unity of faith, and together we shall attain unity of purpose. For behold, how good and how pleasant it is for brethren to dwell together in unity!

I congratulate all the youth members who have sacrificed their

28 St. Theophan the Recluse, *The Spiritual Life and How to be Attuned to It* (Platina, CA: St. Herman Press, 1996), 71.

29 1 Tim. 4:8, 9.

otherwise busy schedules and their holiday time from school to be here for this seminar. I pray that the Holy Spirit guides you to a higher purpose in this life and in the next. Be wary of the ruler of this world, whose sole aim is ensuring that your life lacks meaning and purpose. Free yourselves from trends that benefit not your spiritual and physical health. We are living in dangerous times in which drug abuse is prevalent and the rate of HIV infections is hitting the roof. Say "no" to drugs and be examples to the rest. Don't be intimidated by the flashy, quick trends of the material world. Flee from Satan and his ways and he shall flee from you.

Finally beloved children, let Christ be Lord in your lives. Only he is the faithful and true Captain who steers your ship safely to harbor. The future belongs to he or she who aims at higher spiritual goals. Let that be you. Learn the fear of God, for that is where wisdom starts to grow. Emulate the lives of the many saints of our Church, men and women who conquered the lures of this life and attained the crowns of sainthood.

May God, the Life-Giving Spirit always guide you to that which is spiritually fulfilling. Amen.

MESSAGE
to the Gathering of the Kiambu Orthodox Youth[30]

August 18, 2012

Beloved Children in Christ, I greet you all in the Name of the Father, and of the Son, and of the Holy Spirit. Amen. Grace and peace from our Lord and Savior Jesus Christ be with you.

IT ALWAYS GIVES me astounding joy whenever and wherever I hear of, or witness a youth gathering, in unity, love, and peace. It is a show of a promising tomorrow for our Church. It is a witness that the Orthodox Church is growing and has a future embedded in its youth wing. Today's event is a proof of that fact. Without peaceful co-existence, man lacks even health of body and soul. "A sound heart is the life of the flesh" (Prov. 14:30).

But this is also a wakeup call to train and exercise our whole self, not only the body, but also the soul. Spend your time and energy in training yourself for spiritual fitness. Physical exercise has some value, but "godliness is profitable unto all things, having promise of the life that now is, and of that which is to come" (1 Tim. 4:8).

I also encourage you with these words of Saint Paul to his young spiritual son, Timothy. He knew that Timothy was a youth that could benefit much from physical training, just like you today, yet he encouraged him

30 Given during a youth sporting event.

to cultivate spiritual fitness as well. Forget not what the main goal of our existence is: being like God; attaining divinity. This is the likeness of God that we are to seek after in this life.

I congratulate you on this fabulous festival; I applaud your organizational skills and determination that has yielded fruits in assembling all these majestic and devout youth of our Orthodox Church. I also wish to let you know that even though some win and some don't, this is an opportunity to better ourselves spiritually. The wise learn from today's mistakes and build a better defense for tomorrow. I pray that this spirit doesn't stop here, but will become a blazing torch to illumine all the other bishoprics whose torches have dimmed or have not been lit at all. Be sons of light, doing all that is pleasing to Christ our God.

I wish you blessings from Christ our Lord and Savior.

ADDRESS
on Youth and Leadership in the Orthodox Church

Holy Transfiguration Parish,
Kamangu,
August 27, 2012

Reverend Fathers and Presbyteras, Guests of honor, diocesan and parish Youth Leaders, beloved Children in Christ, I greet you all in the Name of the Father, and of the Son, and of the Holy Spirit. Amen.

Grace and mercy and peace from God the Father, and Christ the Savior, and the Holy Spirit the Comforter be with you all.

Endeavoring to keep the unity of the Spirit in the bond of peace.[31]

IT GIVES ME GREAT joy and pleasure to be with you once more for this very important Orthodox organization of youth. As I have said time and again, the gathering of Orthodox youth anywhere displays unity of purpose, and it's a like a heartbeat that signifies life; yes, life in the body of the Church, life in the youth of the Church. That is why today I wish to base my talk on *syndesmos*. What is it, and what is its importance to the Orthodox Church?

Simply put, *syndesmos* is a Greek term that means "the bond." In the context of the Orthodox youth movement, Syndesmos is an international

31 Eph. 4:3.

fellowship of Orthodox Christian youth that encompasses movements, organizations, and theological schools serving the Church and her unity, witness, mission, and renewal for the life of the world.

History

Syndesmos was started in 1953 by a small group of young Orthodox theologians in Paris, France. However, its origins go back to the very beginning of the century, when Orthodox theologians and youth workers established contacts through which they rediscovered the catholicity of the one Orthodox Church. The genesis of Syndesmos can be traced back to the pan-Orthodox Conference on Youth convened in 1930 in Thessalonica and the Congress of Orthodox Pedagogues of 1936 in Dassel, Switzerland. These two are examples of how pan-Orthodox cooperation had been spread before WWII. A later World Youth Conference in Oslo, in 1947, discussed the idea of a network of Orthodox youth movements. Although there were many obstacles and disagreements among the original organizers, several meetings followed with discussions on Orthodox theology, the ecumenical movement, and youth work. One of the points noted in the meeting of 1949 was that "It is desirable that the orthodox youth movements in all autocephalous churches should enter into direct relation with each other in order to increase their spiritual strength and to exchange their experiences."

Several significant inter-Orthodox events were held in the following three years and in September of 1952, a conference of orthodox youth in Western Europe was held in Sevres, near Paris. During this conference, a constitution committee was formed that included, among others: Father Alexander Schmemann and Nikos Nissiotis. This committee drafted the first constitution and chose for the fellowship the Scriptural term "syndesmos" as proposed by Nissiotis.

It can therefore be said that Syndesmos started as an idea in 1949 and became a reality in 1952. In April 1953, the Second Conference of Orthodox Youth in Western Europe took place in Sevres. This is considered to be Syndesmos' first general assembly. And with that, the wheels were set in motion. Branches were opened in the United Kingdom, Germany, the Middle East, and the United States.

In the following years, Syndesmos was organizing international events with even a pilgrimage to the Holy Land in 1965, with many more meetings in Geneva, USA, Finland, and even Leningrad in 1976. 1977 saw major changes in the fellowship, with its secretariat moving to Finland and for the first time in Syndesmos's history, the Secretary General was employed full-time and had a regular salary.

By 1990, Syndesmos evolved into a well-respected partner of all ecumenical bodies. The festivals, the consultations, the Agape camps and other international events allowed hundreds of youth to experience Syndesmos' life and formed a much more solid understanding of what the work of the fellowship was. So much has happened since then: the constitution has been re-written in 1995, members have been added, and many new bodies have been introduced in its governing bodies. But the bottom line is that all the essential elements of Syndesmos—the pan-Orthodox, the spiritual and missionary aspects—are all bound ecumenically in one: the youth element.

For over half a century, outstanding theologians, church workers, students, and simple volunteers have given their very best to address a variety of key issues in church life. And all this has been possible without a solid financial support or even continued presence of trained staff. The existence of Syndesmos thus far is proof of the power of the Holy Spirit at work. This pan-Orthodox gathering that we have here today is what constitutes Syndesmos—the bond.

Membership

Syndesmos has a membership from almost all Orthodox countries in the world, which is its vision; to realize the catholicity of the Orthodox Church. And it has clearly carried out this vision, which has seen the inclusion of even the Oriental Orthodox into its membership. It has held international forums in many different countries in all the continents and has even held one such forum here in Kenya. It has had the honor to include great leaders of our Church in its steering committee over the years, including, but not limited to, the Ecumenical Patriarch Bartholomew, Patriarch Kyrill of Moscow and all Russia, and Anastasios Archbishop of Tirana and all Albania. By the grace of God, I, as a young seminarian, started participating in Syndesmos meetings in 1971 in Boston, where I had the pleasure of meeting the Patriarch of Moscow, who was by then a theologian also. I have attended meetings in Greece, the United Kingdom, Finland, Cyprus, and Africa, among many other countries. What I can say from experience is that this movement is assisting the youth to be together, to have fellowship, to exchange ideas, and to encourage each other. As I have stated above, most leaders of our Church today were young theologians and participants in Syndesmos and our patriarchate is deeply rooted in this organization.

OCYAK *participation*

As I said earlier, the membership of Syndesmos spans universally. Our very own youth umbrella, OCYAK, is a member and has been actively participating in many Syndesmos gatherings. We have been sending national youth representatives to many such forums to represent Kenya and Africa. Such gatherings have taken place in Greece, Finland, and France, where we have sent our own people to represent us. What's more, in 2006, one such forum was held here in Kenya, where participants from many member countries attended.

I have now opened your eyes to the past. You now know that you are branches of a bigger, universal tree of this Orthodox youth movement. This, however, is not the sole purpose of this meeting. We have gathered here today, and for the next few days, in order to assess the present and the dream for the future of the youth. Soon, many of the dates and figures I have mentioned will be forgotten. What we need to keep in mind is the spirit and vision that constitutes the Syndesmos tradition.

The vision of Syndesmos

Syndesmos is a movement toward the realization of a vibrant Orthodox youth ministry. Some people have always questioned the need or purpose of youth ministry: "Why the youth?" they ask, "when the congregations have been primarily supported by aged?" Some have even gone to an extent of calling our Church: the Church of the old people. But the future belongs to our youth. It is time for the aged to step aside, with our deepest gratitude and thanks, and accommodate the young in the leadership of the Church.

The challenge is this: How might our youth organize for the future while hanging onto the best of the past? Syndesmos is helping us to realize that youth is not a matter of age. Some, though physically young, lack enthusiasm. A youthful attitude must be preserved. The youth must be encouraged so as not to become old before their time. They must be encouraged to work independently to solve their own problems. Ministry can be accomplished only when it is genuine, not artificial. Forming a youth movement must be authentic, from the ground up, not imposed from above.

So, I am calling you as the youth of the Orthodox Church to realize your responsibility and not just linger in the margins. Your future participation in Syndesmos, in helping reach out to the un-evangelized, starts right here at home. This is the accepted time, just as our OCYAK motto reminds us: "This is the time. We are the people."

All of us as young Orthodox, should become aware of the catholicity of the Church. This is not a question of abstract doctrine, listed in catechisms, but of a living reality, without which there is no Orthodox Christian life.

Saint Paul compares the Church to the human body. Like the body, the Church is made up of many "parts" or "members"—the people of God. Each member has a specific and important function, as does each part of the body. The liver, the heart, and the brain have different functions, yet each shares a common goal of working in harmony with the other parts of the body to ensure physical health and growth. In the same way, the clergy and the laity, the young and the old, the active and the contemplative have different functions within the Body of Christ, yet they share a common goal—to work together to ensure the spiritual health and growth of God's people, the Church. Everyone, from the patriarch to the most elderly believer in the remotest part of Turkana, shares in this ministry in different, but equally important ways.

Holding a special place within the Body of Christ are our children and youth. On the one hand, they are the future of our Church. They are the ones destined to carry on the ministry of Jesus Christ well into the twenty-first century, long after most of us are gone. The babies we baptize today are tomorrow's priests, bishops, Sunday school teachers, monastics, parish council members, and faithful Christian parents.

Yet we cannot be content with relegating our youth to a place in the future. That is why Syndesmos is a movement of today, the present. Our youth, especially our teenagers and college-age young adults, have an essential and critical role in the present life of the Church. And this is a fact that we must recognize and accept if we are to take the task of youth ministry seriously. Before delving further into this, however, it is important for us to reflect on the needs and characteristics of teenagers and young adults.

All of us were, at one point, 15, 16, and 18 years old. I'd like to ask you to think back to the time when you were that age. What were you like? With what were you concerned? What were your aspirations and dreams, your fears and needs?

At the age of 15, most, if not all, are faced with many confusing challenges and decisions. Their bodies are changing, growing, maturing. They are worried about how they look. They wonder about life, friendships, what they want to be when they become adults. They are filled with insecurities, questions, hopes, dreams, and ideals. Some of them rebel against their parents, teachers, and the other authority figures they encounter. Often they feel alone and abandoned, convinced that no one cares, that no one is concerned about them. And yet, at other times, they feel that they are the very center of the universe, that they are invincible, omnipotent, and self-sufficient.

Many have contemplated running away from home; some have even run away from home, only to realize later how much they depended on their parents, how much they desperately wanted them to listen to them and to understand them.

The need for love and understanding

Day by day, we are realizing that what the youth really want is an expression of love, a sign of assurance, a sympathetic ear to truly listen to their fears and to reassure them that everything is going to be all right. They crave a way to better understand our faith and its deep roots. They yearn for a bond, for *syndesmos*.

So, as youth ministers, we must first be good listeners. In the Church, we often talk too much. We want everyone to listen to us, but we sometimes fail to listen to others. We remind others that the Church has the answers, but we need to be reminded that we are not always answering the questions youth are asking. I would like to know that during this time that the youth are gathered here, we adults will give them time to speak out while we listen.

The world in which we live is growing more and more complex. We always hear of war in the Middle East, global economic meltdown, devastating effects of global warming, political and ethnic conflicts here at home, and countless uncertainties. Many adults are asking, "What is going on? Where are we going? What will become of us?" Imagine how teenagers react! They confront the same global crises in addition to the countless insecurities and cravings for acceptance, clarity, reassurance, affirmation, direction, and guidance. Add to these the potent draw of secular, vulgar music, pornography in the social media, drugs, alcohol, sex, peer pressure, and fashion. The reason our youth are swimming in a sea of confusion, desperately seeking an answer to "the meaning of life" becomes obvious. Yes, the Church has the answers, but the sensitivity needed to listen to the questions is all-too-often lacking. If we are to effectively address youthful fears, hopes, and needs, we must accept our youth as they are, where they are, rather than where we are, or where we want them to be.

Jesus listened. He accepted people as they were. When Jesus spoke with farmers, he used language they could readily understand. He spoke of God's Kingdom in terms of sowing and harvesting. He spoke in simple terms with the simple, yet he provided sophisticated answers to the well-educated. He knew how to speak because he listened first to those with whom he was speaking. He was the perfect example of someone who became "all things to all men."[32]

Listen to our youth, and listen without prejudice or arrogance. Can you hear their intense need for self-acceptance? Youth, above all, need to love themselves, to discover their strengths, to discern their unique gifts, talents, and abilities, and to feel loved, wanted, and accepted. If these essentials are not experienced at home or in the church, they will be experienced elsewhere. Where the family and the Church fail to provide youth with a positive self-image, a sense of community, or a caring, loving environment, a vacuum is created. The vacuum is filled by gangs, drugs, rock idols, and other elements that promise a definite—even if disastrous and sometimes fatal—identity and sense of community.

Jesus teaches us that everything is based on a single commandment: loving God, and loving others the way we love ourselves. But, before we can love God or others, he says we must love ourselves. I cannot respect you if I am unable to respect myself; I cannot trust a God whom I cannot see if I refuse to trust those whom I can see.

Love heals.

There are many, many young people who need and want healing. Jesus encountered many who needed healing—spiritual as well as physical. He

32 I Cor. 9:22.

once encountered an adulterous woman who was about to be stoned by an angry mob. The Law dictated her death; Love, however, dictated her transformation. After dismissing the crowd by saying, "He that is without sin among you, let him first cast a stone,"[33] Jesus approached the woman. He listened to her heart. He did not lecture her on the evils of adultery, nor did he condemn her less-than-honorable behavior. Rather, he told her simply and lovingly: "Go, and sin no more."[34] Jesus' willingness to accept the woman transformed her. He showed her that, while what she had done was bad, she was, in essence, good. He enabled her to discover this essential goodness and in the process, she changed, repented, and accepted God.

While we, as God's people, are first and foremost a worshiping people who are nourished by the common worship of the Liturgy, it is not enough to say that the only thing we need is the Liturgy. I am not saying that the Liturgy is not important; it is very important. The Divine Liturgy is, historically and by its very nature, a public expression of faith by those who already have "seen the true light, received the heavenly spirit, and found the true faith worshiping the undivided Trinity, who has saved us."[35] There are those who would say, "All we need is the Liturgy," as if public worship is sufficient to fill the needs of our youth.

Before liturgy can become a genuine expression of a young person's faith, he or she must have faith. And this becomes especially challenging when dealing with youth who were raised in a non-Orthodox environment.

The way forward

How might all of this be accomplished? Based on my experience in ministering to the church and youth in Kenya for fifteen years as a lay theologian and for twenty years as an ordained hierarch, I would like to offer the following suggestions:

A need for openness

The Church must provide the setting by which youth will share and discuss their needs and fears. It must help them to "open up." This might take the form of a conference or a retreat such as we are having here—a gathering

33 Jn. 8:7.

34 Jn. 8:11.

35 "We Have Seen the True Light," sung at the conclusion of the Divine Liturgy.

of one to three days at which youth can discuss and share their problems, hopes, fears, and joys, listen to talks by clergy, lay ministers, and peers, and react without fear to what they hear and feel. Such gatherings will build a sense of community and become the model of the Church as the Body of Christ. The atmosphere must be one of trust, mutual acceptance, and love, focused on ministry rather than activity. This kind of gathering is a *kairos*, that is, time spent in conscious awareness that the Lord is present in all that is happening.

In this way, youth are given the opportunity to be heard, as well as to hear, to share their feelings, and to identify with the feelings of others. When youth see that others feel the same way they do and that the problems and fears they face are not theirs alone, they begin to open up. Trust builds. A bond, or syndesmos, is established. The things that unite rather than separate are discovered, as are the ways God reveals himself through others. This will help those who are lost feel found and wanted. That should be our vision: to seek the lost.

The program at a youth camp should also be based on this vision and should include talks, discussions, reactions, sharing, fellowship, and worship. Even athletic activities enable youth to discover their unique roles within a team or community. A lively football game provides enjoyment while teaching the very principle upon which the Church is based: many individuals working together for a common goal and purpose.

Finding qualified leaders

In order to accomplish these things, there must be a core of well-trained youth ministers—clergy, lay adults, and youth—who already possess a genuine experience of God's presence in their own lives that is apparent to others.

Whether we like it or not, we must admit that not everyone has been blessed with the gift of working with youth, and we need to seek out and set apart those individuals who are able to:

- Accept youth as they are.
- Be good listeners.
- Identify with the fears, problems, pressures, and uncertainties youth face, as well as with their joys, hopes, and successes.

- Know when to speak and when to be silent.
- Make youth feel comfortable and not feel threatened.
- Have a genuine faith and experience of the Church.
- Be honest and trustworthy.
- Be sympathetic, open, and willing to share their personal experiences.
- Serve as role models.
- Admit faults, or the fact that they do not know everything, without feeling threatened.
- Sense the pressures youth face in their daily lives.
- Discover and develop the talents and gifts of youth.
- Accept each youth as a unique, special person, and as a genuine gift from God.
- See God's presence in the youth with whom they work.
- See that their ministry is an extension of Christ's ministry, designed to lead youth to salvation.
- Put aside self-interests, ego, pride, and arrogance.
- Possess a sense of humor and a playful spirit.
- Accept a certain amount of freedom by the Church to experiment and to try new methods of youth ministry.
- Display confidence without being boastful.
- Possess a genuine rapport with youth and an understanding of contemporary youth culture and interests.

Above all, youth ministers must love youth and accept them as equals. Nothing is more deadly than youth ministers who see youth as "beneath" themselves. Jesus ministered to prostitutes, tax collectors, lepers, and many whom others had rejected. He accepted them for who and what they were. Never did he reject them as inferior.

Finally, youth ministers must, to a certain degree, be youth themselves, at least in spirit. I saw a man in Subukia who becomes a teenager whenever he is among teenagers. Despite the fact that he is almost forty years old, a part of him is still a teenager! We cannot teach such gifts to those who do not possess them by nature. We can, however, develop the God-given abilities of those whom we know to possess youth ministry skills. A person who does not possess a natural love for youth cannot be taught such love.

Youth must be allowed to lead

Youth must not only be ministered to, but they must also be encouraged and allowed to minister to others as a living expression of their faith and belief in Jesus Christ.

Having served the Lord in the Liturgy, it is necessary to serve one another once the Liturgy has ended, thereby transforming day-to-day encounters and relationships into expressions of God's presence and love.

Our youth must be given the support necessary to:

- Volunteer their services in different spheres of church work, including leadership.
- Offer assistance in areas where charitable service is necessary.
- Teach and assist in Sunday schools.
- Organize activities for younger children and their peers on the premises of our churches, or in other available public locations.
- Participate in the liturgical services as readers, in the choir, altar servers, etc.
- Speak of their faith to others openly and without fear, and speak of it with a genuine joy and warmth.
- Recognize God's presence in others and treat them as they would treat Christ.
- Live and share their faith at school, at work, and in their neighborhoods, thereby offering an experience of God's presence with non-Orthodox and others who might otherwise never come into contact with the Orthodox faith.
- Develop their talents for writing, speaking, and singing for the glory of God and the building up and growth of the Church.
- Use their experience to minister to other youth who are lost, searching, or troubled, with a vision of seeking the lost.
- Invite others, especially non-Orthodox, to camps, retreats, and youth group gatherings.

Supporting these things will see the Great Commission of our Lord being fulfilled from within youth ministry.

There are countless other areas in which our youth can bring a vibrant, living sound to our churches. We, for our part, must encourage and affirm them in all they attempt, thank them for all they accomplish, and assure them of our support in every way.

Conclusion

Finally, we must form local parish youth groups and clubs that meet on a weekly or monthly basis to plan and follow up on realizing the youth's long term strategic plans and all that we have talked of above.

We need dedicated leaders to guide these groups and to ensure that the groups do not become exclusive, cliquish, or self-serving. I also call upon the leaders to work toward unity of the whole fraternity of Orthodox youth in Kenya. Create unity of purpose, and together we shall achieve greater things.

I would like to conclude by saying that this is a commendable step and a great stride toward realization of a vibrant youth ministry, and we must take great care in keeping our vision clearly focused on ministry to and by youth, rather than on merely organizing a self-serving bureaucracy. Our vision must be on the needs of our youth rather than on the needs of an organizational structure, important as it is to be organized. I have witnessed the death of too many Orthodox youth groups due to preoccupation with organizational, rather than human, needs. Many youth are lost in the process.

So let us begin our work, recognizing that our youth are the present as well as the future of our Church, and that their function within the Body of Christ is no less important simply because of their age or lack of experience. Our youth are not the only ones to whom the Church must minister, but without them, something most essential—the future—will be lost.

May God bless you all.

MESSAGE
to the Kiambu Orthodox Youth Association

August, 2012

Reverend Fathers present, different Stakeholders in various church fields, the Faithful and Youth, I greet you all in the Name of the Father, and of the Son, and of the Holy Spirit. Amen.

THIS MORNING I am delighted to have you all attend this crucial and auspicious gathering. As youth, we are called upon by the Church to be in the leading line of evangelism, for indeed we are members of one another in the Body of Christ. The Church at this time is taking us through the great time of fasting, the time of Lent. This is the time of strict self-examination: who are we personally? Who are we to our brothers and sisters? Who we are to our God? This is a time of us-with-God, the best time a person should ever have in his or her lifetime, a time of repentance, a time of God's boundless mercy and endless love, a time of salvation.

Many times, the young people, due to the heightening demands of this transient time in life, are caught up hardly thinking about how much they involve God in their daily chores in the name of seeking happiness. Many do not have the time to ask for God's help, or his presence in their lives. This is the great problem that has affected our Church, the Church of Christ, the Ark of Salvation, here for all who enter it with faith, reverence, and fear of God. So, *kairos*[36] is here: an appointed time for repentance for

36 From the Greek: καιρός, meaning the opportune moment.

everyone who truly loves, and hence wants to save, his own life. When kiaros comes, let no man sleep on in his disease, but rather may he reveal it without fear of shame, for he who confesses his sins truly attains salvation. The greatest miracle that each of us should seek in this short life is the forgiveness of his sin and the attaining of perfection. So, my brothers and sisters in Christ, it is time to see your spiritual father and confess your own sins, in order that you may obtain the great miracle of this life.

Many times a youth may feel kept out of church matters and feel unwanted, thinking his or her opinions are hardly taken seriously by the church leaders, whether in the parish or the top level. However, we are very concerned about the youth and are always ready to help you evangelize at your level, since you also have been granted the gifts of the Holy Spirit. We know how much you sometimes sacrifice for the sake of our Church. Do not think that your efforts are not known; we know them and are profoundly grateful to the Lord for your faith and progress in our life in Christ. So, in your endeavors do not be deterred by anyone, but let your focus remain on the One crucified and blessing will come to and through your every effort.

The wise Solomon, inspired by the Holy Spirit of God, wrote that the bad things you do follow you, and all good things you do come back to you. This is to mean that everything you do is either for your own good, or for your destruction. It is either inspired by the Holy Spirit, or by an evil spirit. So, one must choose what to do. This is the freedom our good God gave us, even though as his creatures were are entirely dependent on him. We choose whether we serve him or not, whether we shall respond to his call or not, whether we shall obey his commandments or not. This is how good our God is. He lets us freely choose our destinies. But it is his will that we be saved and because of his love for us he gave his Only-begotten Son to die for us that we may attain remission of sins and eternal life.

So brothers and sisters in Christ, let this precious moment of Lent not pass you by, but rather take advantage of it and make a good rapport with our Maker, our Father in heaven. Try your best to implement the words of the apostle Paul to Timothy: "Let no man despise thy youth; but be thou an example of the believers, in word, in conversation, in charity, in spirit, in faith, in purity."[37] This is very crucial to anyone who knows and has accepted Jesus Christ as his or her Savior. These words of Saint Paul should find a place in our hearts and lift us up to act on the exhortation he makes

37 1 Tim. 4:12.

to his disciple Timothy. These words are also expressed more simply in one of the prayers of the Lenten Presanctified Liturgy as follows:

> O God, great and praiseworthy, who by thy life-giving death of thy Christ hast translated us from corruption to incorruption: Do thou free all our senses from deadly passions, by setting over them as a good guide the understanding that is within us. And let our eyes abstain from every evil sight, our hearing be inaccessible to idle words, and out tongues be purged of unseemly speech. Make clean our lips which praise thee, O Lord. Make our hands to refrain from base deeds and to work only that which is well-pleasing to thee, fortifying all our members and our mind by thy grace.[38]

This is what we need to pray to God first and foremost, and all other things shall follow.

How do we make use of these great exhortations? We do this by holding seminars that focus on different matters that are affecting the youth of our time, such as HIV/AIDS, alcoholism, and drug abuse. We also visit those parishes that are not active and lift them up with humility and simplicity, without losing the importance of such a visit. Much more important is to faithfully uphold the teaching of the Church in order to present to Christ our Lord a Church without spot or blemish. Issues like alcoholism have really affected us. Let us try to mobilize our brothers and sisters against involvement in addiction. This is because we need a healthy generation of today and tomorrow, a focused people, a people ready to drive the Church forward toward the goal established by Christ.

The wise Solomon also said, "The horse is prepared against the day of battle, but safety is of the Lord."[39] This shows that as we have been saved by grace, we must live in a way that is worthy of our repentance. We must prepare ourselves, our bodies, our minds, and all our thoughts as the horse is prepared for the battle; we must be cleansed, make an effort, a great effort—as much as we can—to show willingness to God and obedience. Hence, we shall freely be granted eternal life, not because of those good actions but because of having faith and confessing him in our actions.

When one is young, one needs to do a lot for the sake of Christ, oneself, and one's neighbor. We must do things that will insure a good earthly future, and the time is today. So, if the future is expecting you, then today

38 First prayer of the faithful, *The Hieratikon*, vol II, 245.

39 Prov. 21:31.

is demanding of you, while yesterday is guiding you. You cannot afford to lose this precious moment of great energy of mind and body. If you lack godly, faithful Christians to guide you in both spiritual and material affairs, seek out such people. Be humble toward God and toward all people; be obedient to God and men; look for peace and pursue it at all times; be gentle to those who are astray and have little understanding, and be considerate. Do all things with prayer and supplication to our merciful God, for the well-being of our Church and all people. Amen.

ADDRESS
at the National Annual Mothers' Union Conference

Holy Transfiguration Church,
Kamangu, Kenya,
April 18, 2013

Reverend Fathers, the national Chairlady, distinguished Mothers' Union Leaders, all present Members of the Mothers' Union, all Visitors, Brothers and Sisters in Christ, I greet you all in the Name of the Father, and of the Son and of the Holy Spirit.

PLEASE ALLOW me to congratulate the leaders and members of the Mothers' Union for their continuous efforts to make the Mothers' Union annual conference possible and successful year after year. These conferences have been great sources of information for all participants who later pass the same to their respective parishes, thus cementing our faith in great ways. Accept my sincerest apology for not being physically present at this year's annual conference opening, due to unavoidable ministerial duties. I pray that my message shall represent me fully and more so to remind you of the place you occupy in my heart.

As we continue with this year's Lenten journey, I would like to share three things with you all: These are repentance, prayer, and philanthropy. The same three are encompassed in the attitude of the Lenten fast, which all Orthodox Christians are called to follow. Great Lent is not only about fasting, but more so, a time to review our past lives in the spirit of repentance and reconciliation with God. It is a time to pray fervently, and above all, a time to share what we have with those who do not have.

> Distanced from you, I am distanced from my homeland; Distanced from you, I am distanced from my friend; Distanced from you, I am distanced from my health and the Healer; Wherefore, I call out to you from a foreign land: O my Victorious Savior, hear my voice.[40]

When man fell into sin, he separated himself from God and paradise, his home. For man to be saved, he had to fix this broken relationship in order to be able to return home. This meant getting rid of sin, the one thing subjecting him to this separation. Christ, the God-man made this endeavor of man's possible by his Incarnation, Passion, Crucifixion, Death, and Resurrection, giving man a chance to repent and reconcile with his Creator. Today, sin has not left the world and thus man continually falls into sin. At the same time, man has a chance to repent and reconcile with God through accepting his sin and, with remorse, deciding to get rid of the same through the auspices of the Church.

"Open unto me, O Giver of life, the gates of repentance."[41] The major responsibility of the Church is to make saints out of sinners, which she does through the sacraments. After being joined to Christ through the sacraments of baptism and chrismation, the neophyte attains the great opportunity of receiving the Holy Eucharist immediately, and when needed, to participate in the sacrament of Confession, and repentance. Those who repent perform the act of *metanoia* (change of mind), meaning that they change their sinful past and adopt new ways of dealing with life, going through a transformation and reformation of their lives by renewing their relationship with God, self, and the other. This is part of the journey in recovering the lost paradise.

"For if ye forgive men their trespasses, your heavenly Father will also forgive you: But if ye forgive not men their trespasses, neither will your Father forgive your trespasses."[42]

Forgiveness is a two-way street. It is not only about you receiving God's forgiveness; it is about offering the same forgiveness to those who have wronged you. Human beings have a tendency not to forgive others, while

40 Ode 5 Ikos of the Akathist to Jesus.

41 Stichera after Psalm 50, Sunday of the Prodigal Son. *The Lenten Triodion*, 115.

42 Matt. 6:14, 15.

they sometimes even demand others to forgive them. Christ puts it very clearly that unless one forgives others, God does not offer that one forgiveness. It is therefore paramount for us to check our past lives and to see who we may have wronged and in the spirit of repentance, go offer them forgiveness, if we want the same accorded to us.

During the earthly life of Christ, he prayed in public and in solitude, teaching us how to pray, and teaching that we can pray for anything that comes from God. Christ prayed in almost every situation. He prayed in words or in thoughts, regardless of whether he was in the midst of love, anguish, or sorrow, whether in joy or depression, whether in thanks or complaint. He prayed even at his point of death. "Prayer is standing before God with the mind in the heart."[43]

In most cases, when we pray to God we use familiar words without thinking of them in deeper ways. The Orthodox Church teaches that the prayer words that come out of our mouths—be they personal or the set songs or prayers used in our liturgical services—should not only come from our mouths as mere words that we are used to reciting, but rather be prayers coming from the deeper parts of our being and engraved in our hearts. In this way, we shall be offering prayer to God not with our human words or thoughts, but through our hearts, where our helper, the Holy Spirit, dwells.

We read in Matthew's gospel: "But thou, when thou prayest, enter into thy closet, and when thou hast shut thy door, pray to thy Father which is in secret; and thy Father which seeth in secret shall reward thee openly."[44] We can only reach the state of praying with the mind in the heart if we keep off all "our worldly cares" when praying. Even in the midst of tribulations and the difficult life of the present world, we should heed Christ's instructions and go in our inner room and shut our doors while praying, that is, being silent before God and away from all distractions. In this state, our prayer is moved by the grace of the Holy Spirit, not by our human will, the mere words disappearing from our prayer, leaving only the heart's wordless unceasing prayer as guided by the Spirit.[45] But prayer is not only when we are alone. Like Saint John Chrysostom says, "It is possible to offer fervent prayer even while walking in public or strolling alone, or when seated in your shop...while buying or selling... or even while cooking."[46]

43 St. Theophan the Recluse in *The Art of Prayer* (New York: Macmillan, 1997) 190.

44 Matt. 6:6.

45 See Rom. 8:26, 27.

46 Attributed to St. John Chrysostom.

As Orthodox Christians, we should maintain the attitude of unceasing prayer for which Saint Paul calls in 1 Thessalonians.[47] You, as mothers, are especially the most suitable persons to teach prayer in your homes by not only leading our children to attend church, but also practicing prayer at home. Whether we be walking, digging, planting, washing, cooking, or any other regular chores at home, in the market, on the bus, or in any other place, we should not cease praying; we should not stop communicating with God. At this period of the Great Fast, let us remember that prayer and fasting complement each other. In fact, fasting without prayer becomes but a bodily punishment that induces spiritual aridity, because without prayer, fasting is just a physical diet exercise. Prayer, on the other hand, is useless if not linked to fasting. Fasting is the burning coal and prayer the frankincense; neither has value without the other. Fasting calms the impulse of the flesh and quenches the fire of passion; it curbs the prattling of the tongue; and more importantly, it prepares us for the work of prayer and the release of the spirit from slavery to the flesh.

"This is my commandment, That ye love one another, as I have loved you."[48] Philanthropy—literally meaning: man-loving—in the Orthodox understanding, emanates from the love that God showed to man by sending his only-begotten Son to come save all those who will accept him.[49] As Christians, we reciprocate this love of God to man, not only by mere words, but also by our attitudes and actions toward our visible fellow man. Christ did a lot of works of mercy to his fellow men. He healed the sick, raised the dead, fed the hungry, and evangelized them, among others. All these, Christ the God-man did out of love for his fellow man.

All Christians, as followers of Christ, are called to offer philanthropic acts to their fellow men in imitation of Christ and in showing their love to God, because as Christ says in Matthew, whatever we do to our brethren we do to Christ himself.[50] Being philanthropic to others therefore, secures us the heavenly Kingdom. Philanthropic acts include, but are not limited to: praying for others, visiting the sick, visiting those in prison, feeding the hungry, helping the aged, and caring for the widowed and orphans. You, as members of the Mothers' Union, should emulate this lifestyle and make it not only your Lenten agenda, like most Orthodox Christians do, but rather make it your way of life as Christians and as mothers. The hospitality

47 I Thess. 5:17
48 Jn. 15:12.
49 See Jn. 3:16.
50 See Matt. 25:31–46

and compassion of women is known to all. You, as the leading mothers of our Church, should utilize this gift in the utmost philanthropic works.

As we open this conference let us practice these virtues of spiritual growth. And now, allow me to ask you to stand up, as I pronounce this conference officially opened in the Name of the Father, and of the Son, and of the Holy Spirit, and may the blessings of the Lord and his mercies, through his divine grace and love for mankind, be with you all now and forever and unto the ages of ages!

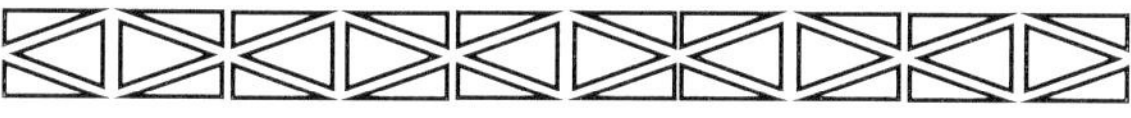

Addresses to Churches & Schools

SPEECH
on the Role of Women in the Orthodox Church

Meru, Kenya,
April 25, 2014

My beloved Daughters in Christ,

WE ARE ALL GATHERED here today to learn, teach, and remind ourselves of one important thing: the role of women in the Church. First and foremost, we need to ask ourselves the following questions. What is a woman? Who are women in the Orthodox Church? Are women a deprived group in the community? Are they the weaker gender? Are they the ones to be led and not to lead? Who are these persons called women? Do they even have any role in their own the Church, and if they do, how can they help build it? The Orthodox Church—as the One, Holy, Catholic, and Apostolic Church—is the full Body of Christ. Thus, she carries the entire congregation, regardless of gender, age, health, status, or ethnic background.

You each have your own personality, temperament, talents, set of circumstances, aspirations, and career goals. You might have differences as individuals, but you have a common experience, especially those of you who are *paphadias*.[1] It is your role to know your faith and to strive to live the Orthodox faith to the fullest by strengthening your relationship with the

1 Paphadia is a title used in the Balkans to refer to a *presbytera* or priest's wife.

Lord, studying the scriptures, and adhering to the teachings of our Holy Orthodox Church. Maintain an active spiritual life through prayer, fasting, and receiving the sacraments, being sure not to neglect the sacrament of confession. Try to locate a spiritual father who can guide you in your spiritual struggles.

As a papadhia, you will be confronted with many challenges. Maintaining an active spiritual life, therefore, will give you the strength to overcome these obstacles, as well as lead you toward a stronger personal alliance with Jesus Christ.

You acknowledged Christ through the sacrament of baptism. You are called upon by the Church to give Christ's love. Through your regular participation in the sacramental life of the Church, our Lord Jesus Christ enters your soul and becomes part of him. You are instructed to listen to the Holy Scriptures and apply its teachings to your daily life. It is your role as women to bring light to the world, enlightening those who are near and far, through your good example in daily life. Many say, "When you educate a girl, you educate the whole nation."

I urge you, my daughters, to devote yourselves out of love to the service of Christ in all aspects of your personal, family, and community lives. In order to succeed, you need to put on your love for Christ within your own family. This then widens to the extended family, neighbors, to your parish community, and then to the whole world. A Christian woman is instrumental in nurturing her children. Women often serve in the society as teachers, nurses, doctors, wives, and mothers. As a wife, she cares for her husband and her children. It is her responsibility to bring the reality of church into her home and lead her household to the church.

If you decide to help or lead in the parish, you should do so because you are an Orthodox Christian, not because you are a papadhia and you feel you must.

My beloved daughters in Christ, I urge you not to try to be someone you are not. Be yourself, with all the wonderful gifts and talents God has bestowed upon you. Bear in mind that your marriage is sacred. Before you were Father and Papadhia, you were husband and wife. Do everything you can to maintain the loving relationship that brought you both together. Make time to do things outside of the social life of the parish. By understanding that church functions and obligations are a part of your husband's ministry, you can lessen the feelings of resentment. Bear in mind that it is your husband who was ordained to the holy priesthood by the laying on of hands, and that it is his responsibility to counsel and advise. Don't feel afraid or embarrassed to talk to another papadhia with whom you can establish a loving relationship. Most likely, she has had similar experiences, and talking to her will be helpful to you.

Priests are not ordained only for their local parish. They may be transferred and given new assignments at some point as part of the life of a clergy family. Because of the diverse needs of the Church, and the fact that there are more parish vacancies than priests available, transfers are inevitable in the life of a parish priest. If you have a career outside of the home, it may be interrupted for a short period of time. If you have children of school age, you will need to help them adjust to a new environment. In any case, moving is a reality, and if you are faced with a new assignment, it is important for you both to discuss concerns with your husband and children. As you all know, the priest is working for the weekend. He prepares for Sunday's Divine Liturgy, which might be followed by other sacraments or events. Usually a day off is taken on a weekday; therefore, the family time together will need some adjusting. Your fiancée or husband will spend many of his evenings in meetings with the various church organizations and in appointments with those who are unable to meet with him during the working day. Flexibility in planning free time is essential to a healthy marriage.

As for you, Papadhia, parishioners will most likely expect you to take on certain responsibilities. The level of your involvement and the way you respond to these expectations depends upon what both you and your fiancée (husband) agree. As you know, being a clergy family sometimes means that you do live in a fish bowl. Curiosity, whether sincere or otherwise, is part of human nature. The amount of privacy necessary to your well being should be determined by you and your husband.

I wish to remind you that Jesus Christ took a revolutionary step in respecting the dignity of women. He glorified their faith and gave them involvement in his ministry. Remember, it was women to whom he entrusted the mission of imparting the good news of his resurrection to the apostles. Christ was fully conscious of the fact that women were sharing the image of God equally with men. Women have a special gift of empathy and compassion, tender care, and sensitivity to pain. We are the Body of Christ, the Church. Each one of us is a part of that Body, dependent on another part of the Body. Men and women have roles to play, and these roles are important in building the body of Christ. Both genders are offered the same opportunities for salvation through baptism.

The Theotokos is an example of a great woman in the history of the Church. She was chosen for a different role than that of the apostles. She was not ordained, yet she holds the highest esteem in our Church as the "Bride of God, the "God-Bearer," and the "Apse of the Heavens." She is an example of purity, parenthood, and apostleship that we should all strive to achieve. The Orthodox Church has a great tradition of honoring female saints, some of whom are considered equal to the apostles, such as Saint Thekla and deaconesses, Saints Tabitha and Priscilla of the early Church.

As part of the Body of Christ—the Church—both men and women are called to listen to God. Being part of the "royal priesthood" means being a servant and sacrificing ourselves for Christ, just as Christ, as the archpriest, sacrificed himself for us. The role and challenge of young women and men is to look beyond some of the misconceptions that exist in the Church and cultivate the gifts that God has given us. When we use them to serve humanity in his Name, then we will have found our special role in the Church. It is important to understand that life in the Orthodox Church is not just attending Sunday services, or teaching in Sunday School, or preparing *prosophora*, or preparing and serving coffee or tea in the church social hall after Sunday service. Orthodoxy is not just wearing a big cross or making the elegant gesture of the sign of the Cross. Orthodoxy is not raising money for some purpose in life. These may be indicators of love and piety. But without Christ's love and teachings, they remain fruitless.

During the times of persecution in the Church, women proved to be true heroines of the Christian faith. They proclaimed the true faith loudly, confessing it before emperors, kings, rulers, and judges. Women guarded the churches and the sacred relics of our faith. Putting their own lives in danger, they moved the holy of holies to safety when it was under threat. Women taught the Christian faith to their children, even when it was dangerous to do so. The special strength women have is a gift from the Lord our God. It is a special grace granted to them by the Holy Spirit to enable them to preserve the true faith.

An Orthodox Christian woman, through faith, finds strength to do what the Lord has chosen for her. She uses the sacramental life of the Church to strengthen her family's faith in the Risen Lord and to practice his commandments. She understands the necessity for Christ to be in her life, and within the life of her family and community, large or small.

When a woman is married into the Orthodox Church from a denomination, she needs a basic idea about the Orthodox faith, rituals, and prayer, to make integration smoother. Otherwise, she may carry her husband to her old faith, or else be unable to participate meaningfully in the Orthodox Church.

It is therefore the responsibility of Orthodox women in the parish to identify such newlyweds and to make them feel welcome, offering to them books and gentle casual guidance regarding the Liturgy, the Orthodox calendar, the importance of the day, attitude toward saints, the use of incense, and other matters. The necessary details regarding childbearing should be explained to the newly married soon after the wedding.

As an Orthodox woman, you are the backbone of the Church in your respective parishes and homes. You need to know that churches cannot continue to be strong unless your families and children—the nucleus of any given parish—are raised and cared for in a Christian manner and according to Christ's teachings. According to Saint John Chrysostom, the home is the little church where all Christian education begins and ends. It is important to recognize that women play an essential and indispensable role in the family. They are caring wives, nurturing mothers, valuable parish leaders and workers. They are hands-on in raising children and keeping the sense of family strong. This doesn't mean that husband or father has nothing or very little to contribute in this field. They, too, have a crucial role to play.

Yet, the wife or mother has a bigger role. God has equipped the female with more qualities than the male in this area of human responsibility. Women have innate ability to comfort and console children when they fall or have a scratch on the knee, thus children will always run to their mothers rather than to dad. Mothers spend quality time with their children to know where the child stands at each moment within his heart. Mothers walk the terrain with their offspring, and they must encourage the awareness that God walks with them.

Parents need to be watching parents as well as listening parents, but never spying or intimidating parents. Their children's friends must be encouraged to visit so that the parents have an idea about the company the child keeps. Parents should know that a child learns first to love and trust his father and mother, and thereby learns to love the Father in heaven. It is therefore the role of each parent to model God's image to their children and only later to shape their parenting style.

Children, who are especially impressionable in the first five years of their lives, receive an invaluable education, not only through the direct teachings from the mother, but also through her actions, behavior, and words. Obedience comes naturally where there is love. Parents need to learn to moderate their expectations, to identify special talents and needs, and to nurture them. Children absorb like sponges the mother's influence on them, even if it is not directly apparent at first. If the mother carries herself properly, adheres to the rules she sets for her children in the house, is polite, and is genuine, then the children will usually follow suit. If the mother, on the other hand, is on drugs, drinks to excess, and does not pay attention to her children, then the children will learn that behavior and eventually practice it. It would seem to the children to be the norm because their mother lived it, and she is the prime example for them. There is an Arabic proverb: "A mother is a school. If you have prepared her well, you have prepared good people."

I wish to request of you, my beloved daughters, to assist parents of the children with special needs who need support from you who have walked the path before them. It is within our power to train our children to face defeat instead of giving up on life out of a sense of inadequacy and unworthiness. As a Church, we urge all women to keep an eye on the sick and the elderly faithful living alone. Visit them in hospitals, and if possible, offer help, including help getting to church.

Saint John Chrysostom instructs mothers,

> "Let everything take second place to our care of our children, our bringing them up to the discipline and instruction of the Lord. If, from the beginning, we teach them to love true wisdom, they will have more wealth and glory than riches can ever provide."[2]

When a child grows up in a home saturated with discipline and the instruction of the Lord, and full of Christian values, and he or she witnesses and experiences sacrificial love, which is the highest virtue, he or she will imitate those patterns and will become a virtuous and productive member of the Church. It is widely known that children learn best through example.

In the Gospel according to Saint John, "Now there stood by the Cross of Jesus his mother, and his mother's sister, Mary the wife of Cleophas,

2 *The Nicene and Post-Nicene Fathers*, First Series, ed. Philip Schaff, vol. XIII (New York, NY: Cosimo Classics, 2007), 154.

and Mary Magdalene."[3] Nevertheless, all of the disciples that followed him, learned from him, and were very close to him for three years, were conspicuously absent at the foot of the Cross, with the exception of John the Beloved. The loyalty that women showed to the Son of God was second to none, which qualifies them to be the backbone of the Church. In the Gospel of Saint Luke, Mary was eager to learn from the Master, so she sat at his feet in humility while Martha served him with love.[4] She complained a little about her sister, but nevertheless, she served him with love. The virtue of knowledge, for which Mary thirsted, strengthens the virtue of faith. The more one learns, the more one realizes that faith is needed in order to accept that which is not understandable, and hence unknowable, like the constitution of the Holy Trinity. At the same time, the virtue of humility, which again Mary exhibited by sitting at the feet of someone, is the beginning of the virtue of wisdom, and one must have wisdom, my beloved daughters, on the narrow road of salvation.

Faith and wisdom are two of the most important virtues on the narrow road toward deification. The virtue of love is evident in Martha's behavior as she served Christ in her house. Despite the fact that she complained about her sister's lack of service, she had obediently served her Master herself. A certain church father remarked that the beginning of love is obedience. If someone is not obedient to anyone, he or she does not love anyone.

The Virgin Mary gives us a perfect example of faith, love, service, humility, and knowledge, among other virtues evident in herself. I urge you to combine the virtues that both Mary and Martha had, namely: faith, love, and service. The Virgin Mary served Christ, her Son, and cared for his needs as would any good mother. She learned from him at every opportunity. Let us not neglect the fact that she had such love for the Master, her Son, and that she was at the foot of the Cross, feeling his pain on the road to Golgotha and at the Place of the Skull. Reflect on how many times you have spent sleepless nights when your children were unable to sleep due to sickness or other complications (how many shed tears when you imagine what others go through, the pain, the sorrow, the anguish). This is similar to the path of the Virgin Mary.

You, as an Orthodox woman, portray the inner life of every Christian. It is unfortunate that some of us still hold onto the old view of the

3 Jn. 19:25.
4 Luke 10:38–42.

German expression, "kinder und küche,"[5] that women are essentially for child-bearing and for cooking, or in Greek, "oikokyrosyne"—the woman of the house. In the Nandi tradition, women are viewed as part of a man's children who need care.

I wish to let you know that women are unique human beings who are willing to sacrifice every notion of their separate and unique identity in order to break the bonds of the presumably man-made social roles that constrain them in their actions and behaviors. It is not unusual for women to deny even their physiological distinctions from the male and to advocate the most extreme form of "gender equality."

As the head of Orthodox Church in Kenya, I wish to firmly state that there is nothing at all truly "traditional" about assigning a certain "nature" to women. It is true: many of the great ascetic fathers warn monks about the wiles of Eve that exist in the female character, but the counterpart of this is the submission of the male counterpart of Adam in sinning monks. Yet, in no sense do we attribute to males a certain "nature," as such, which defines their social roles. Indeed, these images are meant for male and female monastics and are—rather than statements of blame for this or that sin or temptation against one or another of the sexes—practical advice in the pursuit of the angelic life which, after all, transcends human "nature." Men and women are called away from the erroneous "natures" which they have taken on themselves, away from the labor and pain, to deification, to union with God, through the grace of Christ.

Our goals together, as Orthodox men and women, are to make society, as much as possible, an image of the divine. In order to achieve this, our family must be sacrosanct and the parents must fulfill the roles necessary to the preservation of social order. This means that men and women must be caretakers in the home together, that they must be what they are because of a greater goal than fulfilling social roles. If the roles are violated and the spiritual welfare of the family and children are compromised, then we can speak of duty and assigned responsibilities. Saint Paul admonishes the women of the Church to be obedient to their husbands so they don't disturb the spiritual welfare of the family.

I wish to advise you as an Orthodox Christian, not to build prescriptions and proscriptions, but an Orthodoxy in which the Kingdom of Heaven is expressed, and in which that which is worldly reaches up to its

5 German: children and kitchen. The addition of "kirche"—the church—formed the 3 K's.

more heavenly image. Each of us is chastised by the famous Amma[6] of the desert. She hastened to inform a monk, who had crossed to the other side of the road when she and her disciples passed, that had he been a perfect monk, he would not have known that they were women. If we live our Orthodoxy appropriately, we need not define with rigidity the nature of our relationships, men and women, to one another. We will live within that perfect peace by which each knows his role, not out of the imposition of another's will, but out of humility before God. And in this humility, how dare any man think that he is above a woman or a woman above a man, any more than a priest might think himself superior to those of the royal priesthood whom he serves.

We do affirm and recognize an order, meaning, and functional difference in created things. Thus, our faith teaches us that the female is endowed by God with certain characteristics and tendencies that differ from those of men. Our intellects and senses teach us that women and men differ. We cannot deny the biological roles of men and women in procreation. These roles are verified by the external, physical distinctions of gender.

As women, you are called upon to encourage other women to live out an Orthodox lifestyle in their homes because it requires the help of others in the parish. It takes a village to raise a child, and our village is the Church. In many cases there are no grandparents to assist as in the past. Families are separated by distance, and perhaps even faith, since our churches are experiencing an increase in members who have embraced Orthodoxy as adults. The Orthodox faith teaches that, as souls before God, women and men stand equal. Women can and should take an active role in the life of the Church. We believe in the headship of the male and accept the traditional teaching of the Church that reserves the priesthood for men.

Finally, Orthodox women rejoice in the fact that the most perfect expression of Christian life, and the very image of the Church is a woman, the Theotokos. She was devoted to the service of God. She said "yes" to God on behalf of each of us. She continued to say "yes" as she lived out her life, serving as "mother" to the newly founded Christian Church. Now we, too, are called to be devoted to Christ and his Church. With so many areas of ministry in the Church that are available to women, there are more than enough places for women. My beloved daughters in Christ, our devotion requires self-sacrifice, faithfulness to the Gospel and the tradition of the Church, prayerfulness, and the desire to be all God calls us to be.

6 Mother or Eldress—a cognate of Elder, the title given to holy monk-elders.

Jesus said, "Take my yoke upon you and learn from me; for I am meek and lowly in heart: and ye shall find rest unto your souls. For my yoke is easy and my burden is light."[7] Just start slowly and build on the firm foundation that the Church offers. Allow yourselves to be encouraged by each other. Encourage others whose gifts are not being used.

The emotional relationship between the baby and the mother during pregnancy will get stronger during the first weeks after the childbirth through skin to skin contact and by the production of oxytocin, a hormone produced during breastfeeding. This deep biological relationship makes the mother a very important person in the child's life. Mother's care and affection toward the child plays an important role in the psychological, emotional, and verbal development of the child. The enduring patience, unconditional love, and care with which a mother looks after her child, makes a lasting impression on the child's psyche.

May the Lord guide your spirit in the noble task of mothering.

7 Matt 11:29–30.

ADDRESS
at the Opening Ceremony for the Makarios III Patriarchal Seminary

Riruta (Nairobi), Kenya,
September 14, 2010

Reverend Fathers, Lecturers, and Students of our beloved institutions, my beloved spiritual Children, I greet you in the most holy Name of the Father, and of the Son, and of the Holy Spirit. Amen.

> But seek ye first the kingdom of God, and his righteousness; and all these things shall be added unto you.[8]

As we commence a new academic year, 2010–2011, I encourage you to fully embrace the moment, and I urge you to take the time to set your mind on God's Kingdom. Each time one sets his foot in this holy place, he is reminded of the distance he often creates between himself and God, between himself and his brothers. "Be eager to have companions on your way toward God," says Saint Gregory the Theologian. By this statement, he reminds us that we are called to be united in our ascent toward God, our Creator. He reminds us of the spirit we are expected to emulate and live by whenever we come together in this place of worship and learning.

Each year we celebrate this great day of the commencement of a new academic year. At the end of each year, we witness leaps of joy as graduating students rejoice over their success in different academic fields. It is

8 Matt. 6:33.

not an achievement that comes easily! It demands great patience and perseverance. It requires the "knowledge of God," which is "the beginning of wisdom."[9]

Beloved students and spiritual children in Christ, this achievement requires that we all set our minds on the Eternal Kingdom of God. Only by realizing and doing this, can we achieve all else that we desire in life, "and all these things will be given to you as well."[10] Attaining the knowledge of God and the consequential rewards of wisdom can only be achieved through the utmost strict practice of virtue. For virtue is a light and buoyant thing, and all who live in her way "fly like clouds" as Isaiah says.[11]

Every virtue is a good thing, but most of all, gentleness and meekness. Root yourself, therefore, in virtue: in respect, obedience, and humility as you study Orthodoxy as a way of life—the liturgical life. We must, however, not forget that in attaining the knowledge of God, the mercy of God for others is also paramount in our lives both in school and out of school. For even if we have thousands of acts of great virtue to our credit, our confidence in being heard must be based on God's mercy and his love for men. Even if we stand at the very summit of virtue, John Chrysostom reminds us, it is by mercy that we shall be saved.

Let us, therefore, brothers and sisters, beloved children in Christ, approach the new academic year with renewed hope in Christ Jesus. Our Orthodox education center is not only about studying theology or early childhood education or computer studies; here we also learn about life in Christ Jesus. We learn about his love for us and about his greatest command: "that ye love one another as I have loved you."[12]

This is resounded by Saint Paul talking to the Romans when he says, "Owe no man any thing, but to love one another: for he that loveth another hath fulfilled the law."[13] Also, "We know that we have passed from death unto life, because we love the brethren. He that loveth not his brother abideth in death."[14] It is only through this love for one another that we can also realize the best in each one of us. By loving and appreciating each other, we are able to see the image of God in each one of us. We therefore draw near to God and, his kingdom. As priests, lecturers, and students living in the same community, sharing in the same Holy Communion and

9 Prov. 9:10.
10 Matt. 6:33.
11 Is. 60:8.
12 Jn. 15:12.
13 Rom. 13:8.
14 1 Jn. 3:14.

called to the same mission in Christ, let us remember that, "As Christians we are here to affirm the supreme value of direct sharing, of immediate encounter—not machine to machine, but person to person, face to face."[15]

Let us not forget the world in which we are living in today: a world of economic meltdown, political instability, poverty, hunger, and suffering. Therefore, let us desire to change, beginning with ourselves. Everybody desires to see change but no one wants to change. Saint Anthony encourages each and every one of us that, "If you work hard, you can lay a new foundation every moment."[16]

Let us therefore, beloved children in Christ, lay new foundations in our lives this new academic year: foundations worthy of the change we desire to see and to be. This does not mean that we shall be alien to suffering. Suffering will always be there in the life of a Christian.

Declaring the power of salvific suffering, the apostle Paul says, "[I] now rejoice in my sufferings for you, and fill up that which is behind of the afflictions of Christ in my flesh for his body's sake, which is the Church."[17] These words seem to be found at the end of the long road that winds through the suffering which forms part of the history of man and which is illumined by the Word of God. These words have, as it were, the value of a final discovery, which is accompanied by joy. For this reason, Saint Paul writes that he rejoices in sufferings for the sake of his brethren.

The joy comes from the discovery of the meaning of suffering, and this discovery, most personally shared in by Paul of Tarsus who wrote these words, is valid for others. The apostle shares his own discovery and rejoices in it because of all those whom it can help—just as it helped him—to understand the salvific meaning of suffering.

So, dear brethren, beloved children in Christ, these words come to you during this special day of the commencement of the academic year, 2010–2011, that they may be to you a reminder of the obligations ahead of you; both academically and spiritually. Seek ye first the Kingdom of God, and all else will surely be added to you. I beseech you once more to abide in the love of Christ Jesus during your stay here, that he may make your stay fruitful in his great mercy.

May God bless you all.

15 Eagle River Institute, "The Human Person in Orthodox Spirituality," Kallistos Ware (Eagle River, AK, 1998), Orthodox Christian Cassettes.

16 This quote is variously attributed to St Anthony, St. Moses, and St. John Chrysostom.

17 Col. 1:24.

ADDRESS
at the Day of Prayer for the Upper Hill Secondary School

Nairobi, Kenya,
October 14, 2011

I greet you all in the great love of the Holy Trinity.

THANK YOU to the Head Master and members of the school administration for the privilege of joining with you today and for your gracious welcome. And thank you to all of you teachers who work so hard, not only in teaching your subjects, but in modeling with your lives what it means to be good students, good neighbors, and good citizens. And thank you, students, every single one of you. You are the reason that the rest of us are here today. This school—with all of its teachers and all of its staff—exists to help you become the men and women. And for good or for ill, what you learn or don't learn here, and what you do or don't do here will go with you for the rest of your lives. It is an awesome privilege to be teaching and helping a group of young people who have in them the potential to change their world, to make a difference in their homes and communities, and even in this great nation of ours.

Education is powerful. Learning how to read is the key that opens the unimaginably rich world of literature. Learning to multiply and divide opens the door into the universe of physics and astronomy. Reading history opens one's eyes to understanding what really happened and why the world is the way it is. Education can change the direction and therefore change the life of a student. Education opens doors of opportunity, for work and advancement and a career. In education there is a hope for a better life, despite all the challenges that we face in this world of ours. With an education, we are learning the skills we need in order to make us useful in an industry or a market. We are starting to gain the experiences and expertise that will one day allow us to be hired. This is the goal of our system of education: to fashion well-trained and well-rounded men and women, who will take their place in our country's work force and help the nation to take the next steps in her development.

Kenyans have valued education even before the first Europeans built the first school for local children. We have inherited this passion for education from our forefathers and mothers, and can look back with pride on generations of Kenyans who have made education a priority in their lives and then lived to see the transformation of their world.

You are actually a part of a revolution today. Even though class can seem dreary and assignments a waste of time, this process of education is the dynamic behind all intellectual and human development in this world. Education will be the reason that tribalism finally disappears from every corner of this country. Education will be the reason that corruption and impunity are finally chased away as men and women realize that they do not have to put up with corrupt officials and politicians anymore. Education will be the reason that people finally treat the land and water with respect and begin to reclaim the glories of Kenya's land as their heritage. And education will be the reason that men and women realize that it is in their interest to settle for nothing less than justice—justice for the poor and oppressed, justice for the IDPs,[18] justice for the victims of greed.

Education is not just a tool that empowers us, but also a tool that enables us to serve. What we receive here is meant to equip us to serve, to help someone we know who needs help, to give to someone we know who is without. What we learn here is not simply about increasing our knowledge or achieving the highest marks, but becoming the kind of young men and women who think about others first, and who put what we are learning here to use for good. Knowledge is a good thing, but knowledge alone will not accomplish anything worthwhile without character. So, as you are learning your math and algebra, while you are working on your grammar and reading your novels, while you are learning formulas and

18 IDP's: Internationally Displaced Persons.

doing experiments, work on your character as well. Are you growing in your honesty, in patience, in self-control? Are you excelling in humility and compassion and generosity? How are you treating those around you?

You see, our relationships with one another reveal the reality of our relationship with God. By knowing one another and choosing to love the people around us, even the difficult people, we begin to know God himself because each human person is the image, the icon, of God.

Finally, I leave you with these verses from Proverbs: "Get wisdom, get understanding: forget it not; neither decline from the words of my mouth. Forsake her not, and she shall preserve thee: love her, and she shall keep thee. Wisdom is the principle thing; therefore, get wisdom: and with all thy getting get understanding."[19]

We have been thinking about the value and the power of education. But the Bible tells us that there is something even more important that you and I should be about. Education is important, but wisdom is the best of all. Education may fill our heads with lots of facts and ideas. But wisdom shows us how to use them. Wisdom perceives what this world is all about, who God is and what his priorities are, and it helps one to order one's life accordingly. Wisdom enables one to live one's life under God's blessing. There is nothing more valuable; there is nothing more worth having.

Jesus tells two very short parables in Matthew's gospel:

> The kingdom of heaven is like unto treasure hid in a field; the which when a man hath found, he hideth, and for joy thereof goeth and selleth all that he hath, and buyeth that field. Again, the kingdom of heaven is like unto a merchant man, seeking goodly pearls: who, when he had found one pearl of great price, went and sold all that he had, and bought it.[20]

There are many things vying for your attention today, many things trying to win the affections of your heart, many things trying to lay claim to the precious minutes and hours and days of your life. But there is only one thing that is worth such a high price, only one thing that can give you what you are actually looking for, what you were actually created to know and possess. The Old Testament calls this wisdom. Jesus calls this the Kingdom of Heaven. The New Testament calls this new life in Christ. Do not waste your life. Do not spend yourself and your resources on things that will not

19 Prov. 4:5–7.
20 Matt. 13:44–46.

satisfy. There is a treasure in this field. There is a pearl of great price here. "Though it costs you all you have, get understanding."[21]

Thank you again for your warm hospitality and for the privilege of meeting with you here today. Through the love of Christ our Savior. Amen.

21 Prov. 4:7.

ADDRESS
at the Graduation Ceremony of the Makarios III Patriarchal Seminary

Riruta (Nairobi), Kenya,
May 22, 2010

Distinguished Guests, Members of the diplomatic call, Heads of other denominations present here with us, reverend Fathers, the Dean, and Vice Rector, Lecturers and Teachers, the Graduands of both institutions, and all other Visitors present with us here today, I greet you all in the Name of the Father, and of the Son, and of the Holy Spirit.

I TAKE THIS SPECIAL opportunity to recognize the presence of our dignitaries here today, especially the honorable minister, the ambassadors and the representatives from various churches. I welcome you warmly to this auspicious occasion of witnessing the graduation of our students that we have been training within these holy grounds of our archdiocese. First of all allow me to convey my humble gratitude to our beloved pope and patriarch, His Beatitude, Theodoros II, who through his hard work and prayers, has helped us achieve our immeasurable success. I also want to thank the government of Kenya for the support that it has always offered to our Church in all areas necessary, for the growth of the Church and also for the institutions that it has established to offer quality education to Kenyans. We can always conclude that the government's support has been a great help in our development. It is important for me to take this opportunity also to thank our donors, sponsors and well-wishers for their generous contributions to the Church of Kenya. We pray and believe they will keep up their good philanthropic spirit. We also thank, and wish Almighty God's blessings on, all those who have contributed in one way or another toward the growth and the development of the Orthodox Church in Kenya.

Well, it is finally here—the moment we have all been waiting for. For some it is exciting, and for others not. It is almost unbearable for some of you, but for some reason there is part of you and me that doesn't want to let go. We are extremely jubilant because we are finally moving on, but we cannot help ourselves from reminiscing about the good times we had with our colleagues and friends, and thinking how much we will miss everything we had in our institution. And maybe some of you are having some little regrets, too. Perhaps you could have tried a little harder. As all of you look back to your past experiences, you will often have these thoughts, but we must not dwell on them. We must learn from our mistakes and then apply what we have learned.

There are infinite opportunities in life, and your lives have just begun. Brothers and sisters in Christ, let us be women and men of integrity, which happens when we firmly adhere to our standards and values. Integrity is a word not understood by many. Respect for truth and values have been lost over the years. In a world where acceptance by the crowd is desired more than individual integrity, we stand the risk of losing our values and ourselves. Throughout your studies you have seen examples of integrity: A person who was loyal to a friend, the college mate who accepted responsibility for his or her own actions, the individual whom you trusted because never did he give you reason to doubt his honesty, or the steadfastness of someone who, even under pressure, never made an excuse for bad behavior. As the years ahead unfold may these examples inspire, guide, and encourage each of you.

My dear children in Christ, by learning to live a life that is comfortable and true, we could achieve the happiness so many of us seek. This, however, requires us not to accept the norm. Instead we must step outside our comfort zone and toward the integrity so many have abandoned. It's up to you to make these decisions now, to stand up without holding back or being embarrassed by your choice. As you head into the world with all of its influences, please make that choice wisely and with the belief that you possess qualities that will make a difference in this world. Being, in reality, how you wish to appear to others will affirm you.

Today is an important day, in which you will graduate and go from here to the people, not as leaders but as servants. You will be required to serve the people diligently; you will be required to transmit the important knowledge that you have acquired here to serve and enrich those who will be under you. Always keep in mind that there are several people you need to empower on a regular basis. First of all, the people closest to you: your family, your friends, your spouse and children. Secondly, your work relationships: your co-workers, your colleagues and even your boss. Thirdly, all other people that you interact with in your day-to-day life: your faithful, students, and all other people within your neighborhood. In each case, the ability of the people to help you is what will make you a more useful and effective person in your capacity as a priest or an educationist. It is important also to note that the deepest need of all the people who are under you is for self-esteem.

So always give them what you yourself would wish to receive from others, taking into account that the simplest way to make another person feel good or loved is your continuous expression of appreciation for everything good that person does for you, be it large or small. Learn to say thank you on every occasion. Thank your spouse for what he or she does for you. Thank your children for their cooperation and support in everything they do around the house. Thank your students for working hard and attaining high grades. Thank your faithful for their contribution in Church. Thank your neighbor for the smallest act of kindness. The more you thank other people for doing things for you, the more things those people will want to do. Dear graduands, every time you thank another person, you cause that person to appreciate themselves better, you raise their self esteem and improve their self- image, just as our Lord Jesus Christ taught us always to love others as we love ourselves. When we thank people we cause them to feel important and to see that what they do is valuable and worthwhile; we thereby empower them.

Brothers and sisters in Christ, always entrust your destiny to God. Our Church assures us and reassures us again, that the God whom we worship is able to deliver to the utmost those who put their trust in Him; that his power is inexhaustible; that his love and mercy are omnipotent; that his will is sovereign; that he holds our lives in the hollow of his hand. He created dependable laws that govern the surrounding universe. There is nothing of which we need to be afraid; we face the facts with him. In every emergency there is help for us from God. To him we may safely trust the future, and in his confidence we may call upon his reserves as a guarantee of victory. We ought to face daily challenges with stamina and courage. The need to make the citadel of our spirit impregnable demands that we keep our spiritual reserves at their fullest strength, by nurturing a sense of God's presence, by cultivating an attitude of serenity in this chaotic world, and by learning to trust our destiny to God.

Dear graduands, it is important for me to remind you that it is good to have a sense of purpose in life. Having a sense of purpose in life goes a long way toward helping you feel confident, secure, and happy. A sense of purpose is brought about by anything. It can be related to your career, bringing up your family, or even doing volunteer work. It is all about fitting and feeling you are making a difference and that you are achieving something and getting somewhere.

Brothers and sisters in Christ, if you have a sense of purpose in life, then you have something to look forward to everyday, a reason for getting up out of your bed in the morning with a smile. It makes you feel good on the outside and good on the inside. It leads to one becoming a confident person who is happy with his position in life. Almost all of you are still young and I believe that you won't have a problem developing a purpose in life. You are just starting out and the majority of you have had exams to pass, careers to start building, marriages to form, and eventually families to start. Those who are graduating today have a lot to look forward to, and so are right to be filled with a sense of all the possibilities of life in front of you. Because of this great potential which each of you represent, it is of equal importance to strive to develop yourself spiritually, emotionally, mentally, and physically, as this automatically leads to a happier life.

Finally brethren, I wish you all the best, and I promise that I will always be with you in prayers. I thank all those who sacrificed their time for this successful occasion. I thank all of our visitors: the ambassadors, and the representatives of various churches not forgetting the Vicar General, the Deputy Dean, Vice Rector of the Teachers' College and everybody else with us here. I wish you all God's blessings. Amen.

ADDRESS
to the Students of the Makarios III Patriarchal Seminary

Riruta (Nairobi), Kenya,
December 16, 2010

My dear spiritual Children and Coworkers in the vineyard of Christ, Christ is in our midst.

It is marvelous to have a place where you know that God exists, and it is wonderful that he exists everywhere. He is omnipresent. This is the most important assurance to us, as the sons and daughters of God. He is always with those who are chosen to continue with the good work of Christ, those chosen to work in his vineyard. And he is assuring us that his Spirit will always be with us to guide and bless us as we labor to bring people closer to the goodness of God.

It is good to mention that during the Old Testament times, and in accordance with the laws of the Israelites, a shinning cloud called *shekinah* rested between the two winged creatures of the ark. This shekinah was the divine manifestation through which God's people felt his presence. The presence of God is usually associated with glory and light. "God is light and in him there is no darkness at all."[22] It is wonderful to have a shining place where God is present; to be aware of reality behind reality and to be sensitive to the Word of the everlasting God. The ark was placed in the

22 1 Jn. 1:5.

holy of holies of the tabernacle, and a veil was drawn before it, and people were not allowed to enter or even make noise. This ark was a box and inside it was the Law of God, the Ten Commandments. Resting on the box was the mercy seat. Therefore, the law was covered by the mercy seat, and hence, above the law was the loving kindness of God.

We all know the happiness of finding the presence of God on the mercy seat. David felt the happiness when he wrote, "Blessed is the he whose transgression is forgiven, whose sin is covered."[23] Looking at these words, we clearly see that the law is covered by mercy, and thus the crucifixion of Christ signifies that the Cross was God's mercy coming down, covering and resting upon the law that reveals humanity's terrible sin. As Saint Paul puts it: "Where sin abounded, grace did much more abound."[24]

During the Israelites' sojourn in the wilderness, when the ark moved forward, then the people moved forward. They had a shinning cloud directing the way. This, brothers and sisters, is indeed a fascinating story of how the ark led the way for the Children of Israel, and though it may seem as something impossible, yet it is real. It is reassuring to have the presence of God point the way forward for us. This is the main reason for our calling, that of allowing the presence of God to direct us, and to help us lead the people of God and show them the right path, to assist them in their day-to-day life, assuring them that we are always together with them, even when they are facing the most difficult challenges in life. Ours is the mission of hope, assuring the children of God that he is always with them.

My dear spiritual children, it is good to be a priest before the ark and enter the holy of holies where God is—where God covers sin, where the cherubim, the messengers of God, are active, where God speaks in silence—as this was the high priest's privilege and duty. When Jesus came, he became our great high priest. He entered into the presence of God and made atonement for us. When he was upon the Cross, there was a great earthquake and the veil of the temple was torn in two from top to bottom. The significance of this is that there is now no holy of holies where you and I are not permitted to enter, and now it is permitted for us to enter where the shekinah rests upon the mercy seat.

Today, our church building is an ark. The altar on which we are ordained to serve is the place where God is. It is a place where God's mercy is above God's law. It directs men and women forward toward God's

23 Ps. 32:1.

24 Rom. 5:20.

Promised Land, and it should be approached with humility, in reverence, in awe, in love and holiness. It is for all these good reasons that all of you are invited here to this holy institution to learn how to become responsible men of God. You are here to learn how to serve God and people. Your main reason for studying here is to make you priests who are deeply and fully immersed in the mystery of Christ, and capable of embodying a new and a holy style of pastoral life.

Our priesthood should be Christ-centered. This is my main reason for writing you this important pastoral letter, to make you responsible priests of our Church. Remember this is your calling—to serve in the house of the Lord. As we know, the Church participates in the priestly anointing of Christ in the Holy Spirit. We believe that all the faithful form a holy and a royal priesthood, and that they offer spiritual sacrifice through Jesus Christ. And they proclaim the greatness of him who has called us out of darkness into his marvelous light. In Christ, this entire mystical body is united with the Father through the Holy Spirit. It is worth mentioning that, as students of the Ecclesiastical School, you are all chosen and trained to continue with the ministerial work of Christ. The ministerial priesthood finds its reason for being in this important and operative union of the Church with Christ. Our priesthood renders tangible the actual work of Christ, our head, and gives witness to the fact that Christ has not separated himself from his Church; rather, he continues to vivify her through his everlasting priesthood.

My beloved students and co-workers in Christ, our gift of priesthood was instituted by Christ to continue his own saving mission. It was conferred to the apostles and remains in the Church through the bishops and their successors. Through the sacrament of ordination, conferred through the laying on of hands and the consecration prayers of the Bishop, a special bond unites the priest with Christ, the High Priest and Good Shepherd. Therefore, our priesthood is a specific participation in the priesthood of Christ. When one is ordained, one becomes in the Church and for the Church, a real living faithful image of Christ. As priests, we become sacramental representations of Christ, the chief Head and Shepherd, both in and for his Church.

During baptism, each of the faithful becomes united with the Triune God. It is equally true that by the power of consecration received through the ordination, the priest is placed in a particular and specific relationship with God the Father, the Son, and the Holy Spirit. Our identity in our priesthood has its ultimate source in the love of the Father. He sent the Son as our High Priest and we are united sacramentally with the ministerial priesthood through the action of the Holy Spirit. So we can say that the life and the ministry of the priest is a continuation of the life and action of the Christ. This is our ultimate identity, our one and true dignity, the fountain of joy, the certainty of our life.

The grace and the permanent office conferred with the unction of the Holy Spirit places the priest in a personal relationship with the Trinity, since the Triune God is the fountain of the priestly identity and work. Christologically speaking, when we maintain our common priesthood and we are chosen to become part of the ministerial priesthood, we are granted a permanent participation in the one and only priesthood of Christ. This involves the priest participating in the public dimension of mediation and authority regarding sanctification, teaching, and guidance of all people of God. In this unique identity with Christ, the priest must be conscious that his life is a mystery, totally grafted onto the mystery of Christ and of the Church in a new and a specific way. This is the source of his pastoral identity and activity, and the reason for his reward.

"As my Father hath sent me, even so send I you."[25] These words were spoken by Christ when he called the apostles to his own mission. Today he is also calling us as priests to this same mission. When a priest is chosen, consecrated, and sent to carry out his mission of Christ, he becomes an authentic representative and messenger of Christ: "He that heareth you heareth me; he that despiseth you despiseth me; and he that despiseth me despiseth him that sent me."[26]

During the ordination, the priest always receives the seal of the Holy Spirit, which marks him as a sacramental character in order to be the minister of Christ and the Church. He is given the prophetic task of announcing the Word of God and explaining its authority. And the Holy Spirit, whom the Father has sent through Christ, will guide him. The priest is always in communion with the Holy Spirit in the celebration of the Liturgy and other sacraments. This is evident in the Eucharistic prayer in which the priest, invoking the power of the Holy Spirit on the gifts of bread and wine and pronouncing the words of Jesus, actualizes the mystery of the body and blood of Christ, really present through transubstantiation. Through the Holy Spirit, the priest must pray for the unity of the faithful, so that

25 Jn. 20:21.
26 Luke 10:16.

they may be one, in order that the world may believe that the Father has sent the Son for the salvation for all.

Looking at Christ within an ecclesiastical dimension, we see him as the permanent and ever-new origin of salvation. He is also the mystical font from which is derived the mystery of the Church. His Body—that is, his Bride—is called to be a sign and means of redemption through the mystery of Christ. The priest exists in many ministries and is also in the mystery of the Church, which becomes aware in faith that her being comes not from herself, but from the grace of Christ in the Holy Spirit. He is not only made a sharer of the mystery of Christ, the high priest, master and head, but also, in some way, as Christ's servant and spouse of the Church.

The priest should love the Church as Christ loved her, consecrating to her all his energies and giving himself with pastoral charity in a continuous act of generosity. Through Christ, the priesthood pertains in an immediate way to the universal Church, which has a mission to announce the good news "unto the uttermost part of the earth."[27] The demands in the life of the Church in the world must be felt and lived by each priest, above all and essentially as a gift of living within the institution and being at her service. The priest must always remember our Lord Jesus Christ "came not to be ministered unto, but to minister, and to give his life a ransom for many,"[28] and that he bent down to wash the disciple's feet before dying on the Cross and sending his disciples out to the whole world. Like Christ, a priest must make Christ visible in the midst of the flock entrusted to his care, having a positive and encouraging rapport with the faithful. Recognizing them with dignity as sons and daughters of God, he should develop his own role in the Church, offering to all his priestly ministry and pastoral charity.

My spiritual children in Christ, in conclusion, I would like to say that in order for you to perform the apostolic mission that is your responsibility, you will have to bear, engraved on your hearts, the words of the Lord: "Father … I have glorified thee on the earth: I have finished the work which thou gavest me to do."[29]

From these words, as a priest you have the responsibility of dedicating your own life to your brothers, living as a sign of supernatural charity, in obedience, in celibate chastity, with simplicity, and with respect for the discipline in the communion of the Church. As a priest you are called

27 Acts 1:8.
28 Mark 10:45.
29 Jn. 17:4.

to raise up men and women, bringing them to the divine life, and helping them to grow toward fullness in Christ. You should act as a model of Christ in a supernatural way as Christ demands when he says, "For I have given you an example, that ye should do as I have done to you."[30] Your lives should be a living testimony of righteousness to those under you. This qualification constitutes a priest's most convincing sermon. And your ongoing formation as a priest is a task of immense work: open, courageous, enlightened faith, sustained by hope and rooted in charity. In doing all these things, as a priest you should always pray and ask God to help you, and especially ask the Mother of God to intercede on your behalf, as this will provide you with a renewal of your life and the zeal for spreading the Gospel of Christ to the world.

30 Jn. 13:15.

SPEECH

on the Fortieth Anniversary of the Makarios III Patriarchal Seminary[31]

January 19, 2011

Reverend Fathers, Your Excellencies, the Ambassadors & High Commissioners, esteemed Guests, Lecturers, Teachers and Students of our institutions, beloved Brothers and Sisters in Christ, I greet you all in the Name of the Father, and of the Son, and of the Holy Spirit. Amen.

ALLOW ME TO START by quoting some very special words, from the Great Commission of Christ Jesus in Matthew 28: "Go ye therefore, and teach all nations, baptizing them in the Name of the Father, and of the Son, and of the Holy Spirit."[32] One man's mind has the potential to transform not only events, but also people's lives. When Christ was sending out his apostles and disciples, he was seeing beyond the environs of Jerusalem and Judea; he envisioned the Gospel reaching even unto the ends of the earth! He therefore placed that yoke on his apostles and the generations after. This yoke, dear brothers and sisters in Christ, is always on our shoulders: to take the message of Christ beyond our horizons, even unto the uncharted territories. When we do good, we should do it only

31 On the occasion of the fortieth anniversary since His Beatitude, the President of Cyprus, Makarios III, laid the foundation of the theological institute in Nairobi.

32 Matt. 28:19.

because we love it and prefer it to evil, and not because we seek rewards. This way, we will become children of God and not his hired workers.

Today, beloved brothers and sisters, we mark the fortieth anniversary since the laying of the foundations of this theological seminary as well as that of P.C. Kinyanjui Technical. Forty years ago from today, one primate from beyond the African continent set foot here in Kenya, amid some rather unpleasant circumstances. But his predicaments notwithstanding, in a spirit of utter humility and love for the work of God, as well as profound love to fulfill the commission of Christ; seeing a people in search of the true teachings of Christ; he sought to acquire land and actually laid the foundation for the first Orthodox theological institute in Kenya, indeed the only one of its kind in the African continent, as well as the foundation for a training institute for the youth. That foundation, laid forty years ago, by a man from beyond this continent, is the place that we are in today! The primate is none other than His Beatitude, Archbishop Makarios III, President of the Republic of Cyprus. May his memory be eternal!

A person must not be judged by his appearance, but by the purity of his soul and the fineness of his deeds. Not many people at that time could see the vision that the primate had for the entire African continent. There was actually no one to run the institution at that time. Yet, the primate saw beyond the hurdles of trained personnel; he saw beyond the hurdles of financial lack; he saw a hunger and thirst for Orthodoxy and set in motion the wheels that would see that hunger and thirst quenched.

Still, his great contribution didn't stop at that. His great concern, love, and dedication touched on the predicament of the young generation. He desired to give them a technical dimension in life; not only to the potential Orthodox Christians youth, but to all youth across all denominations; irrespective of race, color, or creed. He therefore constructed a technical training institute: the current P.C Kinyanjui Technical. History is faithful enough to testify that many a thousand young citizens of our nation have led productive lives, helped greatly by that institute, and many more will follow for generations to come. These are contributions that we can't fail to recognize and appreciate on this special day.

Great minds do not only discuss ideas; they turn them into realities—realities from visions well-thought out. The archbishop was not only a great man; he was a great visionary, leader, primate and most of all a true statesman.

Our greatest challenge today can only be to ensure that what the archbishop saw comes to maturity. We should ask ourselves how different our lives would be today if the humble hierarch did not initiate these memorable projects. We need to see in the Church and youth of today what he saw. We need to see where he envisioned us to be and work toward that. We need to think of the many theologians who'd otherwise never have heard of Orthodoxy, the many youth who'd never have had access to higher education, the many African nations whose light of Orthodoxy emanated from this institution.

Think of how different life would have been for the many people who have come into contact with these great foundations that were laid some forty years ago. That, reverend fathers, brothers, and sisters, is the change that one's mind and positive action can impart in people's lives, guided by the words of the apostle Paul to the Galatians that as often as we have opportunity, let us do good to all, especially to those who are of the household of faith.[33]

Let us celebrate this day, beloved brethren, with the challenge that even though we've come this far, much is yet to be done, and we are the ones to do it. Let us also be awakened by the great lesson from the deeds of Archbishop Makarios, that the choices we make today will greatly affect generations after us, even decades after our repose!

We also deeply appreciate all of the leaders and staff who have served in these great institutions since their inauguration in 1972, by the late Archbishop of Cyprus Makarios III, together with the late Mzee Jomo Kenyatta. We also recognize and applaud the efforts of those people whose idea it was to start the Orthodox Teachers' College, which is a great and laudable move toward fulfilling the great academic needs of our young generations. We can't fail to also recognize the great contribution of our friends, supporters, and co-workers from Cyprus, Greece, Finland, Australia, the United States, and the countless others who have selflessly supported our mission work here in Kenya. May God always remember them.

Finally reverend Fathers, brothers, and sisters in Christ, Let us always remember and pray for the souls of those dearly departed whose efforts and contributions have led us to this day, and especially the benefactor

33 Gal 6:10.

of these two institutions, Archbishop Makarios III. May his memory be eternal!

I wish you all a blessed New Year in 2011, full of great visions for yourselves, for the Church and for the nation. May God bless you all!

ADDRESS
on the Growth of the Orthodox Church in Kenya the Previous Fifty Years

October 8, 2011

In one of his addresses in the recent past, His Beatitude, Theodoros II, Patriarch of Alexandria and all Africa, remarked that the Orthodox Church in Kenya is truly the heartbeat of mission work in Africa. Indeed it is. With a population of over a quarter million faithful in well over four hundred parishes and close to three hundred priests, its presence is evident in all the corners of this blessed nation.

The beginning of the growth of Orthodoxy in Kenya was earmarked by the generous gesture of the late founding president of Kenya, Mzee Jomo Kenyatta, when he donated land to his counterpart, the former president of Cyprus, Archbishop Makarios III. With great zeal for the growth of the Church as well as the nation, the Church built, together with the seminary, a technical school for the community. Today, that technical school—P.C. Kinyanjui Technical Institute—has grown to tremendous heights and nurtured youthful minds from all over Kenya. And what is more: the institute is celebrating its recent ISO 9001:2008 Quality Management System Standard certification. This is an achievement that gives great pride not only to the institute, but to the Orthodox Church as well.

In addition to the theological studies offered at the Archbishop Makarios III Patriarchal Ecclesiastical School in Nairobi, the only one of its kind in Sub-Saharan Africa, the Church is also engaged in offering different levels of education from kindergarten to the tertiary level. Currently, the Orthodox Church offers free education in her various institutions that include:

- Over twenty-six pre-elementary schools (nursery)
- Eighteen primary schools
- Eleven secondary schools
- Two tertiary institutions: The Makarios III of Cyprus Patriarchal Seminary and the Orthodox College of Africa
- The above mentioned tertiary institutions produce various professionals, including clergy and theologians, teachers, social workers, community developers, information technicians, tailors, and computer technicians.

The church has also engaged in offering ten different feeding programs, offering three meals a day to children from poor families. Among many other philanthropic endeavors, the church also runs the following:

- Six orphanages / children's homes
- Thirty health centers / dispensaries
- Youth movements
- Sunday school education programs
- Scholarship programs
- Help with hospital bills

Under the leadership of Metropolitan Makarios Tillyrides, the current Archbishop of the Orthodox Church in Kenya, these programs have been effectively run despite countless hardships. Many more plans are underway. The foundation for another orphanage has been laid at Woodley Estate by the former First Lady of the Republic of Cyprus and the current European Minister for Health; a proposed girls' secondary school in Aldai, and a nursing school at Riruta. The nursing college, when completed, will help provide ever-needed medical expertise in Kenya.

Apart from clothing and feeding the post-election violence victims (most of whom are still homeless) the church is collaborating with doctors in Cyprus in order to provide dozens of free medical camps around the nation, as well as equipping the new dispensaries. With the help of donors from Orthodox countries, we are engaging in drilling water for the hunger-stricken population of the Turkana region. Some of these boreholes have cost an estimated twenty-five thousand dollars. The current famine in some parts of the nation has been felt by the Orthodox Church, which has moved in to provide relief food to the hunger-stricken. This is in line with the Patriarchate's philanthropic nature of providing relief to the needy in the remote parts of Africa.

At this moment our aim is to expand and extend our programs. However, this is a difficulty since our Archdiocese does not have any sources of income here in Kenya. The funds that we run on are solely from our sponsors and donors and friends abroad.

We would really appreciate consideration from donor organizations and people of good will who could assist and promote our philanthropic efforts. Any assistance whatsoever would be greatly appreciated.

In the meantime, on behalf all the faithful and people of Kenya, I wish to express my heartfelt gratitude to all donors, well-wishers, and friends of the Archdiocese of Kenya from all over the world, who have faithfully stood by us and supported our philanthropic works in different parts of the country. May God bless you all and your beloved families. It is our prayer that the Lord grants us the strength to carry on, and that the government of Kenya, together with those who are near and dear to us, will continue supporting our good work within our beloved country and Archdiocese. We also pray that peace, love and unity will continue prevailing in this country and that God will continue blessing us all.

GRADUATION SPEECH
for Sunday School Teachers

April 28, 2012

Beloved graduates, brothers and sisters in Christ, Christ is risen! Truly he is risen! *Kristo amefufuka! Kweli amefufuka!*

In life, we make so many promises. Some are so easy to keep, others are not so easy, and worse still, there are some that we do not even remember after we have promised. In the Holy Scripture, God is estimated to have made over seven thousand promises. However, unlike us, God keeps all his promises and fulfills all his pledges. In some instances, the promises of God are accompanied by some conditions. In one of Christ's sermons we read:

> Therefore take no thought, saying, "What shall we eat or, what shall we drink or, wherewithal shall we be clothed?" (For after all these things do the Gentiles seek:) for your heavenly Father knoweth that ye have need of all these things. But seek ye first the kingdom of God and his righteousness; and all these things shall be added unto you.[34]

In this promise, God says he will give us all the material necessities we want, if we fulfill the condition he sets, that is, seeking first his kingdom. Trusting in God and focusing all our efforts on attaining his kingdom is the only way to attain all that we need.

34 Matt. 6:31–33.

When you entered this Sunday school program, you all had at least these two things in mind: your goal and your mission. Both of these were the reasons for your being chosen instead of so many others who were not given the chance. You were chosen as the best of them all. After your studies here, you may have said, "I will go back to my home parish and help the Sunday school children and/or the youth do this or that." You were to fulfill your promise once you completed your studies. Your parish priest and his parishioners probably had a vision for you, too. They may have said, "After our spiritual son or daughter finishes his or her pastoral program, then our Sunday school or youth group will have a great teacher." Now that you have completed your studies, it is your time to go fulfill these much-awaited promises. Some people, after finishing similar studies, do a lot of good work in their home parishes, while others unfortunately stop their pastoral activities a few months after their graduation. I urge all of you graduates of this year to work on fulfilling your promises of working diligently for the Church in the capacities your parishes will offer.

"If any man will to come after me, let him deny himself, and take up his cross, and follow me."[35] In this statement, Christ surely asks us freely to follow him. This can only happen if we truly desire and decide to follow him. Christ, in this passage, has preconditions set for us. They include, denying ourselves and taking up our crosses. These are not easy tasks to perform. Nevertheless, all Christians, and in particular those ministering in any form within the Church, must do this. I will not promise you any easy tasks in your ministries as Sunday school and youth teachers.

You will for sure face many new challenges, now that you have been confirmed as official teachers of our faith. You will, in many instances, be stretched beyond normal while working in the vineyard of the Lord. Even in the midst of tribulations and in moments of hardship, do not give up, because the Lord shall remain your Shepherd. In the end, your ministries will always yield many fruits, including some that you will enjoy in this life. In the midst of your challenges and tribulations, I can only adjure you to "be strong and of a good courage; be not afraid, neither be thou dismayed: for the Lord thy God is with thee whithersoever thou goest."[36]

Two secrets of your success in ministry are prayer and the sacraments of our Church. Prayer for ourselves—those with whom we work, those for whom we work, our ministry, our mission, and other areas—is extremely

35 Matt. 16:24.

36 Josh. 1:9.

vital for all of us. Many times, we forget to pray for our ministries, our mission, and ourselves. Prayer connects us with God, the one who has chosen us to serve him. In that case, if we are doing the Lord's work, let us involve him in it, by asking him to guide and guard us through every part of it. That is why I am urging you to not forget to pray before you start preparing your lessons, pray before starting your classes, and also after you end them.

The sacraments of our Church go hand-in-hand with prayer. You have to foster this sacramental life together with that of prayer and make it part of you. Be people who will not miss attending the Liturgy and receiving Holy Communion; be people who will go for confession frequently; be people who receive the other necessary sacraments of our Church; be people who are connected with God. I tell you all this because your success in your ministry as Sunday school teachers depends on this connection with God, a connection that is only given through prayer and the sacraments.

Another thing that will bring about your success is how spiritual you are, and how you live your personal life. Many times we as human beings like telling others what to do but are not doing it ourselves. This is branded "pharisaism" and is continuously condemned by Christ. Your major task will be to teach the children or the youth how to live as Orthodox Christians. I strongly urge you to work extra hard in living the same life that you will be teaching the children. Not only because you need to teach what we believe, but also because it will affect the lives of so many youngsters. As Sunday school teachers in training, you may already have experienced this, but I am still compelled to remind you. The way you walk, the way you talk, the way you behave, the way you react, among other parts of your life that you may think have no connection with your ministry, will affect your pastoral activities in major ways. The most critical one is that the children you will be teaching see you as the best Christian example in their lives and will emulate whatever you do or say. Whether you are in church or outside the church compound, there are chances that you will meet them in different ways. You have to work hard to be the best Christian example, not only for the sake of those children who will lead the Church of tomorrow, but for the sake of your salvation, too.

In many instances, you may be misinformed to think that your position in the Church is among the least, if not already the least, of all others. Sometimes you may even go into thinking that you have the least demanding job within your parish. But, as you will learn with time, you have the most crucial and one of the most demanding positions in the parish. This is because a lot of what you will be doing in your classrooms will help lay the foundation for the Church of tomorrow. Keep in mind that the foundation of any structure is what determines its strength, its ability to hold the future success, and the kind of structure that will be erected on it. In that case, it is through your dedication and efforts to put up a strong foundation of faith in our children that we are assured of a bright and promising tomorrow in the Orthodox faith. In other words, without you we have a very weak tomorrow. You, therefore, encompass the very vital ministries of the Orthodox faith—one that the Church cannot afford to do without.

Education is generally considered as having three F's—that is, informative, formative and trans-formative. I know that you have all been informed of our Orthodox faith, and that you have been formed as resourceful teachers of our faith, and above all, you have been transformed to become better Orthodox Christians. It is these reasons that have led to your teachers and program superiors to recommend you for graduation today. Now you can go and give the same "three 'F's" to others in your local parishes. Please work hard to do this, as your teachers did it for you.

With these remarks, I wish each one of you a blessed life and the very best of success in your ministries.

SPEECH

Offered at the Consecration of the Church of Saint John the Baptist[37]

Lodwar, Turkana,
July 22, 2012

Reverend Father Martin Ritsi, Director of the OCMC (Orthodox Christian Mission Center) American Team, my beloved Children, Parishioners of Saint John the Baptist in Lodwar, I greet you in the Name of the Father, and of the Son, and of the Holy Spirit.

TODAY IS A VERY SPECIAL and significant day, not only to this parish of Saint John the Baptist, but also of the entire Orthodox Church in Kenya. It has been a long journey and we still have a long way to go. The reason I say we have come from far is because maybe nobody would have imagined that they would see this day, given the turbulent history of our Orthodox Church. The parish of Saint John the Baptist is being consecrated in the middle of the desert. Not many people here present know the role played by Orthodox Christians in nurturing and resurrecting the Church after the colonial era. Of course, many of our churches had been shut down by the colonialists just the same way many Turkana people had shut down their faith in the Lord who is always present with us. The love that Saint Paul is talking about kept the faith growing in the hearts of the

37 Also, the occasion of the ordination of Herman Ereng to the holy diaconate, attended by the OCMC missions team from the United States of America.

pioneers of our Church. It is the same love that has made us gather today, Turkana and Americans, as we gathered here some five years ago when we laid the foundation stone for this parish and ordained Father Vladimir as a deacon in a semi-structure. There were only a few people and a deacon without a permanent priest. But as it is written:

> How good and how pleasant it is for brethren to dwell together in unity! It is like the precious ointment upon the head, that ran down upon the beard, even Aaron's beard: that went down to the skirts of his garments; as the dew of Hermon and as the dew that descended upon the mountains of Zion: For there the Lord commanded the blessing, even life forevermore.[38]

Look, how catholic[39] we are here in the middle of Africa, the Turkana people from this sacred place and the Americans representing many Orthodox churches from far away. When God created Adam and Eve they were all naked, and I have always been reminded of this whenever I travel to this place, seeing Turkana people on the road with donkeys and camels; women, children, and men walking naked. It reminds me of God's creation of the Garden of Eden, signified by the Turkana culture.

Blessed are we to be in the presence of the Lord in this newly consecrated church of Saint John the Baptist, and blessed are we to be witnesses of God's divine grace during the ordination of Daniel Ereng who has become Deacon Herman through the laying on of hands. When we ordained Father Vladimir a deacon during the laying of the foundation stone, I know many people wondered how Father Vladimir would work alone. Now see we have managed to ordain four priests: Father Vladimir, Father Makarios, Father Zachariah, Father Moses, and now Deacon Herman.

We have also managed to drill three boreholes, which we can see with our own eyes, and all this is through the efforts of the American team in conjunction with the Turkana people. By the grace of God, we have had unity.

This beautiful cathedral of Saint John the Baptist has now been consecrated, sanctified, and adorned. The entire church has been censed with heavenly fragrance, the oil of gladness, and the relics of saints and martyrs have been placed on the holy table. We are united together in heaven and on earth, the saints, and Turkana people—Sudan, Ethiopia, and Africa.

38 Ps. 133:1–3.
39 Catholic: universal.

Turkana has always been a hub for Sudan, Ethiopia, and the entire continent. Our unity will be a blessing in this remote area, a blessing that will spread to neighboring Sudan, Ethiopia, and other neighboring countries, and will carry the sweet fragrance from the incense and the chrism. The consecration of this parish unites the Old and the New Testaments, the past, the present, and the future. This parish from today has become a symbol of the inhabited world created by God, a symbol of the visible heaven when we send up prayers standing before the church and venerate it as the Garden of Eden.

This is a mysterious Church of the first born, and when we perform the most awesome of all the sacraments, the altar becomes heaven—the center of our salvation. The candles burning on the chandelier show the radiant stars, and the dome, the firmament of heaven. Because of these things, my beloved children of Turkana will be reminded of the beauty of creation. The church of Saint John the Baptist will now signify heaven on earth where all people from different ethnic backgrounds, races, and cultures present their bloodless sacrifices, stream into it and form a unified prayer of glorification to God.

> How amiable are thy tabernacles, O Lord of hosts! My soul longeth, yea, even fainteth for the courts of the Lord; my heart and my flesh crieth out for the living God. Yea, the sparrow hath found a house, and the swallow a nest for herself, where she may lay her young, even thine altars, O Lord of hosts, my King, and my God. Blessed are they that dwell in thy house: they will be still praising thee. Blessed is the man whose strength is in thee; in whose heart are the ways of them. Who passing through the valley of Baca make it a well; the rain also filleth the pools. They go from strength to strength, every one of them in Zion appeareth before God.[40]

In a real sense, we can compare the land of Turkana to a land of slavery, where people live without knowing they are children of God. Like God chose Moses, so God chose Father Vladimir, Father Makarios, Father Zachariah, Father Moses, and now Deacon Herman. All were sent by God to Nairobi to the Archbishop Makarios III Orthodox Patriarchal Seminary to learn theology. Now they return to you as clergy. They will lead you into the light of Jesus Christ in unity and they will live with the living God and be called to share in the Kingdom of Eternal Life in God's presence.

40 Ps. 84.

Christ addresses us as "you," which in English has the same form in singular and plural. When Christ speaks, he speaks to all the people. Christ speaks of the power of the Holy Spirit that he has given to us all. When he refers to Jerusalem, Judea, and Samaria, he speaks to you who are Turkana and you who are Americans. He tells us that we are all witnesses who bear testimony of his being the son of the Triune God.

Orthodoxy has seen many ascetics and many saints who went off into the wilderness or desert—much like Turkana—to pray and to seek God. They felt that being alone would bring them closer to him. In almost every instance, these holy fathers and mothers were never left alone because brothers and sisters sought them out for spiritual sustenance.

Now, Deacon Herman, you have been sent to the desert. Follow the examples of other priests, who have worked in harmony with one another. God has called upon you to be a leader, an anointed leader, to lead your people out of the darkness and the sway of Satan. Keep in mind the fortieth verse from Matthew, chapter twenty-five. You have received training as a catechist, and now you are a member of God's holy priesthood. Being a father to so many children means that you, too, will face judgment as a priest, not just as a man.

"How hardly shall they that have riches inter into the kingdom of God! For it is easier for a camel to go through a needle's eye, than for a rich man to enter into the Kingdom of God."[41] For one to be a faithful servant of God, one must give up his life in this world while living in it. Surely, we have needs that are material and we live in a time when money has an important role to play in life for our basic needs, but remember, life is but a short time and nothingness follows. With Christ, through our spirituality, we can find eternal life and a life without sin, sorrow, sighing, or suffering in the kingdom of heaven.

Deacon Herman Ereng, your service to God is a cross, and no cross is easy to carry. But, "The things which are impossible with men are possible with God."[42] Being a spiritual father, it is crucial not to judge the other, but lead the other to the right way. All people sin and salvation comes through repentance. "Hypocrite, first cast out the beam out of thine own eye; and then shalt thou see clearly to cast out the moat out of thy brother's eye."[43]

I know it is so difficult to face this temptation because we are each a

41 Luke 18:24–25.

42 Luke 18:27.

43 Matt. 7:5.

product of our language, our education, our experience, and our culture. We must not live a double standard. We follow Christ and we must accept that his image is in everyone, regardless of ethnic background, race, and culture. Diversity is positive. We must not allow ourselves to make judgment upon things we do not know or understand. We are all God's children and God calls upon us all to love one another more than ever before. As we approach the election year, I encourage you as my spiritual children and Father Deacon, preach peace and embrace one another not only in Turkana but in your neighborhood.

My dear children, mission work begins in the very heart of one's being, we should begin our mission as evangelizers within our homes and church community. While we are called to evangelize others, we begin by being evangelized ourselves. We are in constant need of being evangelized, of asking ourselves whether the Gospel is effectively proclaimed in our lives and in our parishes. Are we responding to God's presence with the acceptance that expresses itself through conversion? So, in order to evangelize, we must continue to preach what Jesus first proclaimed two thousand years ago: "The Kingdom of God is at hand: repent ye, and believe in the gospel."[44]

The Kingdom of God remains a key experience in evangelization. Although its fulfillment is still to come, the Kingdom has already begun here in Turkana wherever the power of evil, which manifests itself in so many ways, is overcome. Conversion means a change of heart, a complete transformation of one's life, and a turning toward God that results from the proclamation of the gospel. Conversion presents an ongoing challenge that expresses itself in commitment to a new way of life and, ultimately, to discipleship. It is a commitment, without any doubt, to our Lord and God and Savior, Jesus Christ. As it can be seen, Peter was of little faith because his trust in Christ had its limitations and, therefore, instead of walking on the water, as did his Master, he sank from fear and panic. Through baptism, we have been called to proclaim the wonderful deeds that reveal God's plan of salvation. Yet it is only when we have personally accepted the good news and have experienced its power that we are capable of sharing it with others. Those of us who hope to evangelize others need continual conversion by, and to, the Gospel.

Deacon Herman, in the parable of the Last Judgment, Jesus teaches that he will judge us on the quality of our ministry to those in need. "For I was

44 Mark 1:15.

hungry and ye gave me meat: I was thirsty, and ye gave me drink: I was a stranger, and ye took me in … Inasmuch as ye have done it unto one of the least of these my brethren, ye have done it unto me."[45] This is because the ministry is at the very center of Christian life. It is the use of one's gifts and talents for the welfare of another in need.

Many may ask themselves, "How do we minister?" We sometimes minister without knowing it. We minister to others. Perhaps our ministry takes the form of visiting the sick or the elderly. It may be found in the care we take to assist the needy, the homeless, the poor, or the forgotten. Or it may be revealed through sharing of our time and talents for the growth of our parish or the wider community in which we live. And, of course, there are those countless occasions when we minister to others by sharing a kind word, encouraging smile, or offering simple, practical, and loving advice.

Jesus Christ came into the world to save us by serving us. And he calls us to continue his saving ministry by serving others, in order "that God in all things may be glorified" in us.[46] As we start the work of evangelism, we need to be evangelized continually and to experience that ongoing "growth in life and faith and spiritual understanding" for which we pray in the Liturgy. The Gospel must be constantly heard and received, studied and lived.

God's people must continually be "born from above" by the Spirit of God who dwells in the Church, bears witness to Jesus Christ by reminding us of all that he has said and done and guides and confirms us in all truth.[47] Faithfulness to the Gospel, conviction in the faith, and participation in the life of the Church are essential. As evangelized people, we must hear the Gospel and live it by responding to God's presence in our lives and by recognizing his image in others. Only then are we capable of proclaiming the Gospel to others with authenticity, power, and truth without rejecting God's friendship or sinning through presumption and hypocrisy.

As we evangelize, we must recognize the need to know and accept those with whom we hope to share the faith. We need to identify with those to whom the Gospel would be proclaimed. We must become the servants of all "for the sake of the Gospel." To the strong, we must become strong; to the intellectual, we must become intellectual; to the simple, we must become simple; we must hurt with those who hurt and suffer with those who suffer. To the weak, we must become weak, that we might win the weak.

45 Matt. 25:35, 36, and 40.

46 1 Peter 4:11.

47 See Jn. 15:26; 16:13–15.

We must become, as Saint Paul writes, "all things to all people so that by all means we might save some."[48] And, like Jesus himself, we must lovingly bear the faults of others and even be willing to die, if it will bear fruit.[49] We must be prepared to share with all not only the Gospel of God, but also our own selves. "For what we preach is not ourselves, but Christ Jesus the Lord; and ourselves your servants for Jesus' sake."[50] Also, we "seek not yours, but you."[51] God prepares those who evangelize and those to be evangelized; we respond by cooperating with him and allowing his presence to be formed and molded in us, his "earthen vessels."[52]

Let us not run short of faith as the apostle Peter did. We must walk on water, my dear brothers and sisters of Turkana. Let us walk to Sudan and Ethiopia and spread the Good News of Jesus Christ to the yearning souls of our people. It is written in Matthew that we must seek first the Kingdom of God.[53] Without it, we are nothing and can aspire to no accomplishment.

Now that we have consecrated this parish, and now that many of you have been baptized, let us enjoy the holy gifts—the holy Body and Blood of our Lord, which bestows eternal life and the forgiveness of our sins. As we are all sinners, we must repent of our sins. It is right to receive the Body and the Blood of Jesus Christ with sincere confession, with sorrow in our hearts for having gone against the will of God, but we must ask our neighbor—against whom we have done wrong—for forgiveness. As Christ tells us: "If thou bring thy gift to the altar, and there rememberest that thy brother hath ought against thee; leave there thy gift before the altar, and go thy way; first be reconciled to thy brother, and then come and offer thy gift"[54]

As I wind up, I know the American team through your director, Father Martin Ritsi. I know you have many visions for our brothers and sisters of Turkana. It is my prayer that God will enable you to see your dreams come true. It is a noble goal. As I stand here on this special day, I assure you that it is my strong belief that in the very near future we are going to see many activities taking place in this place—many churches being constructed and consecrated as the realities of our visions. All I ask of you is

48 1 Cor. 9:22–23.
49 See Jn. 12:24.
50 2 Cor. 4:5.
51 2 Cor. 2:14.
52 2 Cor. 4:7.
53 Matt. 6:33.
54 See Matt. 5: 23–24.

that you stand united and unshaken, rooted in the faith. Good things take time to come, but they come to those who wait. Patience is paramount in all achievements.

May I leave you with these very strong words of the apostle Paul:

> Only let your conversation be as it becometh the gospel of Christ: that whether I come and see you, or else be absent, I may hear of your affairs, that ye stand fast in one spirit, with one mind striving together for the faith of the gospel.[55]

Allow me to express my sincere thanks to Father Martin Ritsi, Director of OCMC, and others, for the sacrifice they have made for this achievement in Turkana. May God bless you all.

55 Phil. 1:27.

GRADUATION ADDRESS

to the Students of the Makarios III Patriarchal Seminary

May 24, 2014

Reverend Fathers, distinguished Guests, Lecturers and Teachers, Students and Members of staff at the Makarios III Seminary, I extend my warm greetings to you all in the Name of the Father, and of the Son and of the Holy Spirit.

HISTORICALLY, it is a great and a fortunate moment: the official closing of our school year. We should be ready to thank Almighty God for allowing us to be here once again to witness this wonderful and auspicious occasion. It is good to remind all of you that the Orthodox Church has been, and continues to be, on the forefront of providing education to those who thirst for it. The Church has exceeded expectations by supplying quality education within the means of those who are less fortunate. Our institution has proven to be a rich font of knowledge as it delivers quality training to theologians. These great historical achievements and accomplishments could not be realized if it were not for our tireless struggle and zeal to strive to provide quality education to the sons of Kenya and Africa. It is indeed a great blessing for the Orthodox fraternity here in this country.

We cannot forget how far we have come to attain what we witness here today. It has been a long journey and not really as simple as it may seem. All these achievements have been made possible through the assistance and guidance of our Patriarchate of Alexandria, under the patronage of His Beatitude, Patriarch Theodoros II, who through his love for education, has provided us with full approval for all our educational programs here in Kenya.

Today we pay a special tribute to the founder of this holy ground, the late Archbishop Makarios III of Cyprus, who first planted the seed here in Kenya so that we might reap what he has sown. In remembrance, we pray for the first President of Kenya, the late Mzee Jomo Kenyatta, for donating this land on which this precious institution is built. I will also take this opportunity to personally convey my special gratitude to all those who have struggled tirelessly and with humility toward these achievements that we are witnessing here today. We must not forget to thank and pray for our well-wishers and donors for their generous support in funding our seminary and school programs.

Since today we are officially closing our school year at the theological seminary, I would like to take this chance to reflect on some important facts about education. We are all aware that education is not easy. It is never easy because it has to do with life. It involves the lives of the people who send a person to be educated, the life of the person being educated, the lives of those who educate that person, and the lives of the people to whom that person will go after being educated. Thus, any kind of education—be it secular or theological—has to do with a person's life in the widest sense. To add to that, all education must be integrated and holistic so that it will result in service. It must be an education that uses all means available at its disposal to create life where there is no life and renew life where it is decaying and nourish life where it is flagging; it must make use of creative solutions to problems, dream when it seems impossible, not taking place in isolation, but helping and accepting gifts from others. A good education is capable of reaching those who are far and not forgetting those who are near.

Ours is an education that continues to draw nourishment from its roots and pushes them deeper, but it also brings forth fruit to nourish others. It is an education that reflects a sense of the constant presence of God and produces respect and wonder for all of creation. In addition, it is an education that is not content with being religious but is permeated with the presence of God. It is an education that allows individuals to have a reflective encounter with the world. Our institution provides an education that enlightens minds and sets hearts on fire. Brothers and sisters in Christ, you know that we are all connected, so we should help one another so that we may help ourselves.

We widely acknowledge that our great educational achievements can be attributed to our highly trained faculty in both institutions. We should commend them for their good work toward our success. However, it is important to mention that our success can only be attained when we work as a team, struggle together, and join hands in aiming for a common goal. When we work as a team, I believe that each and every individual contribution is important because each person's input helps to achieve our one common goal. We all have responsibilities as leaders, lecturers, and students of this institution. We must all respect our work—and that of others—whether we are administrating, teaching, or studying. We should consider the way in which we conduct our work. When Christ was establishing a rule for his disciples, what did he command of them? Certainly not that they should do wonders, that men might behold them. No, instead he said, "let your light shine before men that they may see your good works and glorify your Father in heaven."[56] To Peter, likewise, the Lord did not say, "If you love me, work miracles," but rather, "feed my sheep."[57]

It is clear that all those entrusted with spiritual education have a very serious responsibility as they teach about the wonders of God and his promises. Everyone has free will, and each will be judged by the care and discipline they exercise in doing their best, not by the results that follow. May all of us continue to be cautious when giving instruction to those who depend on us. Teaching requires great sacrifice and dedication. However, by trusting in God, there is always hope for the future. "For I know the thoughts that I think toward you, saith the Lord, thoughts of peace and not of evil, to give you an expected end."[58]

I know that it is difficult to achieve or fulfill our dreams. At any time, struggles may come our way, and we tend to view their very presence as a sign that something is wrong. We then ask ourselves an important question: "Can all difficulties be avoided by following the commandments in the Bible?" No. God doesn't guarantee us a trouble-free life, an education without struggle, or success without concentrated effort. Truly living for God, serving God, and doing our best to achieve our goals means we

56 Attributed to St. John Chrysostom.

57 Jn. 21:17.

58 Jer. 29:11.

should expect to encounter countless difficulties that may seem like huge mountains. Nonetheless, we have hope and a blessed assurance that God will be with us in every step toward our success and in every struggle toward achieving our goals.

It is true that we can avoid many problems, difficulties, obstacles, and even failure by following God's law. Though we may not be able to control our lives, God always has a plan for our work, our studies, and everything else that we may imagine. This plan is meant to bless, encourage, and provide us with hope for the future. This plan revitalizes us, gives us a new energy, renews the zeal inside us, and acts as fuel to keep us going. We survive with a blessed assurance that we are always in God's care.

I remind you that the theme of our twenty-second graduation ceremony is about mission work. Mission work is not the ultimate goal of the Church; it is worship. Missions exist because worship doesn't. I don't need to tell you how much you've made yourselves part of the community of the parish. You all know it: Only when mission becomes the whole of your life can you become part of the lives of others.

There is a story of a young but earnest soldier student who approached his teacher and asked:

> "If I work very hard and diligently, how long will it take for me to be crowned?"
>
> The teacher thought about this and then replied, "Ten years."
>
> The student then said, "But what if I work very, very hard and really apply myself to learn fast; how long then?"
>
> The teacher again replied, "Well, twenty years."
>
> "But, if I really, really work at it, how long then?" asked the student.
>
> "Thirty years," replied the teacher.
>
> "But I do not understand," said the disappointed student. "Each time I say I will work harder, you say it will take me longer. Why do you say that?"
>
> The teacher responded, "When you have one eye on the goal, you only have one eye on the path."

This is the dilemma I've faced with our beloved seminarians. We are so focused on particular goals, whether it is passing a test or graduating first in the class, that we don't ask ourselves what our ultimate goal is. In this way, we do not really learn. We do whatever it takes to achieve our original objective. Some of you may be thinking: If you pass a test, or become Valedictorian, didn't you learn something? Well, yes, you learned something, but not all that you could have. Perhaps, you only learned how to memorize the simple dogmas of our Church.

School is not all that can be. Right now, it is a place for most people to determine that their goal is to get out as soon as possible. You are now accomplishing that goal; you are graduating. Perhaps you are at the top of your parish and community. Can you say that you are more intelligent than our fellow priests, catechists, or even brothers and sisters?

Are you only the best at doing what you are told and working the system? You may wonder, "Why did I even want this position?" It is so complicated and dynamic, you couldn't have imagined that mission work needs determination and sacrifice: sacrificing time with loved ones, sacrificing money, sacrificing youthful life. Sure, you earned the position, but what will come of it? When you leave the seminary, will you be successful or forever lost? Do you have a clue about what you want to do with your life? Do you have interests, or was every subject of study just work, and was excelling just for the purpose of excelling, not learning? Are you scared?

My beloved sons and daughters in Christ, birds of all kinds can see where they are going. They pick and choose their direction and path. As birds fly by instinct, they head where they are directed. But they can only see what is in front of them. Eagles are known to have vision. An eagle can see up to five miles and oftentimes is able to see well beyond normal sight. The eagle knows where it is going and determines how it is going to get there. While other birds migrate by instinct, the eagle stays in its territory throughout the year, season after season. The eagle is dependable and will hold its place in its territory. When a storm approaches, other birds fly in fear while the eagle is energized by the challenge of the storm. The eagle catches the wind and rises above the storm. The eagle glides through its territory during the storm and will only leave its post if it is badly hurt and must leave to repair its injuries. I believe God is looking for men and women of vision who can see with their spiritual eyes and catch the wind of God's Spirit. These men and women, like the eagle, are dependable, focused, and fearless when it comes to their God-given assignments.

You have to learn the real meaning of mission. Examination is not good enough for you. Education is an excellent tool if used properly, but you should focus more on learning rather than on getting good grades. For those of you who work within the system that I am condemning, I do not intend to insult, but to motivate. You have the power to change. For those of you that are now graduating, I say, do not forget what went on in your classrooms. Do not abandon those that come after you. You are the new future and you are not going to let negative tradition stand. You will break down the walls of corruption to let a garden of knowledge grow throughout Africa. Once educated properly, you will have the power to do anything, and best of all, you will only use that power for good, for you will be cultivated and wise. You will not accept anything at face value. You will ask questions, and you will demand truth.

I personally believe that in each generation God has called enough men and women to evangelize all the yet unreached tribes of the earth. It is not God who does not call. It is man who will not respond. The Gospel is only good news if it gets there in time. Remember the spirit of Christ is the spirit of missions. The nearer we get to him, the more intensely a missionary we become. My sons, never pity missionaries; envy them. They are where the real action is, where life and death, sin and grace, heaven and hell converge.

To me there is no more tragic sight than the below-average missionary. He has given so much, yet not the one thing that counts. He aspires so high, and falls so low. He suffers so much, but seldom with Christ. He has done so much, and so little will remain. He has known Christ in part, and has so effectively barricaded his heart against his mighty love, which surely God must especially yearn to give his missionary. Such is a tragic sight, indeed.

I have but one passion and prayer for you graduates. It is that you possess Christ and Christ alone, and for the world to be the field and the field to be the world, and henceforth that parish, community, and country shall be your home where you can most effectively win souls for Christ.

Don't be like the rich man who did not know why his land produced abundantly, who did not have the intention of giving to others from the abundance. It was so that God's patience could be manifested, since God's goodness extends even to such people. From God comes everything beneficial: fertile soil, temperate weather, plenty of seeds, cooperation of the animals and whatever else is needed for successful cultivation. But human beings respond with a bitter disposition, misanthropy, and an unwillingness to share. These characteristics are what this man offered back to his benefactor. He did not remember that he shared a common nature with his fellow human beings; he did not see it necessary to distribute from his abundance to those in need. He did not keep even a word of the commandments: "Withhold not good from them to whom it is due, when it is in the power of thine hand to do it,"[59] and "Let not mercy and truth forsake thee,"[60] and "deal they bread to the hungry."[61] He did not heed the urgings of all the prophets and teachers.

Maintain purity of heart and body. Purity means freedom from impurities and adulterants, to be full of strength, containing nothing inappropriate or unnecessary. Purity is being total and complete. It is a process of subtracting. Christ lives deep inside our hearts. We become pure by allowing the Lord to remove the admixtures, beginning with our business, eliminating the noise in our lives. The pure in heart will see God, in the *eschaton*[62] as well as here and now, gradually and progressively. The spiritual heart is located in the bodily heart, yet beyond it. Purity is focusing on one thing, one thing at a time.

Society today seems to idolize persons who can do multiple tasks at the same time. The counter-cultural position would be to focus on one thing sequentially. The heart is the earth where the grain of mustard seed is sown, the sanctuary where the fire burns, the field where the treasure is hidden and the inner spring from which comes life-giving water. The heart is the inner chapel where Jesus and I co-exist, where we co-habitate. Jesus and I have the same dwelling place: my heart.

As you leave this graduation ceremony, I wish to remind you that you have one business on earth: to save souls. Go and serve.

59 Prov. 3:27.

60 Prov. 3:3.

61 Isaiah 58:7.

62 Eschaton: From the Greek, ἔσχατον, meaning the last times. The author is using the term to refer to the post-historic age when Christ reigns over earth, as described in Rev. 21:1–22:4.

ADDRESS
at the Consecration of Saint Peter's Orthodox Church

Lodwar, Turkana,
June 21, 2014

I greet you in the Name of the Father, and of the Son, and of the Holy Spirit.

It is a very great pleasure to be with all of you today. Most importantly, we are honored to be together with Reverend Father Martin Ritsi of the Orthodox Christian Mission Center, and our beloved brothers and sisters from America who have been of great help to our Orthodox Church here in Kenya, especially in this Turkana land.

On this historic day on which we have consecrated this magnificent, glorious, and awe-inspiring parish of Saint Peter's Orthodox Church in Turkana that is dedicated to Saint Peter, I wish to share in the rejoicing and joy of the Turkana people and all the faithful living in this land. It is not a day of rejoicing for Turkana people alone but for all Orthodox Christians, in that a new place has been set aside for the worship of our Almighty God in this thirsty and parched land of Turkana, with its hedonistic culture. It will serve as Christ's beacon for all generations to come. Just as Moses raised the snake in the wilderness so that whoever was bitten by a snake could look at it and be healed, the parish of Saint Peter's has been consecrated and raised up in this land of Turkana so that whoever is bitten by sins may look at it and be saved. It will be a living stream that does not dry during any season. It will be a well for all people, not only for Turkana people. From the morning watch even until night, from the morning watch, as we sing during the Vespers, you now need to hope in the Lord.

This parish of Saint Peter's Orthodox Church will serve as the center for your salvation. You have been thirsty for waters to drink, for your animals, and for domestic use for many years. The psalmist sang: "My soul longeth, yea even fainteth for the courts of the Lord: my heart and my flesh crieth out for the living God."[63] You will no longer be thirsty for the Word of God. This because the Lord is God, and he has appeared to you today in this beautiful land of Turkana, and all generations will say, "Blessed is he that cometh in the Name of the Lord."[64]

As a spiritual father, I'd like to point out to you that the people furthest away from God are the people most impressed with themselves. They are trying to believe that they are gods. The people closest to God recognize more their own sin, their own weakness, just as we recognize our physical flaws when we look in the mirror. Without God, nothing is possible. Whenever I visit you, the Turkana people, I have always been impressed with you as you uphold your tradition and culture. It's now time to merge the two cultures—Orthodox culture and Turkana culture. I do not mean you leave your culture, but you need to merge the two together.

My beloved sons and daughters in Christ, eagles fly alone at a high altitude and not with sparrows or mixed with other smaller birds. Birds of a feather flock together. No other bird goes to the height of the eagle. Eagles will occasionally fly with another eagle, but never in a flock. In the same way, when Moses went to commune with God on the mountain, he left the crowd at the foothills. Stay away from sparrows and ravens. Eagles fly with eagles. Eagles have strong vision, which focus on objects up to five kilometers away. When an eagle sights prey—even a rodent—from this distance, he narrows his focus and sets out to get it. No matter the obstacle, the eagle will not move his focus from the prey until he grabs it. My beloved children, have a vision and remain focused no matter what the obstacle, and you will succeed. Whether in dry or rainy season, remain focused.

My beloved brothers and sisters in Christ, allow me to tell you a

63 Ps. 84:2.

64 Ps. 118:26.

parable involving the pumpkin. I know many of you use pumpkins without knowing the spiritual teachings or significance of it to us as Christians. A woman was asked by a co-worker, "What is it like to be a Christian?" The co-worker replied, "It is like being a pumpkin. God picks you from the patch, brings you in, and washes all the dirt off of you. Then he cuts off the top and scoops out all the yucky stuff. He removes the seeds of doubt, hate, and greed, and then he carves for you a new smiling face and puts his light inside of you to shine for all the world to see."

The Word of God is here today, to pick you from your patch of culture and tradition, bring you into his Orthodox culture and traditions, wash away all your sins with the water of baptism, and lead you to his sacraments that will scoop all the yucky sins from your soul, even the sins you don't know about. The Church is the sacrament of salvation. Various forms of consecrated life make visible in concrete ways the inexhaustible richness of this sacramental life, revealing to you and to the world how Christ's heart is in yours.

I wish to remind you how eagles prepare to train their offspring: When about to lay eggs, the female and male eagle identify a place very high on a cliff where no predators can reach. The male flies to earth and picks thorns and lays them on the crevice of the cliff, then flies to earth again to collect twigs which he lays in the intended nest. He flies back to earth, picks thorns and lays them on top of the twigs. He flies back to earth and picks soft grass to cover the thorns, and then flies back to pick rugs to put on the grass. When this first layering is complete the male eagle runs back to earth and picks more thorns, lays them on the nest; runs back to get grass and rugs and lays them on top of the thorns, then plucks his feathers to complete the nest. The thorns on the outside of the nest protect it from possible intruders. Both male and female eagles participate in raising the eagle family. She lays the eggs and protects them; he builds the nest and hunts.

During the time of training the young ones to fly, the mother eagle throws the eaglets out of the nest and, because they are scared, they jump into the nest again. She throws them out and then takes off the soft layers of the nest, leaving the thorns bare. When the scared eaglets jump into the nest again, they are pricked by thorns. Shrieking and bleeding, they jump out again this time wondering why the mother and father who love them so much are torturing them. Mother eagle pushes them off the cliff into the air. As they shriek in fear, the father eagle flies out and picks them up on his back before they fall and brings them back to the cliff. This goes on for some time until they start flapping their wings. They get excited at this newfound knowledge that they can fly and not fall at such a fast rate. The father and mother eagle support them with their wings.

The preparation of the nest teaches us to prepare for changes in our traditional belief to the true teachings of Christ—salvation for our souls. It is our responsibility as the father and mother eagles to ensure that the Word of God reaches into our souls, our community, our village, our county, our country, and the whole world. This can only be achieved through your active participation in the sacraments of our Church. I know sometimes you may be pricked by thorns, as the eaglets, and start crying for God's help. Sometimes, being too comfortable where we are may result in not experiencing life, not progressing, and not learning at all. The thorns of life must come to teach us that we need to grow, get out of the nest, and hear the voice of God that cries in the wilderness to prepare our ways for the coming of Christ. We may not know it, but the seemingly comfortable and safe haven may have thorns. The people who love us do not let us languish in sloth but push us hard to grow and prosper. Even in their seemingly bad actions, they have good intentions for us.

Sometimes you may feel exhausted, thirsty, and weary. Allow me to inform you that when the eagle grows old, his feathers become weak and they cannot take him as fast as they should. When he feels weak and about to die, he retires to a place far away in the rocks. While there, he plucks out every feather on his body until he is completely bare. He stays in this hiding place until he has grown new feathers, and then he can come out. We occasionally need to shed old habits, beliefs, and practices that burden us without adding spiritual value to our lives and our salvation. God created man and woman, each were similar but made differently and for different purposes. God spread the world with people, all of whom were alike, yet different in looks, in language, culture, economic status, and even in religion. Creation was made with diversity. No one element of creation was a replica of the other, and each creation was part of the other, a part of the whole. Each flower, for example, is alike in its whole, yet diverse in its parts.

I am telling all these stories for you to understand how much God has cared for you, taking you high into the cleft of the mountain, to a parched land. And he will teach you to fly in the same way that the eagle teaches its eaglets to do as they seek the hidden treasure. God has now brought this church—consecrated today—to you as a treasure where you will be able to seek the face of God and the salvation of your souls. As the eagle seeks salvation from its parents, you have to seek salvation from God through the active participation in the holy sacraments of the Church. There is nothing we can offer to you except the way to the salvation.

Many times, men and women of this place have walked long distances in search of water and grass pastures for their animals, persevering through the scorching heat of the sun, hunger, and dust in order to ensure good protection for their animals. It is your responsibility to persevere the same way, thirsty for the salvation of your souls. You will now have spiritual long-distance running in search of God's mercy, salvation, and protection. All the time, men and women have been united in one accord to fight the stings of losing their animals. The Lord says, "Seek ye first the Kingdom of God, and his righteousness; and all these things shall be added unto you."[65] Christ was transfigured on the mountain for us to see the God, *as he is.*[66]

"And we know that all things work together for good to them that love God, to them that are the called according to his purpose."[67]

65 Matt. 6:33.
66 I Jn. 3:2.
67 Rom. 8:28.

ADDRESS
at the Annual Opening Ceremony of the Makarios III Patriarchal Seminary[68]

October 16, 2014

Your Beatitude, Pope and Patriarch Theodoros II of Alexandria and All Africa,

ALTHOUGH this is your home and your school, please allow me to welcome you to the Orthodox Patriarchal Ecclesiastical School, Makarios III Archbishop of Cyprus. We as the faculty, staff, and students of this Patriarchal Seminary would like to congratulate you on your tenth anniversary as the Pope and Patriarch of Alexandria and all Africa, and wish you many years and good health, as you continue with your fatherly ministry in the Church of Africa. It is with much love and gratitude that we continuously pray for you and the See of Saint Mark, knowing that we are always on your mind.

Theology remains the consciousness of the Church, where the Church's *phronema*, or mindset, is expressed in detail to those who desire to learn and realize who God is in their lives. Without theology, the Church cannot realize her goal of spreading the Gospel. Just like Christ prepared his apostles for three and a half years before sending them out to evangelize, theological schools are called to prepare those ready for the ministry

68 His Beatitude, Theodoros II, Patriarch of Alexandria and All Africa was an honored guest at the ceremony.

before sending them out. The African continent has shown her zeal in offering theological education since the very first centuries of the Church and it is through such a school as this patriarchal seminary that the same fire as that of our forefathers continues to burn. As a seminary, we will continue working hard to mold our students into prayerful and illumined leaders whose aim is to transform their societies, and prepare them for the Heavenly Kingdom.

As you already know, this school opened her doors in 1982, and has since offered theological education to the sons of Africa who desire to be Orthodox theologians and/or clergy. In the beginning, the school only received students from East Africa, but after the patriarchal decree that the school be elevated to a patriarchal seminary—the only one of its kind on the African continent—the school has since opened her doors for students from all parts of Africa. Although we receive hundreds of local and international applications annually, the school selects and accepts just a few of them, depending on the availability of funds and the performance of students. We usually hold between forty-five to one hundred students annually. This academic year, we accepted only forty students due to the present financial crisis of Cyprus and Greece, from where most of our funds have been coming.

We are continuously indebted to our brothers and sisters from various countries including America, Australia, Cyprus, Finland, and Greece that have continuously helped fund our school. It is through such generosity that our school has opened her doors even in these very difficult financial times. Running a school with the grandeur of our seminary requires a lot of money, as well as expertise. While we have the expertise, we are still short of finances because our students are not able to pay for their education, travel, or upkeep, and thus the need for donors and well-wishers. We pray that things will stabilize financially and that our well-wishers and donors will continue in the same spirit as in the past, as we progress theological education in Africa and look for alternative internal ways of funding theological education in Africa in the future.

Our faculty has continuously grown from just one teacher at the seminary to the present ten lecturers who are all qualified and possess sound theological degrees from Africa, America, Australia, and Europe. Our greatest joy is that some of the members of our faculty are alumni of our very own seminary. The diversity in expertise of our faculty has helped us achieve and offer more to our students. It is such expertise that will continuously help our school compete in the world of theological education, and help upgrade our curriculum to the expected international standards in the near future.

As we continue working on our faculty development agenda, we are working to see that in the near future our seminary offers accredited graduate and postgraduate degrees in theology, education, and other social sciences. This anticipated growth is in answer to the high demand for more educated persons in our Church, and the need to develop and take our Church to the next level. Our goal in such an endeavor will be to prepare our students to be equally competitive with the rest of the world in these challenging times.

The theological authority of the Orthodox Church is bestowed and primarily vested on the episcopate, as expressed in the local and ecumenical synods. At the same time, theologians and teachers are entrusted with the vocation and ministry of practicing theology for the Church. In this case, the faculty of this patriarchal seminary have been entrusted, by your See, with the vocation of instilling Orthodox theological knowledge into young African minds for the progress and growth of the Orthodox faith and church administration in Africa. Therefore, while we teach in this Patriarchal school, we remain under your guidance and blessing as we work to achieve what the Church in general—you and the Holy Synod—and the pastoral fields expect of us.

We want to thank you for your continuous support and prayer, and for your presence as we officially open our school's 2014–2015 academic year. It is with your blessing that we have continuously received students from all over the Patriarchate of Alexandria and all Africa, and we hope that more students will continue coming from different Dioceses of Africa and elsewhere to diversify our theological and academic community.

With this short welcome and remarks, and with your blessing, I beg to welcome you, Your Beatitude, to address the faculty, staff, and students of the Makarios III, Archbishop of Cyprus, Orthodox Patriarchal Ecclesiastical School: as you officially open the new academic year.

GRADUATION SPEECH
at the Orthodox Teachers' College of Africa

October 18, 2014

Brothers and Sisters in Christ, I greet you in the Name of the Father, and of the Son, and of the Holy Spirit.

TODAY MARKS the seventh graduation ceremony of our esteemed Orthodox Teachers' College of Africa, being the eleventh year since the inception of the college. It is an opportune time for all of us to reflect on the responsibilities that each one of you will take on after this graduation and into the future. Today, those of you who are graduating will be tasked with the responsibility to study and do all that relates to your areas of specialization.

We must always remember that responsibility is the cross that you must carry with joy and dedication so as to improve the educational standard of our brethren, and in order to fight against illiteracy, poverty, and disease, and to pursue the fulfillment of Vision 2030. Indeed, it is my duty as your spiritual leader to remind you that you need to be pragmatic in your future endeavors. The humility of a worker is the first trademark of good workmanship. It is closely followed by trustworthiness, firmness, love, and the ability to articulate what you have been taught, to the benefit of those whose parents have entrusted you with the education of their children.

You must always remember to keep a good name for yourself so as to earn the respect of others in the communities that you will be deployed to serve. In the book, *Orthodoxy and the Native Americans*, the most reverend Metropolitan Innocent (Veniaminov) of Moscow and Alaska gave these instructions to the missionaries going to Alaska in 1899: "From the moment when you first enter your duties, you must strive by conduct and virtue to deserve good opinion and respect among all the people. Good opinion nurtures respect, but no one will listen to him who lacks respect."[69]

Everyone is called to holiness. Saint John Chrysostom says:

> You certainly deceive yourself and are greatly mistaken if you think that there is one set of requirements for the person in the world and another for the monk. The difference between them is that one is married and the other is not; in all other respects they will have to render the same account .... For all people must reach the same point! And this is what throws everything into disorder—the idea that only the monk is required to show a greater perfection, while the rest are allowed to live in laxity. But this is not true! [70]

We must therefore aspire to be holy, because the Lord our God is holy. Flee from immorality, abuse of drugs and alcohol, from envy and loose talk. Instead, constantly take stock of the consequences of your pronouncements, for by what you say you will be judged, either as someone respectful or as one from whom everybody runs away.

> For the Lord giveth wisdom: out of his mouth cometh knowledge and understanding. He layeth up sound wisdom for the righteous; he is a buckler to them that walk uprightly. He keepeth the paths of judgment, and preserveth the way of his saints.[71]

Therefore let us always remember to use wisdom for the benefit of humankind, thanking the Lord always for giving us the opportunity to serve others. We are called to be servants and ministers, not masters. A good steward always wants to leave behind a good legacy. Therefore the work before us is great and requires a lot of diligence. Let us make good use of information technology to search for the good things that edify our lives, and let us shun those things that lead to satanic indulgences.

69 St. Innocent of Alaska, "Letter to Hieromonk Theophan" (1853) in *Alaskan Missionary Spirituality*, ed. Michael Oleska (Crestwood, NY: SVS Press, 2010) 247.

70 St. John Chrysostom, "Against the Opponents of the Monastic Life," in *Marriage as a Path to Holiness*, trans. David & Mary Ford (South Canaan, PA: STM Press, 2020) 23.

71 Prov. 2:6–8.

We should take care to avoid the myriad of ailments and viral infections springing up all around us today: the Ebola virus is a danger we all face, like our brothers in the past who died *en masse* due to the Spanish Flu. We must find the right information and disseminate it to our brothers concerning how we can protect ourselves. It is one of our primary goals to be our brother's keeper at all times as we wait for the return of our Savior, the Lord Jesus.

Go therefore, I beseech you, as my own children, to be good ambassadors of the Orthodox fraternity in Kenya and elsewhere, pursuing your careers and also instructing the young ones in the Orthodox Faith as we have continually done here, being one loving, caring, and prosperous family. Ecclesiastes reminds us, "Rejoice, O young man, in thy youth; and let thy heart cheer thee in the days of thy youth, and walk in the ways of thine heart, and in the sight of thine eyes: but know thou, that for all these things God will bring thee into judgment."[72]

Therefore uphold wisdom in all your endeavors, seeking first the Kingdom of God and his righteousness, and all these things you have ever desired will be added unto you. Exercise your free will with great caution so as not to attract the wrath of God.

Be the light of the world. Since education has lifted darkness out of your mind, you have been illuminated with the light of information. Let your light shine before the men you will interact with so that they in turn will glorify God who is the fountain of all wisdom, knowing that we do all things through Christ Jesus who strengthens us. Nothing is beyond your reach. If you continue and remain prayerful, you will overcome even the most difficult challenges. Many people among us have gone ahead, have acquired more knowledge and earned accolades in their education. Emulate them and do not stagnate in one position in life. Promotion will depend on the authentic certificates that you acquire. This will elevate you to vie for positions of honor in society. I am sure you are very much aware of public scrutiny in the full glare of the media for those Kenyans vying for various positions who have to undergo vetting, as it is popularly known today. Let me be the first to congratulate you who will be elected or accepted in those offices. But work hard still, as this graduation is just the beginning and not the culmination of your education. I am sure you can do much better in this regard.

Good students always become better than their teachers. You are our

72 Eccl. 11:9

present, our future, and our hope, and you must work very hard to carry the mantle you now shoulder. All this work must be entrusted to those who are upright, educated, and tested. Saint Paul, in his letter to the Romans, candidly reminds us,

> Let love be without dissimulation. Abhor that which is evil; cleave to that which is good....[Be] not slothful in business; fervent in spirit; serving the Lord. Rejoicing in hope; patient in tribulation; continuing instant in prayer; distributing to the necessity of saints; given to hospitality.[73]

Let us also remain subject to the authorities so that it may go well with us. Remember to assist your siblings and parents; make them glad they are associated with you.

Finally, brothers and sisters, it gives me great pleasure to congratulate our Pope and Patriarch His Beatitude Theodoros II for the continual spiritual support and direction with which he has guided our beloved Patriarchate of Alexandria and All Africa in the last ten years, since his enthronement to the See of Saint Mark the Evangelist. Your Beatitude, we are looking forward to your continued guidance in improving and modernizing the Patriarchate and the Archbishopric of Kenya, as well as this college, which we all hope will be the first Orthodox university in Kenya in the near future, through your guidance and capable leadership. We are very glad that Your Beatitude has found the time to be present in our midst to officiate at this important graduation ceremony. May our Lord and Savior Jesus Christ grant you many years.

Allow me now, with your blessing, to congratulate all our graduands who have worked tirelessly to complete their studies in this auspicious college. May I also commend all the lecturers and staff of the Orthodox Archdiocese as a whole, who have contributed to the graduands' journey through the Orthodox College of Africa. Our benefactors here present and elsewhere, we thank you for standing with us all along the way. We wish all of you health and long life so that you can serve the great Church of Christ for many years to come. May the Lord bless you and keep you, may the Lord make his face to shine upon you and be gracious to you. May the Lord lift up his countenance upon you and give you peace.

In the Name of the Father, and of the Son, and of the Holy Spirit. Amen.

73 Rom. 12:9–13

ADDRESS
to the Students and Staff of the Makarios III Patriarchal Seminary

Reverend Fathers, Lecturers, Students, Staff, and the Archbishopric of Kenya fraternity, I greet you all in the Name of the Father, and of the Son, and of the Holy Spirit. Amen.

I WELCOME ALL OF YOU after the long holiday, which was full of so many activities in various parishes. To our beloved first years students, I wish to inform you that you need now to adjust to the new life and environment—your life in Christ primarily in this larger parish that involves worshiping, chanting, and your personal participation in the Holy Sacraments. From birth to death, the parish is where God raises the infants, guides the young, supports the aged, encourages the faint-hearted, reunites the separated, leads back those who are in error, and joins them to his One, Holy, Catholic, and Apostolic Church.

True knowledge of God comes more through the quality of our lives than through intellectual clarification. Many people today lament the state of our parishes. There are many crises to be dealt with daily, simply because the devil hates and opposes the holiness and unity of a parish community whose life is fully in Christ. I don't mean to despair over these crises, but to rejoice and give thanks for the godly aspects of our community and to enable us to see the shortcomings as challenges and opportunities to grow.

My beloved sons and daughters in Christ, eagles have strong vision, which focuses on something up to five kilometers away. When an eagle discovers prey—even a rodent from this distance, he narrows his focus on it and sets out to get it. No matter the obstacles, the eagle will not move his focus from the prey until he grabs it. Have a vision and remain focused no matter what the obstacle, and you will succeed. The eagle is the only bird that loves the storm. When clouds gather, he gets excited. The eagle uses the wind to rise and is pushed up higher. Once it finds the wing of the storm, the eagle stops flapping and uses the atmospheric pressure to soar to the clouds and glide. This gives the eagle an opportunity to rest. In the meantime, all the other birds hide in the leaves and branches of the trees. We can use the storms of our lives to rise to greater heights. Achievers relish challenges and use them profitably.

In our seminary you will encounter many challenges due to our diverse ethnic backgrounds. Just as we suck the breast of Church, which is the Holy Chalice, let us exchange and share our weaknesses so we may be able to understand and help one another regardless our ethnic backgrounds.

Flying and hunting must be learned, and the adoptive parents play an important part in this. Flying, in a Christian's life, is faith to rise above circumstances. Hunting is searching for the manna or bread from heaven, to grow strong and healthy. At first the role models feed the young. Then they must learn to find food for themselves. "Train up a child in the way he should go: and when he is old, he will not depart from it."[74] There is an old adage, "Give a person a fish, and he has food for a day. Teach a person to fish, and he has food for a lifetime."

Learn to listen. The young learn by watching someone older; then they mimic the action or speech themselves until they develop their own skills. Listen, my children, to what your lecturers and leaders will teach you. Don't neglect their advice. Many a time, I have seen people gather around unprofitable issues. My dear children, don't be like chickens who are crowd followers. If a hen sees a flock of other hens running across the yard, she will take off after them. It doesn't matter that she doesn't know where they are going or why they are going there. She follows along because she doesn't want to miss out on anything they are doing. Hens just naturally "squabble and fight" over things in the chicken yard. If one finds a nice juicy bug to eat, suddenly they all want it. They will chase each other all over the chicken yard, trying to take it away from each other. They are funny that way. They can walk all around a bug or a grasshopper and not pay any attention to it, but the moment one decides she wants it, at that moment,

74 Prov. 22:6.

they all decide they want it and the chase is on. They have no interest in the heavenlies. They are content to live in the chicken yard, walking around with their eyes on the ground, scratching in the dirt, looking for something to eat. Most of them will never try to fly. They are earthbound birds.

Eagles, from birth, have very unique physical characteristics. They are born with their mouths open and their eyes looking into the sun. They have a tremendous hunger and constantly cry for food. In the same manner, the moment we get baptized, we start having a tremendous hunger for God's Word. The newly baptized, or converts, in the Lord need to be constantly and sufficiently fed with the Holy Sacraments of God, and have great love in their respective parishes.

I know that some of you had to make a very tough and bold decision when you saw an opportunity that other parishioners did not see—an opportunity to serve God As you know, eagles can see what other birds do not see. They can see a tiny lizard on a rock at a thousand feet. They can see the movement of a fish underwater.

As we open our learning today, learn to go beyond the lecturers and the expectations of your home parishes. Try to excel in everything you do to bring glory to the Church of God and yourselves as Orthodox young men. Never give up in education. A time will come when you will be required to give an account for what you have learned. As you know, the real training is in the field, so equip yourself with all necessary armors.

Homilies

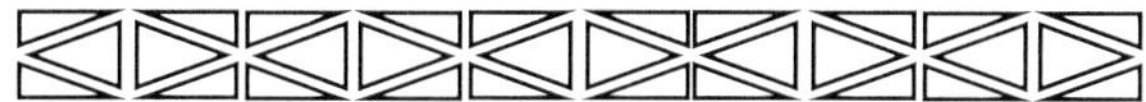

HOMILY
on Ephesians

October 5, 2010

> But speaking the truth in love, may [we] grow up into him in all things, which is the head, even Christ.[1]

In the Name of the Father, and of the Son, and of the Holy Spirit.

TODAY, brothers and sisters in Christ, we will be treated to a very unique and inspiring message from Saint Paul's Letter to the Ephesians. This message is very important to us as it is talking about some important aspects of our daily spiritual lives. It also explains why there is diversity of persons and gifting in the Church, which can be seen in the following important reasons: for the unity of the Church, for the preservation of truth in the Church, and finally, for the operation of love, which is the primary quality of Christian growth. Our Church, in which we develop as Christians, is not primarily an organization but an organism whose members receive their edifying power from Christ to grow up into Christ. Paul does not view a Christian as an isolated individual walking toward perfection, but as a member of the body, striving to reach the perfect faith

1 Eph. 4:15

and full knowledge of the Son of God. Therefore, unity of faith cannot be separated from the knowledge of the Son of God.

My dear brothers and sisters, I believe each one of you knows that growth is a process, and when a child is born, he does not become an adult immediately. It is also believed that the weakest and the most helpless of all newborn creatures is a human baby. It has to be taken care of completely and totally by its mother and father or it would die. In most cases other young mammals are able to feed themselves after being born, but human babies are absolutely helpless. Human babies will, of course, grow rapidly and accumulate a great deal of knowledge and experience with each passing day.

Today's sermon is encouraging us to grow. It is not assumed that we have all the knowledge of God to grow in Christ. It is not that we understand all the biblical principles; we do not have all the wisdom. We simply know very well that these things accumulate over many years of living. The truth is never to give way to false doctrines, but truth must be spoken in love. At times we cling to the truth tenaciously, but forget to speak it in love and grow up in Christ in all things. Today we are advised that in all our growth, there should also be a growth of Christ's character in us, a growth into his likeness. This is so that we will be like him.[2] The process of identifying ourselves starts here. It is our responsibility as Christians to do what we can to submit ourselves fully to God and live as Christ does.

Brothers and sisters in Christ, God expects us to grow from the point of receiving his Spirit, so he provides us with sufficient time after our calling so that we can grow. We are all in a race, or more like a marathon, just like Israel's marathon that lasted for forty years. We should never be discouraged, but be full of thanksgiving because God is merciful and has promised us enough time to grow in him through Christ Jesus. As Christians, we are told we must continue to request God's presence in us—our daily bread of life—by his Spirit. We must ask, seek, and knock constantly, pursuing God and his kingdom and his righteousness.[3] If we do this, he promises to us to add all things, that is, our daily needs. Jesus Christ, just before his arrest declared: "I am the vine, ye are the branches: He that abideth in me, and I in him, the same bringeth forth much fruit: for without me ye can do nothing."[4] It is true that if we request his presence in us each day and obey

2 See 1 Jn. 3:2.

3 See Matt. 6:33.

4 Jn. 15:5.

him in faith, then we will, by his power, yield astonishing spiritual growth and bear his fruit in our lives.

My dear sisters and brothers, as we know, reaching perfection is not an easy task. It requires our total sacrifice. The Holy Scriptures always encourage us to strive and reach perfection. "Perfection" in the Scriptures means being mature and complete. We can certainly attain an increasing level of spiritual maturity, yet we cannot truly complete the process until changed into God, until our human nature has been totally transformed. It is only then, my fellow Christians, that one can reach the stated goal of being perfect as our Father in heaven is perfect, having the mind of Christ, bringing all our thoughts into captivity and never uttering a wrong word. Saint Paul admonishes us to "put away childish things,"[5] and that love must grow, must be perfected. What we have now is partial. Therefore, God does not give it to us in one huge portion to be used until we run out of it. In this sense we must always see ourselves as immature and needing to grow. But, a time is coming when love will be perfected, and we will have it in abundance like God.

In the meantime, while we are living this life, we are to pursue love. Paul encourages us to be "always abounding in the work of the Lord," and by using the words, "your labor," the apostle draws attention to our responsibilities. Our labor, brothers and sisters in Christ, refers to whatever energies and sacrifices it takes to yield to the Lord so he can do his work. The Holy Scriptures refer to God several times as a potter, and we are the clay he is shaping. The difference between the earthly clay and us is that the clay God is forming is alive, having a mind and a will of its own. It can choose to resist or yield. After our initial repentance, finding motivation to use our faith and yielding to him in his work—not just agreeing mentally—is the most important attitude of all. Real, living faith motivates conduct in agreement with God's purpose. My dear sisters and brothers, God's purpose for us is that we grow and change and become as much like him in this life as time allows.

Finally, Saint Paul is saying to us that a new convert is a child, unstable in his ways, who really does not know which end is up spiritually. He can easily be tricked and deceived. Someone who is grown, on the other hand, is someone who is stable, someone who will not be swept aside by persecutions, trials, deceitful teachings, or false doctrines. He or she can fight these because he knows and understands, is convicted, and continues in

5 1 Cor. 13:11.

truth. However, he or she does not get to this point without also going through a process of growth. One has to pray, and study, and obey, and make choices, and analyze and compare the options, and look at the fruit produced from all the different choices, and so on. One must set his will, and her will, and change. As he or she does these things, growth will take place. May we be inspired and motivated to grow in Christ. Amen.

HOMILY
on Worship and Prayer in the Orthodox Church

October 19, 2010

THE BASIC PURPOSE of Christian public worship is to enable the mystical body of Christ to take palpable form in the liturgical assembly; the Liturgy reveals the Church. Therefore, in the Church, all power and grace comes from liturgical activity, and conversely everything is directed to the sacred Liturgy. This Liturgy that I am talking about today is the point of departure, the generative power, and the well-spring of vital energy for all the activity in the Church, and at the same time, the goal toward which all this activity is moving. In the liturgical assembly the faithful are called together by the Father in the spirit of the glorified Christ by the means of the shepherds whose function is to be the voice, here and now, of the Holy Spirit. Once called together, the liturgical assembly puts into mind the wonderful things that God has done for it with praise, thanksgiving, and petitions to the Father, who then expresses his overflowing goodness of love for it in his Son. One of the changes that take place in the lives of people as a result of the release of the Holy Spirit by the Father is a new dimension and intensity in the experience of worship and prayer on both an individual and collective basis.

The Orthodox Church has much to offer through the reality of worship, her experience of which has accumulated for nearly two thousand years. Out of that treasury of experience, our Church seems to have a prayer or service for everything. Even so, worship is simply that which brings out the life of the Church. The Scriptures and the daily life of the Church have, through ages, always understood the priority of worship in our approach to God. Christianity means fullness of life in Christ in all aspects of life, be it intellectual or emotional. As we worship together in Christ, we are all transformed. Worship is therefore the priority for all who profess Christ. Our corporate worship is when he manifests his love, power, and glory. In the New Testament we read account after account of the worship and transformation that occur when men and women encounter Christ face to face.

Worship gives expression to our intimate and yet awesome relationship with the Lord. During New Testament times, one's faith was known not simply by what he believed regarding God, but by how he worshiped. One's worship demonstrated one's allegiance and commitment to his or her God. In our Church, of all types of worship and prayers that exist, the one that remains central in the life of the Church is the Divine Liturgy.

Liturgy simply means "service of the people." Another way of putting it is that the liturgy is our "work." Worship and prayer, in Spirit and in truth, do not come easily. Worship and prayer take effort. It is good to realize that our relationship with the Lord is based on truth, not on our emotions. If we believe something is true, we will adhere to it regardless of how we feel at any given moment. Likewise, when we trust in the Lord, we will always do what he wants us to do, even if the feelings are not there. This goes for worship and prayer as well, along with doing what that entails, for example: singing, lifting our hands, prostrating, kneeling, or offering praise and supplication. This is what God wants, and in the long run, we benefit from his blessings as a result of expressing our intimacy with the Lord. We then grow into a deeper union in our relationship with him.

Our liturgy entails participation, and in order for us to have a relationship with God in worship and prayer, we must participate fully. Since our liturgy expresses and facilitates our relationship with Christ and each other, there must be a full participation for all those involved. The fathers of the Church emphasized the issue of worship time and again; namely, it is much better to talk to God, than simply think about him. When we worship, we are not just an audience, but part of the divine drama itself. We are meant to be fully engaged in what is happening in front of us, around us, and within our hearts. The whole Christian, with his or her whole body and mind, is to be standing before the Lord. In order for us to participate fully, I would like to encourage the clergy and the laity to move into fuller corporate worship. We must also include men to act as altar boys in the altar; more readers must be tonsured in order to serve in church prayer services like Vespers. We ought to encourage people speaking a foreign language to be actively involved in our worship and prayers.

An active participation is all that is required of all the worshiping members of the Church. Our priests should be able to encourage mature worship, which includes having prayer meetings, using clear and helpful teaching. This attitude of mature worship is becoming increasingly evident in the liturgical life of many of our churches. Our priests should aim to involve all the members of the Church in a tangible way. God would have us participate fully and put ourselves into his kind of life, as he fully puts himself into ours. Blessed Augustine, referencing 1 Corinthians, wrote, "If you receive them well, you are yourselves what you receive."[6] Christ is in us by reason of his flesh, and we are in him.

"Abide in me, and I in you."[7] This is a verse that calls us into a profound and mutual relationship with Christ. The risen Lord walked with the disciples on their way to Emmaus, and when they urged him to stay with them, the Savior responded by giving them a much greater gift: the Sacrament of Eucharist. Receiving the Eucharist means entering into a profound communion with our Savior Jesus Christ. This Eucharistic Communion is given to us so that we can be united with God here on earth, in expectation of a much better life in heaven. The Church is the body of Christ. We walk with Christ to the extent that we are in a relationship with his Body. Jesus Christ has provided for the creation and growth of our unity with him by pouring out his Holy Spirit on us. Through our prayers and worship, Christ is revealed in his Eucharistic presence. In the one Eucharist, "we being many are one bread, and one body: for we are all partake of that one bread."[8]

Paul further states that, "Is it not the bread we break a communion in the body of Christ?" We do not simply participate; we commune with him in unity. Paul goes on to say, "For we being many are one bread, and one body: for we are all partakers of that one bread."[9] Why then simply talk of communion? He says: "We are this very body. After all what is the bread? It is the body of Christ." Saint John Chrysostom adds that, "We have become

6 St. Augustine, Sermon 227, *Works of Saint Augustine*, part III, vol. 6 (New Rochelle, NY: New City Press, 1993), 254.

7 Jn. 15:4.

8 1 Cor. 10:17.

9 Ibid.

a single mass with him and a single body in Christ, and a single flesh."[10] Saint Cyril of Alexandria sums it all by saying, "We have become co-corporeal with him and with one another. This is why the Church is called the body of Christ, with us being her members. Since we are united to the one Christ by means of his sacred body ... we become co-corporeal with him through reception of the mystical eulogy."[11] Saint Cyril, commenting on the Gospel of John,[12] says, "Christ does not say that he is in us by a relation of an effective kind, but by a physical participation."

It is worth noting that, throughout the Scriptures, God is seen relating to a people, not just individuals. It is true that though we pray as individuals, we nevertheless relate to each other, as do the persons of the Trinity. Each one of the persons is fully God, yet see themselves as part of the other two. It's amazing that most of the private prayers of the Church use "I" and "we/us" in the same sentence. We always pray and worship as individuals who are part of the people of God. In our daily prayer, though each and every one of us experiences the "full Christ," no one can express the fullness by himself. That is the main reason it is said, "Where two or three are gathered together in my Name, there I am in the midst of them."[13]

The Orthodox Church has a special approach to prayers and worship. Unlike other traditions, one priest can never celebrate the Eucharist alone; there must be at least "two or three." The Eucharist is a communion that must be shared, and it is also a life that can be known to "persons." Our fellowship is the life we share that is not done alone. The God of Trinity shares his life by nature, which he "fleshed out" in Christ. The same is true with us. We must be sharing this new life of ours in Christ by having right relationships with one another. This shared life lies at the base of our worship.

Saint Paul gives us a guideline for maintaining order in worship and prayers in his letter to the Church in Corinth.[14] He also advises them on the effective use of gifts of the Spirit. A good and real disciple is one who is disciplined. The best thing a Christian can do is to set aside time for daily prayer, and make sure that he sticks to it. This will facilitate his daily, constant relationship with God. If this relationship is not cultivated or maintained, then the results will be unhealthy, stunted spiritual growth. So it is

10 St. John Chysostom, Homily XXIV on I Corinthians.

11 Attributed to St. Cyril of Alexandria.

12 Jn. 6:56: "He that eateth my flesh, and drinketh my blood, dwelleth in me, and I in him.".

13 Matt. 18:20.

14 See 1 Cor. 14:40.

always wise to give the Lord the best of your time in worship and prayer, so that you may maintain this special closeness with God.

The place of worship must be approached with fear and reverence. It is important to be aware of whose presence we are coming into. We should express our attention, love, and respect, even physically. In the Orthodox Church, things are expressed physically. This is why "posture" during worship is taught. Standing instead of sitting not only looks like we are attentive but also helps us pay attention. It also gives us more freedom to move—to kneel and make prostrations. This whole approach to our prayer is evidence enough to demonstrate that Christ is always present in our prayer and worship practices. These prayers, which are a service to the Lord, indeed require even our physical efforts. This is the main reason why the fathers of the Church, speaking in the context of the whole person being saved, teach that this can only be seen as the whole self participates in prayer and in the life of God. Amen.

HOMILY
on Hebrews 4:12, 9:26 & Acts 4:32

October 22, 2010

In the Name of the Father, and of the Son, and of the Holy Spirit.

BROTHERS AND SISTERS in Christ, Is there any meaning to our work in this world? We may ask ourselves this important and yet disturbing question, but surprisingly enough, often instead of seeking a sound answer to this query, we end up adding another question: Is there a time when we will rest from these labors? Today, we will find answers to these questions that will act as an encouragement to us that, in the Word of God, we can always find solutions to the challenges we may come across in our daily living. The Word of God reassures us, and is full of unimaginable hope. Scripture is full of wisdom, and carries within itself the message of salvation for all mankind. It is good news and a source of relief to those who are laden by the heavy burden of sin. This Word is a guide for all of us Christians who are living under the grace and mercy of God. It is a map for those who have strayed in sin and would like to use it to lead them back to God's glory. God's Word can also punish; it can see through every heart and soul: "For the Word of God is quick, and powerful, and sharper than any two edged sword, piercing even to the dividing asunder of soul and spirit, and of the joints and marrow, and is a discerner of the thoughts and intents of the heart."[15]

15 Heb. 4:12.

After man had sinned and fallen short of the God's glory, God did not hesitate to send his son, Jesus Christ, to come and lift him back to his glory. By doing so, he expressed his great and unending love. He went on and promised everlasting life to everyone who accepts Jesus Christ as his or her Savior and continues living according to his will. Our God never fails in his promises. But as human beings we often fail. He does not lie, but at times we lie. His word is true, living, and powerful. The Word of God that was there in the beginning, is here now as our Lord and Savior, Jesus Christ. Our Savior, Jesus Christ is the Word that conquers all. It is the Word that has given us salvation, and it is through him that we are going to see God's eternal kingdom. He has assured us that if we believe in him and let his word guide us, then we will live with him forever. It was not by mistake that our Lord and Savior Jesus Christ was put on the Cross. His crucifixion was purposeful. The Word came as a man and was put on the tree for the sake of saving humanity. He saved us by reconciling us with God and restoring the relationship that had existed between God and man in the beginning.

The Word of God is living and powerful. Without God's Word, man would languish in the darkness of sin; he would be blind and not able to see the light of salvation and the eternal kingdom. The Word of God has saved us, and has continued to guide us all through our spiritual journey—the journey of salvation. So, the reason that we struggle and labor is to work out our salvation, and to maintain and deepen our good relationship with our heavenly Father, so that we might be able to live with him in eternal glory. God, through his Word, knew us from the beginning and even while we were still sinners. The Psalmist says with wonder, "For thou hast possessed my reins thou hast covered me in my mother's womb."[16] He continues and says:

> My substance was not hid from thee, when I was made in secret, and curiously wrought in the lowest parts of the earth. Thine eyes did see my substance, yet being imperfect; and in thy book all my members were written, which in continuance were fashioned, when as yet there was none of them.[17]

It is amazing that God's Word is so powerful that it knows all our weaknesses, all our strengths, and even what we think. We cannot hide

16 Ps. 139:13.
17 Ps. 139:15–16.

our sins from God, because his Word penetrates even deep into our souls and minds. We have all been weakened by sin, and it is through accepting Christ as the only Word of God that he comes and heals us from all our infirmities. He is the only person who can search deeply into our souls and minds, as the psalmist says: "Search me, O God, and know my heart: try me, and know my thoughts: And see if there be any wicked way in me, and lead me in the way everlasting."[18]

Brothers and sisters in Christ, it is worth noting that each one of us is known by the Lord. Our duty as Christians is to follow the guidelines that are set for us by the Word of God. We should strive to do whatever is righteous before him, because he already knows us, including our deep secrets. This is why he sent his son to save us from sin, as Hebrews says, "For then must he often have suffered since the foundation of the world: but now once in the end of the world hath he appeared to put away sin by the sacrifice of himself."[19]

Brothers and sisters in Christ, the Word who is Christ and who was present from the beginning, accepts to suffer so that we might obtain rest in the eternal kingdom. Thus we are his disciples for good reason. We therefore strive to be close to God. If Christ suffered for us in order to save us, then beloved in Christ, we will want to strive to keep ourselves pure. And since we have come to know the saving power of our Lord, we must stand firm and never reject God's grace. Instead, we will always want to please our God. We serve and please him through participation in his once-for-all sacrifice, tasting of the heavenly gift, and sharing in the Holy Spirit. Our Christian faith should be one of faith, one love, and good works, as described here in the book of Acts: "And the multitude of them that believed were of one heart and of one soul: neither said any of them that ought of the things which he possessed was his own; but they had all things in common."[20]

Since we have a common goal of obtaining rest in the of the Kingdom of Heaven, we must at all times help each other so that we can emerge victorious together. We should combine our energies and resources to fight our common enemy, the devil, and resist his wicked ways. This is why we attend church every Sunday, for common prayer, and for giving our energies and resources to support the ministry. We do not go to church just for

18 Ps. 139:23–24.
19 Heb. 9:26.
20 Acts 4:32.

communal fellowship, but to make ourselves available to do what is necessary for the good of the community of God. "Christian sharing" should be our motto, and helping the less privileged is a good way of achieving our goal, which is salvation for all. When we meet together as a community in the church where the Holy Spirit abides as God's Pentecostal gift, his presence is experienced again and again in the liturgical assemblies of the church, as recurring Pentecostal outpourings. He gives us both boldness and confidence, as a Church that is worshiping and living in his presence. This verse in Acts reminds us that we should always be ready to care for each other's needs as Christians, and regard all our possessions as belonging to God. Our churches should always be filled with love unity and joy, like the Church of Jerusalem.

My dear brothers and sisters, let our labor lead us to experience salvation and to see the eternal kingdom. Our Lord and Savior Jesus Christ came into this world so that we can be saved. Never let go of the grace of God, which he has poured into our lives. Let us instead pray together and help each other as the community of God's people, and let us ask God to give us courage and to open our hearts to the Pentecostal outpouring of his Holy Spirit, who promises to be with us in our labor until we see the kingdom of God. Amen.

HOMILY

on John 17:21, 16:24 & I John 4:8

October 26, 2010

In the Name of the Father, and of the Son, and of the Holy Spirit.

My spiritual children, one of the most difficult of the challenges that we face in our everyday lives is how to maintain our oneness with God, how to maintain a constant closeness with the Creator and to avoid falling into sin as much as possible. The story of the Garden of Eden tells us that everything was fine between God and man, until somebody with a different opinion showed up. Adam and Eve foolishly believed in that different thought, they put it into action, and it immediately produced a division that has not healed to this day. In this particular case, these divisions produced two separations. First, it separated Adam and Eve from the presence of God and the Garden of Eden. Second, it separated them from their own lives.

Here we see the serpent's full intention to separate man from the unity of God and from life. It was not the intention of Adam and Eve to sin against God and cause disunity, but the serpent, with its cunning, hit them and persuaded their minds in a devious manner. At first, it seemed reasonable and enjoyable to them. Thus, they went along with it, and the consequences were devastating. So the unity of God and man was destroyed. God had to restore this unity through Jesus Christ. In order for us to understand this unity fully, I will cite Christ's words from the Gospel of John:

"That they all may be one; as thou, Father, art in me, and I in thee, that they also may be one in us: that the world may believe that thou hast sent me."[21]

We Christians enjoy two kinds of unity: vertical with the Trinity, and horizontal with one another, the latter rooted in the former. It is very easy see that God's plan is being worked out to produce unity, but we absolutely cannot excuse ourselves from doing our part. It is required that we cooperate; there is no escaping. It is we who are going to be held responsible for doing our part in the work that God is carrying out. Unity, brothers and sisters, does not happen by magic; it is made; it is created. Every married couple will note that even their unity must be worked on. The father and the mother have to work hard to produce unity. This must be done in God's family as well. Everybody is responsible. We cannot justify our inaction nor our unconcern. The first step toward unity is to recognize what it takes to produce it. The second is harder: doing it!

Brothers and sisters in Christ, our daily living often affects our relationships, not only with God, who is our Creator, but also with each other as his children, for we are members of one another. The moral standard for a new humanity is the life appropriate for a child of God, of the Father, and of the Son, and the Holy Spirit. This child of God fulfills two general commandments: love of man, as demonstrated in the self sacrificing service of Christ, and the love of God, manifested in worship, which is an offering and a sacrifice to God. We are all one in Christ, bound together in one unity. This is what Saint Paul expresses in his epistle to the Galatians, "There is neither Jew nor Greek, there is neither slave nor free, there is neither male nor female; for you are one in Christ."[22]

We all share our human nature with Christ Jesus. Therefore, valuing people based on opinions and ethnicity, pride, social status, and gender has no place in the Church. All are one in nature and so are equal in dignity. "If I do not the works of my Father, believe me not. But if I do, though ye believe not me, believe the works: that ye may know, and believe, that the Father is in me, and I in him."[23] These words describe how relationships should exist between us, God, and his Son and Savior Jesus Christ. Our relationship with Christ determines our relationship with God, the Father. If we reject Christ, then we will not find the Father, but if we believe in Christ and follow him, then we ourselves become "sons of God," living

21 Jn. 17:21.
22 Gal. 3:18.
23 Jn. 10:37–38.

eternally in the love of the Father. Brothers and sisters, we must believe in Christ because the Father has sent him. "And when the day of Pentecost was fully come, they were all with one accord in one place."[24] By these words, we see that the Church began in unity.

Shortly thereafter, as God announced the beginning of the Church, he gave them the gift of tongues. The purpose of this gift was to unite others with the Church. This unity helped the Gospel to spread. Hearing, understanding, believing, and acting upon God's truth produced the exact opposite effects of Adam and Eve's sin recorded in Genesis. Their sin separated them from God and unified them with the world. Sin unifies and separates at one and the same time. Obedience and sin move in different directions. There are things that God wants, and there are things that God detests. Sometimes, choosing is very difficult, but you can see that God's intention is clear; he does this on purpose. He wants us to be united with him, but we must decide whether or not to go with him. "Hitherto have ye asked nothing in my Name: ask, and ye shall receive, that your joy may be full."[25]

God's love for us is clearly visible through his son Jesus Christ. Even though we come across challenges, Christ is asking us to try him, and that we shall reap the benefits as a result. The Father and the Son, who are united and are already one, are our leaders in this greatest of all challenges. Here is what we must do: We must follow their examples. Both of them have shown us what we must do to create unity. Notice the very clear pattern of life exhibited by both of them. The Father shows his leadership in that he gave his Only-begotten Son. He loves us while we are sinners. Since this same love exists between us, we have gifts with which to work. Because love is the only one of the major positive qualities that works to produce unity, we need to seek him for more. Let us ask, and we shall receive. "He that loveth not knoweth not God; for God is love."[26]

Brothers and sisters in Christ, these particular words that sum up my homily are very crucial in defining our exact relationship with God the Father. "God is love" is not a definition of who God is, but rather a description of his relationship with us as our Father. Since God is the source and origin of all love, and all true love comes from him, then it stands to reason that everyone who loves—that is, who loves either God or a neighbor with a selfless devotion, which according to Saint John's teaching alone is true

24 Acts 2:1.

25 Jn. 16:24.

26 1 Jn. 4:8.

love—knows God. God, who loves us, expressed his love by sending his son to earth. While the origin of love is in the being of God, the manifestation of love is in the coming of Christ. Since God loves us, we ought also to love one another. The reason for this reciprocal love is enforced not merely by abstract truth that God is love, but by the concrete fact that he showed his love among us by sending his one and only Son into the world for us. This concept of God sending his Son into the world for us shows Christ's preexistence and divinity. Amen.

HOMILY

On Ephesians 1:3–10 & Romans 5:20, 21

October, 2010

Grace to you and peace from God, our Father, and the Lord Jesus Christ.

> Blessed be the God and Father of our Lord Jesus Christ, who hath blessed us with all spiritual blessings in heavenly places in Christ.[27]

THIS VERSE FROM PAUL'S letter to the Ephesians shows as an opening theme the preeminence of God's initiative. Day after day, in our lives, we always say, "Blessed is the Father, and the Son, and the Holy Spirit." In these precious words we find more details. In this passage we find that the Father has all the power, the Son all the rule, and the Spirit all the care-taking responsibility. Brothers and sisters in Christ, God blesses and so is blessed. Our lives on this earth are a response to God's initiative, not only that of the Father, but also that of the Son, our Lord and Savior Jesus Christ. Spiritual blessing is primarily the work of the Holy Spirit. We can only be in the heavenly places, where the risen Christ ascended, when we begin our new life, which is joined with Christ through the sacrament of baptism. What Christ accomplished on the Cross is the actual death to sin. Likewise is baptism to us: an actual and real death to sin and liberation from it. Thus, in our union with Christ through baptism, in his death and Resurrection, lies the power and victory over the law, the power over sin.

27 Eph. 1:3.

For us, baptism is an exact likeness of Christ's death on the Cross. Baptism is a reality through which we gain access to Christ's Cross, which is the power of God for overcoming sin. Baptism is where we get the power of God to say no to sin's commands and temptations. We may ask ourselves, "If Christ was buried with us, then how are we buried with him through baptism?" Jesus Christ accomplished an actual and a real burial of sin by his death, and it follows that, through baptism, we also accomplish an actual and real burial of sin. Our old nature is replaced by a renewed nature capable of living righteously. We are united in Christ: meaning that when we are baptized, we become like him in his death. We are planted in the ground of his death so that we can grow together with him through baptism, so we achieve a real unity with Christ's death. For the Holy Spirit unites the reality of being immersed in water with the reality of Christ going to the Cross and the grave.

Dear brethren, in the creation of humanity, God breathed into Adam and Eve his own life, making them in God's own likeness and image, making them children of God. This image of God, the original condition of son-ship and daughter-hood, which was lost by sin, is being restored through regeneration and adoption. To men and women who believe, he gives them the renewed right to be heirs in his family, "the right to become children of God."[28] If anyone is formed in Christ, he is formed into a child of God.[29]

Brothers and sisters in Christ, everything comes from God, and everything should be drawn back to him. God's original intent for incarnation was not redemption from the fall but adoption as sons of God, and that adoption is deification. When God thought of creating the world, he planned on bringing it into union with himself through the incarnation of his son, through his son's union with human nature. That's why Saint Athanasius, reflecting of the same matter, said, "God become man that man might become god."[30] The adoption to which he refers here leads us to introduce three other terms: justification, regeneration, and adoption; all of which are correlated. By justification, we are pardoned for our offenses against the Father; by regeneration, we are given a new life in the Spirit by adoption, we are permitted reentry into the Father's family. Those of us who are justified become heirs. By adoption, we are no longer foreigners

28 Jn. 1:13.

29 Attributed to St. Cyril of Alexandria.

30 St. Athanasius, *On the Incarnation* (Crestwood, N.Y.: SVS Press, 1989) 93.

and aliens, but fellow citizens with God's people and members of God's household.[31] Through regeneration, we are born anew into a present resurrected life with an incomparable future family inheritance. As it is written, "According to his abundant mercy, [he] has begotten us again unto a lively hope by the resurrection of Jesus Christ from the dead, to an inheritance incorruptible, and undefiled, and that fadeth not away"[32]

"But when the fullness of the time was come, God sent forth his son, made of a woman, made under the law, to redeem them that were under the law, that we might receive the adoption of sons"[33] Following these words from Paul's letter to the Galatians, we see that the Father chose us in Christ. Jesus Christ, the Son, who is God by nature became a man by choice. If we choose him, we, who are human by nature, become gods by grace. If we are in Christ, the Son of God, we become sons of God. Saint Paul does not here address the role of our human will on salvation, but instead focuses on what God does. God chooses us; we are chosen and thus greatly loved. Brothers and sisters in Christ, we are not sons by creation but by the "new creation." We became sons not by natural birth but by spiritual birth, not by generation but by regeneration; not by being born but by being born again: born from above, born of the spirit, born of God. This is the adoption we are talking about. It has redemption beneath it and divine life in it. Even so, God does not nullify the human will. In everything God is the originator, the initiator; we merely respond. But our response is necessary. Becoming a Christian does not solely mean inviting Christ into our lives, but rather getting oneself into Christ's life.

In Saint Paul's letter to the Romans, we see that the Law of Moses was a temporary measure on God's part to reveal sin and to lead us in faith to Christ. But instead of decreasing, sin abounded and got worse, not because of God's law, but because of human weakness. This necessary remedy came through God's grace in Jesus Christ. It follows that sin and death, righteousness and life, are paired. Therefore, Christ did not come to save us only from human weakness, but also to give us the gift of life.

Brothers and sisters in Christ, the sacrament of baptism, which signifies redemption, and the Eucharist, which is his blood, are alluded to as the necessary foundation for drawing near to God. Redemption frees us from slavery—that is, bondage to our sins. And the act of releasing us is

31 See Eph. 2:19.

32 1 Pet.1:3–4.

33 Gal. 4:4–5.

forgiveness. The price of redemption is blood. Christ gave his human body over to death for the sake of our new life. The mystery in today's sermon is the plan of salvation, the Gospel, the kingdom of God, and the Church. This mystery centers on Christ himself, from his incarnation and his crucifixion to the culmination of all things. It is the fullness not only of humanity, but of the whole creation. The mystery is revealed through Christ and is presently experienced in the sacraments of the Church called "Mysteries."

Finally, brethren in Christ, let's take heed of these words, that we are joint heirs only in union with the Son, for it is written, "He that hath the son hath life; and he that hath not the Son of God hath not life."[34] Amen.

34 1 Jn. 5:12.

HOMILY
on Luke 8:41–56

November 7, 2010

In the Name of the Father, and of the Son, and of the Holy Spirit.

BELOVED BROTHERS AND SISTERS in the Lord, the Gospel today recounts two important miracles that were performed by Christ in his earthly ministry. These two miracles—the healing of the bleeding woman and raising Jairus's daughter from the dead—lead us to pose the question, "What is the purpose of the miracles, signs, and power manifested by our Lord Jesus Christ during his earthly life?" This question should be answered in general terms as follows: To bring human souls through instruction by action, to bring them to a knowledge of the good news of Christ, and to concentrate the attention of those surrounding him on the mystery of his personality. In other words it is to evoke in people a faith awakening, and thus, new life through the action of God in man. My dear brethren, the two miracles we are witnessing today are a call to both faith and mercy. It is a manifestation of a power not of this world that enters this world and interrupts—or otherwise directs—the natural, casual order of things. A miracle should not be explained. It can only be known by those who perceive it.

> And behold, there came a man named Jairus, and he was a ruler of the synagogue: and he fell at Jesus' feet, and besought him that he would come into his house: For he had one only daughter, about

> twelve years of age, and she lay a dying. But as he went the people thronged him.[35]

My dear brethren in Christ, faith lead Jairus to the Lord to beg him to heal his ailing daughter. The ruler of the synagogue had faith that Christ had the power to heal his daughter. He knew very well that Christ, while preaching the Gospel, often went to places where his help was needed and worked miracles among the sick and those afflicted. Jairus fell down and begged Christ to heal his daughter. Little did he know that, when human help is powerless, the almighty power of God is made manifest. The Lover of mankind and the Savior of the world who came to free man from death and hell and to bring him comfort and blessedness is always prepared to help those who are suffering or in trouble. This is the only hope that Jairus had, and this is our living hope today as Christians—that Christ will always be with us during our suffering here on earth. He is always ready to bless us and clear our afflictions. As Christians full of hope, we should not despair, however much sorrow comes into our lives. This is because despair does not belong to the Christian spirit. Christian sorrow comes to act as a means of bringing us back to our senses and helping us along the path of our goal, that is salvation.

Brothers and sisters in Christ, we must not see sorrow as something terrible, but we must be willing to accept it with Christian humility and patience. And it is only then that humility and patience assist us toward spiritual renewal and salvation. Our Lord and Savior already warned us that our path to salvation is narrow and comes with many tribulations. But, it is through that path that God's deliverance is witnessed. Jairus had learned that, as a Christian, he should accept all sorrows that he experienced as coming from the hand of God Almighty himself.

When our Lord and Savior Jesus Christ was preparing to go to Jairus's house to heal his daughter, he was confronted by the occasion of the second miracle cited in the following verse:

> And a woman having an issue of blood for twelve years, which had spent all her living upon physicians, neither could be healed of any, came behind him and touched the border of his garment: and immediately her issue of blood was stanched. And Jesus said, "Who touched me?"[36]

35 Luke 8:41–42.
36 Luke 8:43–45.

My spiritual children in Christ, the faith expressed by this woman is unimaginable. Her long-suffering leads her to touching the border of Christ's garment, full of hope and faith that she is going to be healed. The suffering that she underwent is a great lesson for us today; that no matter how long we suffer or are felled by afflictions, through our strong faith in Christ, he will heal and deliver us. Our long wait will be rewarded. This woman believed and hoped that a new day would dawn, and that she would be able to receive her healing. We now see Christ rewarding her patience. She believes that by touching the garment of Christ, she will be healed. Her faith has no doubts, and she knows that a miracle is going to happen to her. "Who touched me?" Christ replied, after realizing something might have happened to him and he said, "Somebody hath touched me: for I perceive that virtue is gone out of me."[37]

It is amazing how the healing power flows from Christ. That which Jesus touches, or that which touches him, is sanctified. The power to heal comes from the garment of Jesus, though it originates within him. Similarly in our Church, we always use physical things in our daily worship, because in the context of faith and prayer, the power of Christ works within them. There is power in the paint or wood of an icon or in the metal of the cross, or in oil or water, but only if they are sanctified by Christ. Our Lord and Savior taught that one thing sanctifies another. He said, "Ye fools and blind: for whether is greater, the gold, or the temple that sanctifies the gold?"[38] Therefore, to trustingly touch the border of his garment was to touch him. Other people in the crowd might have touched Christ, but not like this woman's touch that through faith drew his power, and she was healed. Jairus was told, "Thy daughter is dead; trouble not the Master." But, when Jesus overheard this request, he replied, "Fear not: believe only, and she shall be made whole .... Weep not; she is not dead, but sleepeth."[39]

In this miracle, Christ calls the parents of the young girl to believe. Christ is also encouraging us to believe, even when it appears there is no hope. By these parents' maintaining their trust, finally their daughter is made well. It is evident that Christ's divinity also works together with humanity to accomplish his miracles. The restoration of Jairus's daughter's life is an act of Christ's divinity, while Christ's taking the girl by the hand and calling her to arise is an action of his humanity. These two actions of

37 Luke 8:46.

38 Matt. 23:17.

39 Luke 8:49; 52.

Christ cannot be separated because he is one undivided person, and thus he says, "I am the resurrection, and the life: he that believeth in me, though he were dead, yet shall he live."[40]

Christ's victory over death is final, and it was won in the dark abyss leading to non-existence by the one whom tomb and death could not keep. Death still fights, but in Christ it has sustained a crushing defeat. Death has lost its power, and faith, which has overcome the world, has become our birth into life eternal. When we depart from this world, we leave our mortal bodies and pass into life, to be garbed in the new spirit-bearing of the transfigured world. In the gospels, the three miracles of raising people from the dead are actually the miraculous returning of life to the same corruptible bodies, to await the inevitable second death. Interrupted existence is resumed, but decay is not eliminated, for they will meet death again.

In two instances of Christ raising the dead—of the daughter of Jairus and of Lazarus—one cannot help but notice a sort of claim emphasized by the Lord that the person is not dead, but sleeping. The best lesson to be learned from these episodes is the Lord's compassion for the sorrow of people who have lost their relatives—compassion that prompts him to carry out these miracles. These are the people whom he awakened from "sleep" to return them to the same mortal life. Today, brothers and sisters in Christ, we see the Lord's consolation in his love that he extends to human sorrow, for he is always there for us. He is not cold toward us, and he reveals to us the living personal God, who is close to us as his children and who is guided in his actions by the love he has for all of us. These miracles of the resurrection are a preliminary blow to death. The real defeat of death by Christ will come through his Passion, Crucifixion and Resurrection, so that "He that believeth in me, though he were dead, yet shall he live."[41] Amen.

40 Jn. 11:25.
41 Ibid.

HOMILY
on Isaiah 65:24

December 10, 2010

In the Name of the Father, and of the Son, and of the Holy Spirit.

BROTHERS AND SISTERS in Christ, we are all living in a world of unknowns, and every day we are confronted by new things and unexpected problems. We face many challenges daily, which though we struggle to solve them, at times they prove to be really difficult. These daily challenges weaken our dedication to our faith, and at times, lead us onto shaky ground along our path to salvation. They may present themselves as sickness, poverty, persecutions—you name it—and they all discourage us to the point of leaving us hopeless in our spiritual journeys. And in the long run we end up having a bad feeling—a feeling of being lonely and alienated from God's care. We can even be tempted to believe that God has forsaken us, that he has left us and that the power of the Trinitarian God does not exist in us anymore. All these things I call evil illusions sent to us by the evil one in order for him to gain advantage over us and reclaim us for his camp.

But, my dear brethren, God today is giving us hope; he is providing a solution to our endless challenges. Our Creator is here with us, and he is listening to us. He is omnipresent. This can be proven by the following words that illustrate his presence and his willingness to listen to us. He says, "And it shall come to pass, that before they call, I will answer; and while they are yet speaking, I will hear."[42]

42 Is. 65:24.

Today God has given us a quick response to our distress call. He wants to prove us wrong. He wants to assure us that no matter what we go through, whatever challenges would come along our path of salvation, his eye is always watching and guarding us, and his ears are listening to our call. He is assuring us that he is our Creator and will never forsake us. His one and only request is that we should strive very hard to communicate with him through our daily prayers. That is his only requirement. We ought to pray daily, cry to him, present all our challenges to him, because he already knows our problems. God is aware that we are facing spiritual warfare, and he knows that we are prone to frequent attacks from the devil. He is already aware that we are suffering daily and need urgent help, be it in our family life or our spiritual life. God's plan for us is not that we just sit down and wait for him. We ought to show instead that we are fighting the evil one. What we are going through is not just like a walk in the park, as indicated by the following passage from the epistle to the Ephesians:

> Finally my brethren, be strong in the Lord, and in the power of his might. Put on the armor of God, that ye may be able to stand against the wiles of the devil. For we wrestle not against flesh and blood, but against principalities, against powers, against the rulers of the darkness of this world.[43]

My spiritual children in Christ, all those who stand for good must wage a constant battle with the forces of evil. For demons still have power in the world until Christ comes again in glory to judge the living and the dead. This is shown clearly in the prayers to conclude the Orthodox service of baptism. It is important to know that we Christians fight back this evil power with God's arm, which is his uncreated, divine energy, given to us and actively used by us. The conquering power is not ours but God's. In our Church, we believe that at baptism we put on all the qualities described by the apostle Paul as armor in Ephesians, chapter six, and these qualities must be exercised in conflict, for we know that if we do not struggle, then there is no deification. In addition, just as our spiritual armor is important in our Christian readiness and alertness, so also is our diligent prayer and watchfulness in submission to the Holy Spirit.

My dear brethren, it is worthwhile to keep in mind that spiritual strength and courage are needed for our spiritual warfare and suffering here on earth. The spiritual strength and courage that I am emphasizing here can only be witnessed in a life of continuous prayer, a life of constant

43 Eph. 6:10–12.

communication with our Creator. Those who would prove themselves to have genuine grace must put on the whole armor of God, which he prepares and bestows upon us. The Christian armor is meant to be worn and there is no putting off our armor till we have fought our battle and finished our course. The fight is not against human enemies, or against our own corrupt nature only. We have to deal with an enemy who has many ways of beguiling our unstable souls.

The devil always assaults our souls, and he labors tirelessly to deface the heavenly image in our hearts. My dear brothers and sisters, we must resolve, by God's grace, not to yield to Satan. We must resist him, and then he will have no option but to flee. If we give him a way, he will get ground on which to attack us continuously. If we distrust either our cause, our Leader, or our armor, we will give the devil the advantage.

The different parts of the armor of heavily armed soldiers, who had to sustain the fiercest assaults of the enemy, are here described in this verse. There is nothing in Saint Paul's description that talks about going back; it says nothing about defending those who turn back in the Christian warfare.

Truth—or sincerity—is the girdle in this warfare. This girds on all the other pieces of our armor, and is first mentioned. There can be no religion without sincerity. The righteousness of Christ that is imparted to us is a breastplate against the arrows of our enemy's wrath. The righteousness of Christ implanted in us fortifies the heart against the attacks of Satan. Resolution must be as greaves—that is, armor—on our legs. The feet must be shod with the preparation of the gospel of peace in order to stand their ground, or to march forward on rugged paths. Motivation for obedience amidst trials must be drawn from a clear knowledge of the Gospel. Faith is vital in the time of temptation.

Saint Paul, in his epistle to the Ephesians, continues to encourage us in our spiritual readiness by saying, "And take the helmet of salvation, and the sword of the Spirit, which is the Word of God; praying always with all prayer and supplication in the Spirit, and watching thereunto with all perseverance and supplication for all saints."[44] Faith, which means relying on the unseen, and receiving Christ and his benefits of redemption, is like a shield; faith is our defense in every way. As we know, the devil is the wicked one. Violent temptations, by which the soul is set on fire by hell, are darts that Satan shoots at us. Faith, applying the Word of God and the grace of Christ, quenches the darts of temptation. Salvation must be our helmet. A good hope of salvation, an expectation of victory, will purify the soul and

44 Eph. 6:17, 18.

keep it from being defiled by Satan. To the Christian, armed for defense in battle, the apostle recommends only one weapon of attack: the sword of the Spirit, which is the Word of God. It subdues and mortifies evil desires and blasphemous thoughts as they rise within us, and it provides answers to unbelief. Single verses—well understood and rightly applied—at once destroy our temptations and help to protect us from all evil and subdue the most formidable adversary.

Prayer must fasten all the other parts of our Christian armor. We must use holy thoughts in our daily lives and always remember that a vain heart will be vain in prayer. My dear brothers and sisters, we must pray with all kinds of prayer—public, private, and secret; social and solitary; solemn and sudden—with all the parts of prayer: confession of sin, petition for mercy, and thanksgiving for favors received. God has already promised that he is more than willing to listen to us, and we must do it by the grace of God the Holy Spirit, in dependence on, and according to, his teaching. We must persevere in particular requests, notwithstanding discouragements. We must pray, not for ourselves only, but for all the saints. Our enemies are mighty, and we are without strength, but our Redeemer is almighty, and in the power of his might, we will overcome. Wherefore, we must stir up ourselves. Have not we, when God has called, often neglected to answer? Let us think upon these things, and continue our prayers with patience.

Finally brothers and sisters in Christ, I will end my sermon with the parable in the book of Luke about a tenacious widow, who prayed to God diligently against a city judge who never believed in God. This is indeed a good example of how prayers can uplift us and save us from wicked forces. This story, which only occurs in the book of Luke, illustrates the results of persistent prayers. It teaches us that to pray and not to lose heart is a vital step in preparation for the coming of our Lord and Savior Jesus Christ. If this helpless widow wins her case by a persistent pleading before a callous judge, then how quickly will God's chosen people find justice before a loving and righteous Father? And will Christ, upon his return, find people of faith on earth? So, my dear children in Christ, let each one of us take care so that we can be part of the faithful remnant. "Watch and pray" is a key to Christian spirituality and our struggle against temptations. Since our bodies and souls are united, a lethargic body paralyzes the spirit. Our willing spirit, after recognizing the weakness of the flesh, knows it needs God's help and power. True faith, my dear children, is nourished by ardent and vigilant prayers. Amen.

HOMILY
on Eternal Life

June 22, 2011

In the Name of the Father, and of the Son, and of the Holy Spirit.

What shall I do to inherit eternal life?[45]

BROTHERS AND SISTERS in Christ, in our daily Christian lives here on earth, this is the question that lingers in our minds when we wake up and engage ourselves in our activities. Our activities are in relation to the eternal life promised us by our Lord and Savior Jesus Christ. We often ask ourselves, "What shall we do to inherit eternal life?" We are branded as "fallen" due to the sins of our first parents. But, in our belief in the true God and his qualities, and his action in creating the universe, the Lord's intention remains clear for us to attain eternal life according to his design. The reconciliation of sinful man with God by the sacrificial Cross brought man's salvation and makes man to be the center of the Gospel of Christ. The apostle Paul states three steps that should be taken by the faithful: namely, repentance, justification, and sanctification, to the glory of God. Our Christian calling is attained through the Gospel of Christ, with which the power of grace is linked.

Our constant pursuit of a state of joy and happiness has become our intimate desire and a never-ending search. Each one of our individual efforts

45 Luke 18:18.

to fulfill the desire of this state has led us along various roads in the hope of finding it. Choosing the right path has been our never-ending challenge. The desire in us to choose the right road that leads us to the ultimate state of happiness is the fundamental task of every human being. This road to happiness is not always wide and well-kept. It is important to note that men who have chosen the straight, narrow paths through their imaginations have realized great achievements. These people were among the first in looking for happiness beyond earthly riches, concluding that there was and is no lasting reward on this earth.

Brethren in Christ, the right path is one that can be reached with the illuminating torch of revealed truth and total belief in Almighty God. This unparalleled road leads man to the ultimate state of happiness and joy. When we become pious Christians, we discover a state of bliss, made vivid by the grace of God. This is the crowning gift of man's salvation. A good Christian is seen in light of his faith in everlasting life. Whatever he does or says, or wherever he worships, the believer evaluates him by his faith in the kingdom of God. For a good Christian should readily know that, in this life, he has found the source of meaningful life on earth, and everlasting life in the Kingdom of God.

Brothers and sisters in Christ, we all end up asking ourselves, "What shall I do to inherit eternal life?" This question is expressed in silence, lived in vividness, and considered with fear. We often try to answer this question, but, in truth, it cannot be answered with human endeavors or achievements. God himself reveals the answer. We find the answer doesn't deal primarily with good works done, but is our expression of trust in God. The answer is an expression of trust in God through good works. It reflects the deepest conviction of man and his faith in the almighty God. We humans require assistance from forces from without and within our environment. We need assistance from the grace of God to attain eternal life—what we seek by nature. As Christians, we are supposed to keep undefiled the true faith, from which the grace of God and good works come. "For as the body without the spirit is dead, so faith without works is dead also."[46]

The Christian first should have the faith, and through it, the inspiration to do good in the Name of Jesus Christ. We as the faithful are members of the mystical body of Christ because of our faith and conviction in Christ. By virtue, we are stewards of the riches of God. "But without faith it is

46 James 2:26.

impossible to please [God]: for he that cometh to God must believe that he is, and that he is a rewarder of them that diligently seek him."[47]

Therefore, those of us who desire eternal life must first have true faith in God in order to plan our lives according to the principles of faith. Our true faith in Christ is the foundation on which true worship and prayers depend, and in which good works are interwoven in such a way that faith presupposes the others.

"Now faith is the substance of things hoped for, the evidence of things not seen."[48] This verse explains what true faith is. It means believing with one's heart and to confess one triune God. Our Orthodox faith tells us that all issues concerning faith were handed down by Jesus Christ, through his apostles, as can be witnessed in Saint Paul's letter to the Thessalonians: "Therefore, brethren, stand fast, and hold the traditions which ye have been taught, whether by word, or our epistle."[49]

My dear brethren, true faith is nourished in the Gospel of Christ, both by that which is written, and that which was handed down orally to the Church through the apostles—that is, the sacred tradition. Our faith should not be silent but should be confessed and widely spread. The Nicene Creed, which was formulated during the times of the early Church, was used as a basic confession of all the commandments of the Lord. It was formulated to pronounce our doctrines against new heretical teachings. In it is embodied the truth which we should know and believe in for our salvation. We should be able to follow and study our creed as it was determined by the early Church. The first article refers to the Father, the second through the seventh relate to the Son, the eighth to the Holy Spirit, the ninth to the Church, the tenth to baptism, the eleventh to the resurrection of the dead, and the last, eternal life.

In order to be a good Christian, one should believe in one true God and Father of all, who is above all, and through all, and in you all. It is sufficient for us to know what has been revealed to us for our own salvation in the Scriptures. The holy fathers of the Church believed in the Holy Trinity as revealed in the Holy Scriptures and taught likewise: The Lord is one in substance and nature, but is also *tri-hypostatic,* existing as three Persons. The Holy Trinity is one in substance, but three in *hypostases*: persons. The three Persons in the Holy Trinity have distinct attributes, by which each is

47 Heb. 11:6.
48 Heb. 11:1.
49 2 Thess. 2:15.

distinguished: The Father begets the Son, the Son is begotten of the Father, and the Holy Spirit proceeds from the Father.

It is important to know that God's attributes are important for our salvation. They are not limited to the act of creation. He is found everywhere, and at the same time, fulfilling everything. Another attribute of God is his knowledge of all thoughts and the deepest secrets of the heart of every one of us. He knows what we are thinking and whether we are genuine in our repentance. So we can never lie to God or ourselves. When we are living our lives here on earth, let us follow the right path, and God will reward us with eternal life. This is the moment we will all be waiting for—a joyous moment, a time when our important questions will be answered, a time to reap the harvest of our labors! Amen.

HOMILY

at the Consecration of Saint Kyriake Orthodox Church

Chepkwesis, Kenya,
June 25, 2011

Beloved Presbyters, Brothers and Sisters in Christ, I greet you in the Name of the Father, and of the Son, and of the Holy Spirit.

Today being a very important day for all of us who are gathered here, I find it worthy for me to give you a brief history of Saint Kyriake, the saint for whom this Church has been named. She was the daughter of Dorotheus and Eusebia, who were devout Christians. Her parents were wealthy and had remained without a child for a very long time, but as they were unceasing in prayers, God blessed them with a child. Since this child was born on a Sunday—the day of the Lord—she was given the name Kyriake. From childhood, this child was dedicated to God, until the time she was mature and became unnaturally beautiful. During this period, many suitors approached her for marriage, but she refused them all saying that she had chosen to dedicate her life to God, and that she desired nothing but to die a virgin.

There came a time when the magistrate in Nicomedia tried to betroth Kyriake to his son, but as she declined. So the son betrayed Kyriake and her parents to Emperor Diocletian, stating that they were Christians. The emperor was angered and ordered Kyriake and her parents to be tortured.

Dorotheus was beaten until the soldiers grew tired, but nothing could change his stand for Christ. The saint's parents were exiled and later died due to much suffering. The emperor proceeded to send Kyriake to Nicomedia for a thorough interrogation by Maximian, who was his son-in-law and co-ruler. Kyriake was whipped after refusing to renounce her faith. It is said that on one night while she was languishing in prison, God spoke to her and said, "Don't be afraid of torture, Kyriake; my Spirit is with you." It was after Maximian had tried his best to change Kyriake that he decided to send her to Hilarion, the eparch of Bithynia. He instructed him to convert her to paganism or send her back to him.

Hilarion tried on her all the best torture methods known to him, but was not successful. He then ordered her to be thrown into a cell where she suffered from the pains of the wounds on her body. Later that night, Christ appeared to her, and healed all her wounds. This miracle led many pagans to accept Christ, and they were later beheaded. Apollonios, who succeeded Hilarion, came into power and decided that Kyriake should be killed. This was after trying to throw her into fire, only to have the flame immediately die. He also instructed his soldiers to put her inside a den of wild beasts, but the animals became gentle and tame. It was after all this that Apollonios decided to sentence her to death by the sword. She was allowed to pray, whereby she asked God to accept her soul, and then she was beheaded.

Brothers and sisters in Christ, the story of Kyriake is an inspiring piece for us who are gathered here. It is a lesson for us amid the challenges that we might undergo when we are doing the work that Christ left us to do. The story encourages us to be strong even when we are about to die for Christ. It is a lesson for us to continue persevering in faith, not giving up at any moment. Our Lord has promised never to leave us alone, but to walk with us in our spiritual journeys. Saint Paul's epistle to the Hebrews encourages us in a similar way:

> But call to remembrance the former days, in which after ye were Illuminated, ye endured a great fight with afflictions; and partly whilst ye were made a gazing-stock both by reproaches and afflictions, and partly whilst ye became companions of them that were so used.[50]

Brethren in Christ, the epistle admonishes us about the advantage of persevering and why it is important to continue doing so, just like in the life

50 Heb. 10:32, 33.

of Saint Kyriake. The writer warns us that it is impossible to abandon Jesus and return to spiritual life. Though some of us are in danger of doing that, the writer of Hebrews hopes that we will repent before crossing the line. This is the same reason that we are invited to remember the days after our conversion, when our actions proved that our faith was real, and when our salvation could be seen from the changes that took place in our attitudes and behaviors. The advice in Hebrews is that we look back and see the promised miracles of the New Covenant, for God is living inside us, even though we sin, and our most terrible steps have been forgiven and forgotten.

> For ye had compassion of me in my bonds, and took joyfully the spoiling of your goods, knowing in yourselves that ye have in heaven a better and an enduring substance. Cast not away therefore your confidence, which hath great recompense of reward. For ye have need of patience, that, after ye have done the will of God, ye might receive the promise.[51]

Brothers and sisters in Christ, the words above emphasize the way we should react when facing afflictions for the sake of our Lord and Savior, Jesus Christ. Afflictions may come in the form of difficult challenges, persecutions, hatred, or even our crops and goods being destroyed because of following Christ. How are we to behave when these things happen to us? The words of the writer become our new hope. We are encouraged that during such trials we ought to remain calm and at the same time rejoice, because the reward kept for us in heaven is greater than anything on earth. The spiritual riches that we can receive from Christ are worth far more than those things that would be lost. We are also warned against losing confidence. Having started well in our Christian lives, our zeal should not decline to the point of abandoning Christ, no matter what happens. "Cast not away therefore your confidence," because when we do not throw away our confidence, our reward in heaven is great.

Beloved of Christ, we are told that for us to actually receive the fulfillment of God's promises, we must continue to do God's will until the moment when see Christ's face, whether through death or at his physical return. Otherwise the promises will be lost. Our faith must endure until he who is coming will come. God assures Abraham that, although the fulfillment of His words might appear to take long time from a human

51 Heb. 10:34–36.

perspective, events would happen at the appointed time. Then God said to him, "The just shall live by faith"[52]—that is, those who would patiently wait for him to do what he said he would do, and who would not shrink back from obeying him, would be counted as righteous. This means they would attain eternal life.

Brethren in Christ, the Hebrews were getting weary and fed up with the troubles they were experiencing. But, instead of God telling them that their hardships were over, and that it would be smooth-sailing, he told them that it was going to get harder. The same applies to us. God is not promising us a smooth sailing life if we follow him, but one that is full of discouragement and challenges. The only hope we have is that he will never forsake us, but will always come to our rescue when needed. We should live a prayerful life, which is the only way to keep evil spirits at bay. We should go to church often, because when we meet our fellow brothers and sisters, we encourage each other to keep on with our struggles. Let us not throw away our confidence, but continue doing what is good in God's eyes, and he will bless us and guide us.

May God bless you and give you strength to carry on with his good work! Amen.

52 Heb. 10:38.

HOMILY
at the Consecration of Saint Irene Orthodox Church

Maseno, Kenya,
June 27 2011

Venerable Presbyters, Brothers and Sisters in Christ,

WARM GREETINGS in the Name of our Lord and Savior Jesus Christ. Praise be to God for this wonderful chance to gather here at Saint Irene Church. It is a great opportunity to witness yet another consecration of a church of God. Today this is our humble calling to spread the good news of Christ to all corners of the world. It is in this church, and under this same roof, that such noble work will take place, and it is also under this shelter that our holy services will take place and the sacraments will be administered. Let us rejoice today because Christ is in our midst. He is with us, as he has said, "where two or three are gathered in my Name, there am I in the midst of them."[53]

Let us increase our faith and trust in the Master, who alone is able to understand our inner beings and offer us blessings according to his mercies. Today is the day we realize the fruits of our labor, a day that clearly shows that we are still strong spiritually and continuing with the work that Christ left us, that of spreading the good news. I believe that our labor shall not

53 Matt. 18:20.

be in vain, and that our trust in the Lord shall not be a mere formality, because we have kept all that has been passed on to us by the apostles, by the help of the Holy Spirit, and we will go on with our missionary duties.

Brothers and sisters in Christ, you might ask yourselves why this church was named after Saint Irene. What kind of person was she? Saint Irene was born during the reign of Constantine the Great in the Persian city of Magidus. She was the daughter of Licinius, the governor of the region. At the age of eight, she began attending school. She studied for ten years under Apelianos, an educator renowned for his wisdom and intellect. According to Apelianos, an angel appeared to Irene in a dream and told her that she had been chosen to be the voice of the Messiah among her own people. When she told Apelianos about the dream, he warned her of the awaiting obstacles if she decided to take that direction, but Irene knew in her heart that her faith would sustain her.

Brethren in Christ, we are told that Licinius at first could not believe his daughter and he attributed her new interest in Christianity to the whim of youth. He advised her to give up this madness, but Irene failed to comply. He went on and threatened to have her trampled in the arena by wild horses. Apelianos related that while Licinius was arranging the arena for his daughter to be killed, wild horses somehow trampled him. Irene rushed to her father's side, prayed to the Lord, and her prayers healed her father. He, in turn, repented and was baptized into the Christian faith.

The Persian king, Sedecian, heard what had happened and asked his soldiers to arrest her. The king then commanded Irene to disavow Christ, but she declined and was put into prison. She was tortured and then released after the king's death.

Saint Irene regained her health and continued with her work of carrying the message of Christ throughout the land and through her activities thousands of people were converted to Christianity. The successors of King Sedacian tried once more to stop her missionary efforts, but in vain. At last, one of these kings resolved to kill her and she was beheaded.

Brethren in Christ, what a great lesson of humility we learn here today. Although Saint Irene lived after the great heroes recorded in the Bible, her nature is a lesson for us today. Her life is an expression of the Scriptures in every way. She was not only humble, but also led her father see the light of Christ without fearing the consequences.

While carrying on with her mission work, she encountered the ever-present dangers that we experience today, and yet managed to outlive three kings. She is a triumphant mother-figure and an encouragement for us to continue with the good work of Christ no matter what we are going through. Her story rejuvenates our zeal to continue with the wonderful work of today: The work of building more churches—our mission stations for spreading the good news of Christ. My ardent prayer is that God may give us the courage and strength required to keep on with this noble task. Saint Irene inspires us. No matter what the obstacles, no matter what hardships we face in doing what Christ commanded, we will always triumph, and our good work will always come back to us as blessings. We must accept hardship for Christ's sake, as our reward is kept in heaven.

Brothers and sisters in Christ, today's epistle is a good example of what we are supposed to do when giving in the Church. The apostle Paul says:

> But this I say, he which soweth sparingly shall reap also sparingly; and he which soweth bountifully shall reap also bountifully. Every man according as he purposeth in his heart, so let him give; not grudgingly, or of necessity: for God loveth a cheerful giver.[54]

Saint Paul's advice to us is that we should not simply have the recipient in view when showing our generosity in almsgiving, but we should consider who we emulate when we show kindness to the poor person, and who promises to recompense us for the favors we do for them. We should direct our attention to God while showering all our zeal in giving with complete happiness. We are urged to sow generously in season, so that we may reap generously. When the day of harvesting comes, we may gather the returns of what we have planted here on earth and be regarded with loving-kindness by the Lord. Paul's purpose in the verse above was not only for money to be contributed to the poor, but for it to be contributed with great eagerness.

God chooses giving not only for sustaining whoever is receiving, but also for blessings to the giver, and hence, the reason the giver should be cheerful while giving—giving with pleasure. Blessed, then, is almsgiving that both renews the recipient and rejoices the giver. Paul is encouraging us not to pray for abundance, but for enough to live on. Why is this? It is because he wants us to have enough of this world's goods, but more so an overflowing abundance of spiritual blessings. He adds:

> As it is written, 'He hath dispersed abroad; he hath given to the

54 2 Cor. 9:6–7.

> poor: his righteousness remaineth forever.' Now he that ministereth seed to the sower both minister bread for your food, and multiply your seed sown, and increase the fruits of your righteousness; Being enriched in every thing to all bountifulness, which causeth through us thanksgiving to God.[55]

Beloved of Christ, when we give cheerfully, we attract many blessings and favor from God. The things that we give generously do not remain, but the effects of giving them do. As we are able to experience them through blessings, therefore, we should not be mean and calculating with what we have, but give with a generous hand. We always give a lot to our worldly pleasure. Why not give just half as much to Christ? If God rewards those of us who till the earth with abundance, how much more will he reward those of us who till the soil of heaven in caring for our souls?

Finally, brethren in Christ, God has allowed us to dispose of great things and reserve smaller things for him. Our bodily nourishment belongs exclusively to him because he can control rain and seasons. But, our spiritual nourishment he has left as our own responsibility, since by our own wills we decide whether or not our harvest will be abundant. We are the ones who can decide while we are here on earth, because whatever you plant is what you will harvest. Let God give us strength and wisdom to make the right decisions.

In the Name of the Father, and of the Son, and of the Holy Spirit. Amen.

55 2 Cor. 9:9–11.

HOMILY
on the Life of Saint Ephraim

Kayole (Nairobi), Kenya,
July, 2011

Venerable Brothers in the vineyard of Christ, Brothers and Sisters in Christ,

IT GIVES ME GREAT JOY to meet you on this occasion of consecrating Saint Ephraim Orthodox Church here in Kayole. I would like first of all to take this opportunity to express my deep gratitude to all those who have devoted their time and energy to the service of this church. As I thank God for the fruits already gathered, I encourage you to persevere in your commitment to the service of the Church, and God will reward you abundantly. On this great and special day, we have given our church the name of a very important person in the history of the Orthodox Church. This person was known as Saint Ephraim the Syrian. He was born early in the fourth century in the ancient city of Nisibis in Mesopotamia. The reason he was called "the Syrian" was because at one time, Mesopotamia belonged to Syria, and he was born there by his Christian parents before the Edict of Milan was issued in the year AD 313.

When Saint Ephraim was young, his parents had a dream. In it, the boy's tongue sprang a lush vine that produced an abundant cluster of grapes. The more the bird ate the fruits, the more it multiplied. Later it was revealed that these clusters were his sermons, the leaves of the vine, his hymns. However, through his youth, one could never judge his future greatness, and despite the fact that his parents had brought him up in Christian teachings, he was impetuous, wild and unruly, and his life nearly convinced him that life is ruled by chance. He once killed a cow that belonged to a poor old man, and later he was also suspected of arranging a robbery for sheep. This act caused him to be taken before a magistrate and imprisoned. He was released upon the magistrate seeing that he had stayed enough in the prison and had already learned his lesson. Saint Ephraim, just like David, entreated the Lord to overlook his youthful folly. True to his vow, upon his release he went straight away to the hermits living in the mountains where he became a disciple of Saint James, who later became the Bishop of Nisibis.

Saint Ephraim, born again in repentance, began to train as an athlete of virtues, exercising himself in the study of the Bible, prayers, and fasting. This lesson is important for us faithful because we see how the power of God can transform a person from bad to good, and from being unworthy to worthy and useful. The passionate wayward youth was transformed into a humble, contrite monk, weeping day and night for his sins, having entirely surrendered himself to God through his decision to leave the sinful, worthless life. The Lord was pleased with him, and he was rewarded with gifts of wisdom. Grace flowed from his mouth like a sweet spring, streaming the fulfillment of his parents' dream.

In spite of all the gifts that were bestowed upon Saint Ephraim, he remained humble. He even feigned madness so as to avoid being consecrated bishop and the glory that accompanies the position. His humility was guarded by his constant remembrance of the sins of his youth and by his contrite spirit. While tears of repentance constantly flowed from his eyes, Ephraim's face was bright and shone with joy. As Saint Gregory put it, "Where Ephraim speaks of contrition, he lifts up our thoughts to the Divine Goodness and pours thanksgiving and praise to the Most High."

Saint Ephraim, after a brief illness, reposed from his labors and was received into the heavenly habitations. The people of Edessa called him "the lyre of the Holy Sprit."

Today, brothers and sisters in Christ, we face the challenge of leaving our old ways and adopting the new life in Christ. This will mark a happy ending for us here on earth, and at the same time a happy beginning of our lives in heaven. We should learn to persevere in the incarnate Son, who came down and died for us so that we attain salvation. Jesus Christ is superior to the prophets, angels, Moses, and Aaron. He offers to us a superior priesthood, sanctuary, and sacrifice, for in worshiping him we enter heaven. Therefore, I urge you today to hold first to him, as he will never let us down. Today's Epistle according to Hebrews warns us against willful negligence. It begins with the following words:

> For if the word spoken by angels was steadfast, and every transgression and disobedience received a just recompense of reward; How shall we escape, if we neglect so great salvation; which at the first began to be spoken by the Lord, and was confirmed unto us by them that heard him; God also bearing them witness, both with signs and wonders, and with divers miracles, and gifts of the Holy Ghost, according to his own will?[56]

Brothers and sisters in Christ, these words are an admonition to us against willful negligence and carelessness by a slow process of attrition. We are warned against drifting away from our incarnate Lord and following our own sinful ways. We at times fall short of faith and start to drift away hopelessly in sin. But why do we drift away? All the teachings are clear, the prophecies have been given to us, and what is more, Christ came as a human being to be with and die for us. What excuse can we give for living sinfully? Yet, Christ is right here with us. The writer of the epistle gives us a conditional statement: If Israel was to obey the words of the created angel or suffer punishment, how much more must we heed what God incarnate has said through his apostles, especially when the words have been confirmed by many miracles of the Spirit, to prove that the Kingdom has come upon us? This is the same reason why in our Liturgy we ask for "pardon and remission of our sins and transgressions," and a "good defense before the dread judgment seat of Christ."[57] When we mention these particular words, then we affirm that there is just reward or retribution, a very real judgment.

> For unto the angles hath he not put in subjection the world to come, whereof we speak. But one testified in a certain place, saying, 'What is man, that thou art mindful of him? or the son of man, that thou visitist him? Thou madest him a little lower than the angels; Thou crownest him with glory and honor, and didst set him over the

56 Heb. 2:2–4.

57 *The Hieratikon*, vol. II, 140.

works of thy hands: Thou hast put all things in subjection under his feet.'"[58]

Brethren in Christ, the Jews expected the Messiah to be an earth-conquering king, a political success story, and not a failure. At times they would honestly ask, "If Jesus is superior to the angels—indeed a divine being—then why did he die, especially in such a degrading way?" Today's epistle tries to answer this important question. Christ's humiliation is only temporary; it is the only way of redeeming mortal man, and finally it re-establishes that God intended for man to have dominion over all creation, including the angels. Hebrews applies an extract from Psalms in order for us to understand Jesus Christ, the perfect man: "But we see Jesus, who was made a little lower than the angels for the suffering of death, crowned with glory and honor."[59]

Here we see in Hebrews that Christ was, "made a little lower than the angels." Simply referring to his incarnation, the Son become man for our salvation. When Christ was incarnated, he suffered and later died. His suffering and death has highly exalted him. The Cross, which was thought to have brought shame and reproach, has brought Christ glory and honor. Christ tasted death; he experienced death fully and knew it intimately. His death was a real death. He died for us. He died for everyone, for the whole world, so that salvation may be realized, not because he owed us anything, but as a gift. He was "made perfect through suffering." These words are not to suggest that there was imperfection in Christ before the crucifixion; rather it shows that Christ voluntarily took on human nature—human nature that can be saved and perfected only by the suffering of death.

Brothers and sisters in Christ, this is a great lesson for us today, that Christ is the pioneering captain of the narrow path to God in his suffering for sin, going through death, the descent into Hades, resurrection and ascension. In conclusion, beloved brethren, in salvation we take Christ's way of suffering. Our perfection requires growth that is manifested in suffering. Let us today, like Saint Ephraim, put down our own evil past and embrace Christ. Even though we might go through suffering, we will be perfected and attain eternal life.

In the Name of the Father, and of the Son, and of the Holy Spirit. Amen

58 Heb. 2:5–8; quoting Ps. 8:4–6.
59 Heb. 2:9–10.

HOMILY
on the Life of the Apostle Andrew

Kathima (Meru), Kenya
July 18, 2011

I greet you in the Name of our Lord and Savior, Jesus Christ.

TODAY, BROTHERS AND SISTERS in Christ, we stand here to witness the holy and historical service of consecrating this beautiful church of the Apostle Andrew. This moment is very important to us all, as it reminds us of the labor and passion of holy apostle Andrew, who was also known as the first-called. We may ask, why is his life is important to us in our daily lives as modern Christians?" The answer to this vital question lies in his life, work, and unquestionable trust and loyalty to our Lord and Savior, Jesus Christ. There was not any single moment that he stooped down to deny Christ, but he walked with him even to the point of death. We are told that Saint Andrew, a native of Bethsaida, was the son of Jonah and a brother of the apostle Peter.

The apostle never married, and after listening to the teachings of John the Baptist, he decided to forsake all things and become his disciple. It was when John the Baptist pointed to Jesus as he was passing, "Behold the Lamb of God," that Andrew and another disciple, presumed to be John the Evangelist, left the Baptist and followed Christ.[60]

The apostle Andrew then hurried to find his brother, Simon Peter, to whom he declared, "We have found the Messiah," which is interpreted,

60 Jn. 1:29.

"the Christ." It was afterwards while he and his brother were fishing at the sea of Galilee that Jesus called them, saying, "Follow me, and I will make you fishers of men."[61] So, Andrew dropped his nets without delay, obeying the Lord's summons, and he followed Christ together with his brother Peter. This is the reason for which he is usually referred to as "the first called"—simply because he became a follower of Christ before any other apostle.

After the Lord's passion and resurrection, Saint Andrew started spreading the Gospel in the land of Bithynia and the Papontia in Chalcedon, Byzantium Thrace, and Macedonia, as far as the Black Sea and Danube, as well as Thessaly, Hellas, Achaia, Amisus, Trebizod, Haraclea, and Amastors. It is said that at one time the people of the city of Sinope cast him to the ground, bound him hand and foot, and dragged him about and beat him. They also severed his fingers and shattered his teeth, but to the amazement of his persecutors, he was completely made whole by the grace of God. He continued with his missionary journeys, instructing many in faith, ordaining presbyters, and consecrated Bishop Stachys, whom Paul had mentioned in the Epistle to the Romans. Saint Andrew later suffered greatly at the hand of the worshipers of pagan gods. He was later crucified and died after a light came down from heaven in the form of lightening. His spirit departed and went to stand in the light of the Lord.

Brothers and sisters in Christ, having seen the life of the apostle Andrew, who sets a very good example for us to follow, we should be able at all times to sacrifice ourselves for the sake of Christ and the Gospel. We should be able to go an extra mile for the sake of defending and spreading the good news. The suffering of Andrew marks a new beginning for us; it opens to us the door of martyrdom. This proves that in order for us to be glorified, we have to pass through all kinds of tests. The great lesson we learn here is that at the heart of Christianity suffering and glory are intimately related. There can be no glory without suffering. Saint Paul says,

> For those whom he did foreknow, he also did predestine to be conformed to the image of his Son, that he might be the firstborn among many brethren. Moreover whom he did predestinate, them he also called: and whom he called, them he also justified: and whom he justified, them he also glorified.[62]

61 Mt. 4:19.

62 Rom. 8:29–30.

Brethren in Christ, we are predestined to be transformed into Christ's image. The apostle Paul tries to explain the centrality of Christ in God's plan, saying that the purpose was to make Christ "the firstborn among the brethren." The "firstborn" here means not only that he is the example for all others, but also that they belong to his family. Paul later continues his teaching on God's action: God predestines, he justifies, and he glorifies. By doing so, he presupposes that we have responded to our calls in faith. Paul's word for us here is that our eschatology is founded on the awesome saving will of God, and his love for us is our assurance.

> What shall we then say to these things? If God be for us, who can be against us? He that spared not his own Son, but delivered him up for us all, how shall he not with him freely give us all things? Who shall lay any thing to the charge of God's elect? It is God that justifieth, who is he that condemneth? Is it Christ that died, yea rather, that is risen again, who is even at the right hand of God, who also maketh intercession for us.[63]

Beloved brethren in Christ, if God is for us, who can be against us? The apostle Paul sums up all our privileges: "God is for us." He is not only reconciled to us and not against us, but in covenant with us. He is engaged for us—all his attributes and promises are for us. All that he is and has and does is for his people. He performs all things for them. He is for them, even when he seems to act against them. And, if so, who can be against us, so as to prevail against us, so as to hinder our happiness? Be they ever so great and strong, ever so many, ever so mighty, ever so malicious, what can they do? While God is for us, and we keep in his love, we may, with holy boldness, defy all the powers of darkness. Let Satan do his worst; he is chained. Let the world do its worst; it is conquered. Principalities and powers are spoiled and disarmed and triumphed over in the Cross of Christ. Who then dares fight against us, while God himself is fighting for us?

My brothers and sisters in Christ let us observe what God has done for us—he spared not his own Son. When he was to undertake our salvation, the Father did not withhold his only-begotten Son. He did not think him too precious a gift to bestow for the salvation of poor souls. The Father delivered him up for us all as a sacrifice to atone for our sins. Though he was his own Son, yet, "it pleased the Lord to bruise him; he hath put him to grief: when thou shalt make his soul an offering for sin,"[64] as writes the prophet Isaiah. Christ Jesus took upon himself our sins. By this we know

63 Rom. 8:31–33.

64 Is. 53:10.

that he loves us. Furthermore, the apostle Paul offers the following assurance:

> Who shall separate us from the love of Christ? Shall tribulation, or distress, or persecution, or famine, or nakedness, or peril, or sword? As it is written, for thy sake we are killed all the day long; we are accounted as sheep for the slaughter. Nay, in all these things we are more than conquerors through him that loved us. For I am persuaded, that neither death, nor life, nor angels, nor principalities, nor powers, nor things present, nor things to come, nor height, nor depth, nor any other creature, shall be able to separate us from the love of God, which is in Christ Jesus our Lord.[65]

Beloved children in Christ, absolutely nothing can separate us from the love of our Lord. Shall they, can they do that? No, it is impossible. All these things cannot cut the bond of love and friendship that is between Christ and us who are true believers. Christ does not, will not, love us less for all these things mentioned above.

All these troubles are very consistent with the strong and constant love of the Lord Jesus. They are neither a cause nor an evidence of the abatement of his love. When Paul was whipped, and beaten, and imprisoned, and stoned, did Christ love him in a lesser way? Was his fellowship with Christ interrupted? Nothing of that sort happened to him. These things only separate us from the love of our friends, but not from Christ. When Paul was brought before Nero, all men forsook him, but the Lord stood by him. However our persecuting enemies may try to rob us, they cannot rob from us the love of Christ; they cannot intercept his love-tokens; they cannot interrupt nor exclude his visits. They may try to do the worst things, but they cannot make a true believer miserable.

We cannot pretend that we love Christ less because of persecutions. Charity thinks no evil, entertains no misgiving thoughts, makes no hard conclusions, no unkind constructions. It considers all to be good that comes from love. A true Christian loves Christ, though he suffers for him. He does not think negatively of Christ, even if he loses everything for his sake.

May God bless you all. Amen.

65 Rom. 8:35–39.

HOMILY
at the Consecration of the Church of the Holy Pantocrator

Micii Mikuru, Kenya,
July 19, 2011

Greetings in the Name of the Father, and of the Son, and of the Holy Spirit.

ONCE AGAIN, we assemble here through the blessings and grace of our God. This is a great day that we are gathered to celebrate the consecration of Holy Pantocrator Orthodox Church. It is indeed a memorable day because you will always remember it when you hold your prayers, as the church now has a holy altar and holy marking on its wall. This holy practice that we bear witness to today has been passed on to us from the ancient Church by the apostles of Christ. The Altar table is an important part of the interior of the Orthodox Church building. It is actually the place where Christ is enthroned, both as a Word of God in the Gospels and as a Lamb in the Eucharistic sacrifice. Around the table are the angels and saints: the servants of the Word and the Lamb who glorify God the Father in the perpetual adoration that is inspired by the Holy Spirit.

Brothers and sisters in Christ, we are all aware that our God is a mighty God. He is all-powerful and has the ability to do all things because he is the creator of the heavens and earth. He also created us according to his own image. He is the one who sustains us and controls all that happens under the sun. He is the Pantocrator—that is, the omnipotent ruler of all.

This word represents the divine majesty of our Creator and Redeemer, who presides over the destinies of the world under the human features of the incarnate Son. "Come unto me all that labor and are heavy laden and I will give you rest, for my yoke is easy."[66]

Today's occasion of consecration gives me the opportunity to address you on church issues as presented by the apostle Paul in his letter to the Church of Corinth. In this epistle, we see Paul rebuking those who had divided the Corinthian church and at the same time trying to hide their wickedness by ironically suggesting that they were teaching more perfect doctrines, as these people also pretended to be wiser than others. In this letter, we see Paul attacking the root cause of this particular problem before dealing with the issue of division. The epistle begins by saying:

> Paul, called to be an apostle of Jesus Christ through the will of God, and Sosthenes our brother, unto the Church of God which is at Corinth, to them that are sanctified in Christ Jesus, called to be saints, with all that in every place call on the Name of Jesus Christ our Lord, both theirs and ours: Grace be unto you, and peace, from God our Father and the Lord Jesus Christ.[67]

Brethren in Christ, these words are not addressed to those who are already cleansed from their sins, but also to those still looking toward the fuller reception of sanctifying grace. Their instruction is not limited to the Corinthians, but is applicable to all Christians, everywhere, including us who are present here today. These words should reflect to us the new message and new instructions on how we are to conduct ourselves as true Christians. In this epistle, Paul continues to tell us that he is an apostle by the will of God, alluding to those false apostles who had not been sent by Christ, and whose teaching was not true. Why, we may ask, did Paul say these words? The reason lies in the fact that during that time there were many of sects that had emerged and that were preaching Christ according to their own teaching. Paul opposed heresies, and he confirmed that he was a true preacher sent by Christ, according to God's will. Here Paul sets a good example for us, that we should stand tall as good missionaries of the Word of God, and strive to shun all false teachings that go contrary to the teaching of God and our Church.

Beloved of Christ, today we witness Paul casting down the Corinthians'

66 Matt. 11:28.
67 1 Cor. 1:1–3.

pride by speaking of himself as "called." For what he has learned he did not discover himself, but while he was persecuting the Church, he was called. It was God who willed that he should be saved in this way. The apostle says that we have done nothing good by ourselves, but by God's will we have been saved. We were called because it seemed good to him—not because we were worthy. This verse warns us that the Church ought to be united because it belongs to God. It does not exist only in Corinth, but all over the world the Church is one, and that is the reason it is referred to as the *ecclesia*, meaning "assembly." This name does not stand for separation, but for unity and concord. This oneness is brought about by the grace of God and humility. A certain church father asks, "If our peace comes from God's grace, why are you so proud, since you are saved by grace? How can anyone find grace with God except through humility?"[68]

The apostle Paul says, "I thank my God always on your behalf, for the grace of God which is given you by Jesus Christ; that in every thing ye are enriched by him, in all utterance, and in all knowledge; even as the testimony of Christ was confirmed in you."[69] Brothers and sisters in Christ, here Paul begins with praise, in order to prepare the Corinthians for the admonition that is to come. The apostle puts himself in the position of a father who is thankful for his children all the time, whatever they have done. Saint John Chrysostom, who cites these words, observes that the praises are not only uncritical as the rest of the epistle makes clear, but are inserted to prepare the Christians for the criticism that is to come. For Saint John reckons that whoever starts out with unpleasant words antagonizes his hearers. The apostle continues to say,

> So that ye come behind in no gift; waiting for the coming of our Lord Jesus Christ; Who shall also confirm you unto the end, that ye may be blameless in the day of our Lord Jesus Christ. God is faithful, by whom ye were called unto the fellowship of his Son Jesus Christ our Lord.[70]

This verse tries to show us that Paul is confident that the Corinthians will persevere in righteousness until the Day of Judgment. Following the apostle's belief, we may ask ourselves "Do we have this confidence? Are we going to persevere till the day of judgment, or we are a giving up?" Today

68 Attributed to St. John Chrysostom.
69 1 Cor. 1:4–6.
70 1 Cor. 7–9.

Paul is encouraging us that people, who could not be shaken in spite of so many turmoils and disagreements, proved that they could remain faithful to the end. So, we too should not be shaken. In praising the Corinthians, he challenges those who had been corrupted by the errors of the false apostles. In proclaiming the faith of the righteous, he is calling on the false prophets to repent. The apostle Paul concludes by telling us that fellowship is brotherhood, just as he also declares God's unfailing faithfulness toward us in this regard, so we ourselves must not be found to be faithless or dishonorable with respect to an adoption. Rather we must remain faithful in it.

Finally brethren, as I conclude my sermon, I would urge all of you to love your Church just as Christ loved you, defend your faith always and avoid unwanted divisions. Let us look at Paul as our model, as we leave our old habit of sin and false belief, and instead embrace Christ our Lord and Savior. Let us shun evil doctrines coming from false prophets, and at the same time defend the good teachings of Christ. We ought to put our trust in God because he is faithful, and this means that we can trust in his self-revelation. His Word reveals him. He is God who is faithful.

I leave you my paternal blessings. Amen.

HOMILY
at a Marriage Service

Church of Saints David & Nectarios,
Nderi, Kenya,
March 17, 2012

OUR CHURCH is a Church of sacraments. We need the Holy Spirit and we need to accept each other, for we are all the image and likeness of God. There is so much joy when we are celebrating our sacraments.

Today, we have come to witness the new life of Harun and Tabitha. They have decided to come to the church and participate in one among many of our sacraments: Holy Matrimony. In most cases, people decide to stay together and have families, but in reality, the only time a couple can be known as husband and wife is when they come to the church and accept this special service. We congratulate the newlyweds, and we know that, as Christians, you will remember this day. You also have obligations to honor, respect, and love each other, accepting that you have different characters and therefore it will be very important for both of you to cultivate the Spirit of God in you through patience, love, humility, and obedience.

Make a new home, a home of God our Creator. Pray always and remember that God is always with those who pray together, for in doing so they create a bond of unity. When there is love between you, God abides in your midst and therefore your home will be a home of love, humility, patience, and peace. When you had not decided to be together, you used to do whatever you wanted alone, but now that you have joined your lives, you should be near each other, listening and working with each other. And as you do so, Jesus Christ will be at the center of your marriage.

I pray that God will give you, who have now become one, a spirit of growth and that the Holy Spirit will guide you to find godliness in whatever you undertake to do. May God bless you and give you a lot of joy.

I also take this opportunity to congratulate your parents. I am sure they are happy and proud of you. Continue to love, respect, and listen to them, for they are the ones who know you and understand you better. For the rest of you who came to witness this marriage, keep the couple in your prayers. May our prayers always be with them. What else do we need?

May God bless you all. Amen.

HOMILY
at the Sacrament of Holy Baptism

Makarios III Patriarchal Seminary Chapel,
Nairobi, Kenya,
June 16, 2012

LET US AGAIN SAY, blessed is God, "who alone doeth great wonders,"[71] who does all things and transforms them. Before yesterday you were captives, but now you are free and citizens of the Church. Lately, you lived in the shame of your sins, but now you live in freedom and justice. You are not only free, but also sons; not only sons, but also heirs; not only heirs, but also brothers of Christ; not only brothers of Christ, but also joint heirs; not only joint heirs, but also members; not only members, but also the temple; not only the temple, but the instrument of the Spirit.

> Blessed is God who alone does wonderful things. You have seen how numerous are the gifts of baptism. Although many men think that the only gift it confers is the remission of sins, we have counted its honor to the number of ten. It is on this account that we baptize even infants, although they are sinless, that they may be given the further gifts of sanctification, filial adoption, and inheritance; that they may be brothers and members of Christ, and become dwelling places for the Spirit.[72]

71 Ps. 136:4.

72 St. John Chrysostom, *Baptismal Instructions*, 3rd homily (Mahwah, NJ: Paulist Press, 1963) 56.

baptism in the Orthodox Church means new life in Christ. New life in Christ carries not only the forgiveness of sins, but also filial adoption and inheritance. This makes the neophytes brothers of Christ and members of the Body of Christ. Christ is the Son of God, but through baptism and chrismation we become sons and daughters in the Kingdom, sharing and participating in his life. The neophyte is clothed with Christ and becomes the dwelling place of the Holy Spirit.

Baptism is the first sacrament that a person receives to become an Orthodox Christian. Orthodox baptism entails several rites: the reception of the catechumen, baptism by immersion, chrismation, and receiving of the holy Eucharist. Baptism has so many symbols: oil, water, triple immersion, anointing, procession, and tonsure, each with its own meaning. Regardless of the age of the candidate, the rite of baptism is the same. When baptism is meant for adults, the Church recommends a formal catechumenate period, which entails instructions on the fundamental doctrines of the Orthodox faith, life, and worship. This entire process is correctly called the sacrament of initiation in the Orthodox Church. Just before his ascension, Christ commanded his disciples to baptize all nations, a mission continued even today by the Church, as we all have witnessed.[73]

Baptism is a passage through which one enters the realm of salvation in the Church. This sacrament is absolutely necessary for salvation. The candidate—or a sponsor on their behalf—makes the decision to unite with Christ, just like Christ went to his passion and death voluntarily. Baptism is a personal Pascha, through which the candidate passes from the domain of evil into the domain of the risen Christ and his people.[74] Through the triple immersion, the candidate is buried in the imitation of the death of Christ in order to become a partaker in the Resurrection of Christ.[75] The candidate dies to sin and is reborn through water and Spirit.[76] This very central theme of Pascha is the principle that unites and illuminates every stage of the process of initiation. In the same way that Christ changed the meaning of the cross through his Crucifixion so did he change the meaning of water through his baptism in the river Jordan. The Holy water blessed in baptism reminds us not only of the regeneration (new birth) of the

73 See Matt. 28:16–20.
74 See Rom. 6:3–11.
75 See Rom. 6:3–5; Col 2:12.
76 See Jn. 3:5.

baptized, but also the renewal of the entire creation. We are liberated to be a new humanity in which we transcend sin and sinful barriers.[77]

After the elimination of the candidate's sins through baptism, he or she is then anointed with holy chrism. The descent of the Holy Spirit on the candidate is just like the descent of the Holy Spirit after Christ's baptism. Here, the candidate experiences his or her personal Pentecost and, at the same time, this imitates Christ's anointing in the Jordan. The candidate then becomes the anointed one of the Father, following in the footsteps of Christ. Just like Christ's ministry started after his baptism in the Jordan, so does the ministry of royal priesthood for all Orthodox Christians start after their baptism and chrismation. Through chrismation, the baptized person receives the gifts of the Holy Spirit, and their charismata is revealed henceforth strengthening them and helping their lives in Christ. The same Spirit helps to make the Trinity a reality in the life of the neophyte. Saint Irenaeus reminds us that it is through the Holy Spirit that the human person ascends to the Son, and through the Son, to the Father.

May the Holy Spirit lead and comfort your entire Christian life. Please don't forget to come for Communion frequently, and for those above seven years to renew your baptism through holy confession regularly. Amen.

77 Gal. 3:27–28; 1 Cor. 12:23.

HOMILY
at the Sacrament of Holy Matrimony

Patriarchal Cathedral of the Holy Anargyroi,
Nairobi, Kenya,
July 28, 2012

Your Excellency Right Honorable Raila Amollo Odinga, Her Excellency, Ida Odinga, Mr. and Mrs. Bekele, the newly married couple, Mr. and Mrs. Makarios Fidel Odinga, Family Members, Friends, and all invited Guests, I greet you in the Name of the Father, and of the Son, and of the Holy Spirit.

TODAY IS A VERY SPECIAL and significant day, not only for the newly married couple, but also for historical remembrance. Marriage is one of the seven major sacraments in which the grace of the Holy Spirit is bestowed through the blessing of a priest or a bishop, with the purpose of sanctifying the union of a man and woman who freely and willingly agree to marry. It is God blessing your love. "Without me you can do nothing," said Jesus.[78] Marriage, my dear sons and daughters in Christ, was established by God himself, who joined Adam and Eve as husband and wife for the begetting of new people on earth. God did not start by making an individual, but a community, a marriage. Remember, Mr. and Mrs. Makarios Fidel Odinga, that a person is a person because of people. God said, "It is not good for man to be alone .... So God made them male

78 Jn. 15:5.

and female."[79] And later, God said, "Therefore shall a man leave his father and his mother, and shall cleave unto his wife and they shall be one flesh."[80]

The apostle Paul compares the relation of husband and wife to that of Christ and his Church. "Wives, submit yourselves unto your own husbands, as unto the Lord. For the husband is the head of the wife, even as Christ is the head of the Church: and he is the savior of the body."[81] The Church has an obligation to and before the whole community, which is to provide the framework for the beginning, growth, and fulfillment of a marriage. The service of holy matrimony is evidence of the humble willingness of the couple to be in union with the entire Body of Christ. In turn, it is an assurance from God and a testimony of the Church recognizing this union.

The sacrament of holy matrimony in the Orthodox Church has its beauty and richness of the service that is steeped in tradition and symbolism and has remained unchanged through the centuries. The rituals that you observed have special meaning and significance. Each is performed three times to honor the mystical presence of the Holy Trinity. It is God who unites the couple, as we have witnessed with Makarios and Lwam to become one and, in mutual love, understanding, honesty, sincerity, obedience, and order, to listen to one another and to live together happily, until the next life.

To the newly married couple: Without God, true love is impossible. It cannot be what it was created to be. With God, love is perfected, completed, transfigured, sanctified, blessed, resurrected, and ultimately saved. This does not mean that having a church wedding will automatically guarantee a successful marriage. It only gives Christ an opportunity for completion and the perfection of your love as husband and wife. In holy matrimony, a man and woman are united by the Holy Trinity. Mr. and Mrs. Makarios Fidel Odinga, your conjugal union has now been blessed by our Lord Jesus Christ. God's grace has been imparted to you to live together in his love, mutually fulfilling and perfecting each other.

We are all gathered here today to witness Mr. and Mrs. Makarios Fidel Odinga acknowledge publicly this life-long commitment. They stand before God and the world—represented by this congregation—to pledge their commitment to each other, not until some other prettier face comes

79 Gen. 2:18; 5:2.
80 Gen. 2:24.
81 Eph. 5:22–23.

along, but "until death do you part." You have bound yourselves together by way of joining your hands and by saying, "I have chosen you. From now on, my aim will be not to search for someone who will please me, but to please you, the one I have chosen."

In marriage, Mr. and Mrs. Makarios Fidel Odinga, husband and wife do not love because they are perfect or because they complement one another. Rather, their unconditional forgiving love enables them to grow toward perfection. True love, my beloved son and daughter, entails a lifelong commitment to the person loved.

Real love never says, "I'll love you for a day, or a month, or a year, or ten years." True love is forever. Love is the burning part of life, embracing joy and sorrow alike, encompassing both loyalty and loss. In love, there is everything—the fullness of God and the fullness of life. Love is a gift from above; it is God himself. The power of love is the seal of the image of God within us, the seal of the gift of the Holy Trinity. That is why in marriage, the marriage partner is the life-giving personal revelation of Christ. To love the other person is to love oneself, to love one's own flesh. Many people say love is blind, but in fact it would be more correct to say that genuine love enables one to see and accept the other person as he or she is. It is a statement between God and humanity. One's marital partner is the covenant of faith and way of union with God himself.

Through the sacrament of marriage, a man and a woman are publicly joined as husband and wife. They enter into a new relationship with each other, God, and the Church. Marriage is not merely a social institution; it is undertaken in the presence of God before his holy altar. It is an eternal vocation of the Kingdom. A husband and a wife are called by the Holy Spirit not only to live together, but also to share their Christian life together so that each, with the aid of the other, may grow closer to God and become the persons they are meant to be.

The rings have been given. These rings are blessed and sanctified by the bishop. The rings which you are wearing now are the symbol of betrothal. In married life the weaknesses of the one partner will be compensated for by the strengths of the other, the imperfections of one by the perfections of the other, thus the reason the rings were exchanged three times denoting the Holy Trinity. By yourselves, you are incomplete; together you are made perfect. The exchange of rings gives expression to the fact that in marriage you will constantly be complementing each other. Both of you will be enriched by the union. You have also been entwined as one by the grace of the Holy Trinity.

Mr. and Mrs. Makarios, the candles you were given are a reminder of the light of Christ that is with you throughout the sacrament and your coming life together. Hold on to them as you did during the wedding service. The candles are like the lamps of the five wise maidens of the Bible. The maidens had enough oil in their lamps, as you have enough love for each other, to be able to receive the Bridegroom, Christ, when he comes in the darkness of the night. The candles are also a symbol of spiritual willingness to receive Christ, who will bless you through this sacrament and guide you throughout your life together.

Crowns will allow you, as a man and a woman in your union with Christ, to participate in his kingship. They are a symbol of martyrdom, since marriage is not a bed of roses. Every true marriage involves immeasurable self-sacrifice on both sides as the married couple bears witness to the presence of Christ between them. They represent the giving of one life totally to the other, and through the other, to Christ. You saw the crowns removed and returned as a symbol that God will receive your crowns in his Kingdom. They are signs of the glory and honor with which God crowns you during the sacrament of your holy matrimony. Makarios, you have been crowned as a king and you, Lwam, have been crowned as a queen of your little kingdom, the home, the domestic church, which you will rule with fear of God, wisdom, justice, and integrity.

The common cup is a reminder of the marriage at Cana of Galilee, which was attended and blessed by our Lord and Savior, Jesus Christ and for which he reserved his first miracle. There, he converted water into better wine and gave it to the newlyweds. In remembrance of this blessing, wine is given to you. This is the common cup of better life denoting the mutual sharing of joy and sorrow, the token of a life of harmony, from this moment on you will share everything in life—joys, love, pain, sorrows. You are to bear one another's burdens. Your joys will be doubled and your sorrows halved because they will be shared. Just as wine was drunk at the wedding in Cana, you also shared unconsecrated wine, symbolizing the sharing of all that life will bring. You will always drink from the same cup of life, with faith in God, and honor and fidelity to one another.

The procession recalls the joy that the Prophet Isaiah felt when he envisioned the coming of the Messiah. Do you remember, Makarios Fidel, the joy you had when you proposed marriage to Lwam? And you Lwam, do you remember the joy you had when Makarios proposed marriage to you? It is the same joy the Prophet Isaiah had. That is why we led you in a circle around the table on which are placed the gospel and the cross, with your hands joined together. This is a symbol of redemption by our Savior, Jesus Christ. You have taken the first steps as a married couple with my leading you in the way that you must walk. This movement expresses the fact that the way of Christian living is a perfect orbit around the center of Jesus Christ our Lord. You are required to walk through life with the Gospel and the Cross as your center. You will be supported throughout your married life by your best couple, who accompanied you in the procession. As a newly married couple, there is a need for sacrificial love for each other in marriage, a love that seeks not its own, but is willing to sacrifice its all for the one loved.

The joined hands symbolically meant the appeal to God to make you one in flesh and spirit and to grant you the joy of children in oneness.

In today's readings from the Saint Paul's epistle to the Ephesians, in a way the apostle is advising you, Makarios, to love your Lwam even as Christ also loved the Church, and gave himself for her. Christ and the Church express the strength and sacrifice required of you, Makarios, as a husband, and you, Lwam, as a wife. He is advising you to have unconditional love and service to one another by keeping your marriage holy and without blemish. And in Saint John's Gospel, Christ, at the wedding in Cana of Galilee, blessed the institution of marriage and performed the first of his miracles, transforming water into wine. Christ will also perform miracles in your marriage and transform your weaknesses into strengths.

It is only the Word of God that should come between you, as you saw when your hands were separated by the Bible.

Allow me to mention one important event that happened in 1957, when the late pioneers and Mau Mau fighters met with Makarios of Cyprus. The meeting occurred by the providence of God, and the focus was fighting the British colonial regime. The meeting was held with Oginga Odinga, who is the grandfather of Makarios Fidel Odinga. During the meeting, Makarios said one thing that kept their candles burning: "Never give up." We are also meeting here today to tell the newly married couple, as your late grandfather fought with Mau Mau in the wilderness, you have to fight Satan, who will come all the time as a colonist to tempt you, and we also tell you: "Never give up." My dear son, Makarios, I am sure your grandfather is rejoicing as his fight has been fulfilled and will be fulfilled through his grandson. What a coincidence it was that your grandfather was told by Makarios of Cyprus to never give up in fighting. I, Archbishop Makarios of Kenya, also tell you to never give up.

Finally, allow me to express my sincere thanks to Mr. and Mrs. Makarios for the sacrifice they have made for this achievement. You are now a married couple, and may God lead you in all blessings and keep your crowns of immortality until his second coming.

Bless them, Oh Lord our God, as you blessed Abraham and Sarah, Isaac and Rebecca, Jacob and all the Patriarchs, Joseph and Asenath, Moses and Zipporah, Joachim and Anna, Zachariah and Elizabeth. We beseech God to grant you a long, happy, and fruitful life.

May God bless you all and grant you good health. Amen.

HOMILY
on Christian Unity

August, 2012

OUR COMMON WISH is that every Christian soul should come together in prayer and in action, even though we belong to different Christian bodies. At this moment, for a while, let us consciously raise up our hearts together and give thanks to the Lord for this great day of our meeting.

A continuous presence for our spiritual nourishment is the reading of the holy words of our Lord Jesus Christ. The presence of our Lord is in us, especially today. This presence remains as an expression of his infinite love toward us, his children, and servants of his Church. It is not an empty or vague presence; it is something we experience daily in our work, in our lives, and in our pastoral responsibilities as shepherds of his flock. It is a reality that the great love of Jesus Christ is extended through us toward our people—to the lives of our Christian brethren. And in order for that love to achieve a real place in our daily lives in a way that will become a witness, we need to follow the commandment of our Lord Jesus Christ to love one another.

Our prayer, therefore, or expression of love toward our God, is a personal relationship of a man or woman with God, which has a *doxological* character. It is the goal of our confession of true faith and true *orthopraxia*, which finds its full expression in the phrase, "Love one another." The Cross of Christ is a strong sign through which we know his love toward us. Through his sacrifice, Jesus Christ, on the one hand, fulfilled the will of God and sanctified himself through his obedience to his Father. On the other hand, he saved humankind and became for us righteousness, sanctification, and salvation.

We should remember that our prayer has a continuous and sincere meaning and is moving according to the speed of our God, because if we ask God, with full awareness in our daily devotions, then God will answer our prayers.

If, therefore, we are nostalgic for the unity of the Church and our common understanding of fellowship, then we should not work for our personal interest, but that of the whole of the body of our Church. Therefore, we are called today with humility, not in human understanding, but according to the will of God and in obedience to him.

We should also remember to come back to the roots of our Church and to be reconciled in humility and repentance, with open hearts and thoughts in the spirit of God. Then we will realize the sacrifice of God and the spirit and the heart: *syntetrimmenes*.

We are looking for the work of our Church in the Middle East, and that means we have a responsibility to see the way open. That means that each of our actions should be authentic. Our mission is to give the love of God to the world. Therefore, the aim of our service should be the projection of that love of God, because the One who is sending us is himself the aim and goal of that mission. That service and goal is realized in the world by the Church, which is none other than the Body of Christ. Unfortunately, along its path the Church has not been able to be one body. Human weakness, passion, and egoism erase the Spirit of God. We as people have repeatedly refused to be subjected to his will and have not allowed the Holy Spirit to govern our lives. Therefore, with sincere hearts and love, let us come together and become imitators of God. Let us walk in love in order to live in the mystery of Christ.

Christ is inviting us again and again to become more and more human. Amen.

HOMILY
on Peace, Love, and Forgiveness

August, 2012

My beloved Children, Priests, Papadhias, and Parishioners, I greet you in the Name of the Father, and of the Son, and of the Holy Spirit.

How good and how pleasant it is for brethren to dwell together in unity.[82]

We need to recognize and acknowledge angry feelings. It takes humility to do this, but if we will get on our knees and ask our heavenly Father for a feeling of repentance and forgiveness, he will help us. The Lord requires us to forgive all people for our own good because hatred retards spiritual growth, and turns away the comforts that the Lord would put into our hearts. Of course, societies and families need to be protected from hardened criminals, because mercy cannot rob justice.

Forgiveness is a source of power. While forgiveness does not relieve us of consequences, when tragedy strikes we should not respond by seeking personal revenge, but rather by letting justice take its course and then letting go. It is not easy to let go and empty our hearts of festering resentment. The Savior has offered to all of us a precious peace through his death on the Cross, but this can come only if we are willing to cast out negative feelings of anger, spite, or revenge. For all of us who forgive those who trespass

82 Ps. 133:1.

against us, even those who have committed serious crimes against us, the blood of Jesus will bring peace and comfort.

A good marriage does not require a perfect man or a perfect woman. It only requires a man and a woman committed to strive together toward perfection. Sometimes I feel puzzled when young men and women approach me to speak about divorce. This is a sensitive issue because it evokes such strong emotions from persons it has touched in different ways. Some see themselves as the victims of divorce. Others see themselves as its beneficiaries. Some see divorce as evidence of failure. Others consider it an essential escape hatch from marriage. In one way or another, divorce touches our children, parents, relatives, and most of all the Church. The weakening of the concept that marriages are permanent and precious has far-reaching consequences. Influenced by popular notions that marriage is a ball and chain that prevents personal fulfillment, some young people shun marriage. Many who marry withhold full commitment to each other. In the Church, couples are married for all eternity. But some marriages do not progress toward that ideal. That is because of the hardness of our hearts.

We know that divorced couples look back on their divorces with regret at their own partial or predominant fault in the break-up. All who have been through divorce know the pain, and the need the healing power and hope that come from the crucified Lord.

If we can find forgiveness in our hearts for those who have injured and hurt us, we will rise to a higher level of self-esteem and well-being. We all need to speak one language, a language of caring, a language of unity, a language of love, a language of forgiveness, and a language of service. Through love and forgiveness, we shall be able to help and love our families, friends, our Church, and be able to provide the healing that people desperately need. The prayers, smiles, and the gifts we offer unto our loved ones, including priests and parishioners, touch hearts in a way no words can describe. Our compassionate love reaches beyond our family, beyond our community, and beyond our parishes. In everything we do, let love manifest itself through forgiveness, which is part of our inner beings.

Forgiveness is not always instantaneous. Especially when our loved ones hurt us, most of us do not think first about forgiveness. Our natural response is anger. We may even feel justified in wanting to get even with anyone who inflicts injury on us or on our family. Forgiveness is freeing up and putting to better use the energy once consumed by holding grudges, harboring resentments, and nursing unhealed wounds. It is rediscovering the strengths we always had and relocating our limitless capacity to understand and accept other people and ourselves. Most of us need time to work through pain and loss. We can find all manner of reasons for postponing forgiveness; one of these reasons is waiting for the wrongdoers to repent before we forgive them. Yet such a delay causes us to forfeit the peace and happiness that could be ours. The folly of rehashing long-past hurts does not bring happiness. Some hold grudges for a lifetime, unaware that courageously forgiving those who have wronged us is wholesome and therapeutic, and the better way.

Forgiveness comes more readily when we have faith in God and trust in his Word. Such faith enables people to withstand the worst of humanity, enabling them to look beyond themselves. More importantly, it enables them to forgive. All of us suffer some injuries from experiences that we cannot understand or explain. We may never know why some things happen in this life. Only God knows the reason for some of our suffering. But because suffering happens, it must be endured. God knows what we do not know and sees what we do not see. Some of our suffering has a purpose. Every calamity that comes upon us comes to us in order to prepare us to enjoy the presence of the Lord. Every trial and experience we pass through is necessary for our salvation.

Forgiveness will help us to become less angry, more hopeful, less depressed, less anxious, and less stressed. Forgiveness is a liberating gift that you can give to yourself.

I strongly advise you, for most marriage problems, the remedy is not divorce, but repentance. Often the cause is not incompatibility, but selfishness. The first step is not separation, but reformation. Divorce is not an all-purpose solution and it often creates long-term heartache. It is easier for someone to recover happiness after the natural death of a spouse than after a divorce. Spouses who hope that divorce will resolve conflicts often find that it aggravates them, since the complexities that follow divorce—especially when there are children—generate new conflicts. Think first of the children. Since divorce separates the interests of children from the interests of their parents, children are its first victims.

If you are already descending into a low state in your marriage, I urge you, as your spiritual father, to plead for the help and healing power of Jesus Christ, who was crucified in order to heal your drowning marriage. Your humble and united pleadings will bring you closer to the Lord, to each other, and will help you in the hard climb back to marital harmony.

Even those who think their spouse is entirely to blame should not act hastily. Sometimes the power of hope, expressed in love and forgiveness, is rewarded with repentance and reformation, but sometimes it is not. Personal circumstances, my dear children, vary greatly. We cannot control and we are not responsible for the choices of others, even when they impact us so painfully.

I am sure the Lord loves and blesses husbands and wives who lovingly try to help spouses struggling with long-term consequences of childhood abuse. When you suffer afflictions and much sorrow from the actions of other family members, I want to remind you that God knows, and he shall consecrate your afflictions for your gain. The apostle Paul assured us that "all things work together for good to them that love God."[83]

Two individuals approaching the marriage altar must realize that to attain the happy marriage they hope for, marriage means sacrifice, sharing, and even a reduction of some personal liberties, that it means long and hard economizing. It also means children, who bring with them financial burdens, service burdens, care, and worry burdens. But it also it means the deepest and sweetest emotions of all.

True repentance blesses our lives. We feel God's forgiveness and his peace, and our guilt and sorrow are lifted away. The essence of forgiveness is that it brings peace to the previously anxious, restless, frustrated, and perhaps tormented soul. If you have done all within your power to overcome your mistakes, and have determined in your heart that you will never repeat them again, then peace of conscience can come to you, by which you will know that your sins have been forgiven.

I know Satan will try to make you believe that sins are not forgiven because we can remember them. Satan is a liar; he tries to blur our vision and lead us away from the path of repentance and forgiveness. God did not promise that we would not remember our sins. Remembering will help us avoid making the same mistakes again. But if we stay true and faithful, the memory of our sins will be softened over time. This will be part of the needed healing and sanctification process.

For our own good, we need the moral courage to forgive and to ask for forgiveness. Never is the soul nobler and more courageous than when it forgives. This includes forgiving ourselves. Each of us is under divine obligation to reach out with pardon and mercy and to forgive one another. There is a great need for this Christ-like attribute in our families, in our

83 Rom. 8:28.

marriages, in our communities, in our parishes, and in our nations. We will receive the joy of forgiveness in our own lives when we are willing to extend that joy freely to others.

Lip service is not enough. We need to purge our hearts and minds of feelings and thoughts of bitterness and let the light and the love of Christ enter in. As a result, the Spirit of the Lord will fill our souls with joy accompanying divine peace of conscience. Yes, there is hope. Hope is linked to repentance. You can change. You can come unto Christ and be perfected in him. The natural man is an enemy to God, and has been from the fall of Adam, and will be, forever and ever, unless he yields to the call of the Holy Spirit, puts off the natural man, and becomes a saint through the sacrament of confession, therein gaining the forgiveness of the Lord. He must become like a child: submissive, meek, humble, patient, full of love, willing to submit to all things that the Lord sees fit to inflict upon him, even as a child submits to his father. When you forgive somebody who has wronged you, you're spared the dismal corrosion of bitterness and wounded pride. For both parties, forgiveness means the freedom to be again at peace inside their own skins and to be glad in each other's presence. Peace is not possible without forgiveness. Martin Luther King, Jr. once said, "Forgiveness is not an occasional act; it is a constant attitude."[84]

The only way children can learn the habit of forgiveness is by seeing their parents forgive others and forgive themselves. We relinquish this freedom when we hold onto anger and resentment. Enormous amounts of energy are wasted when we hold back our love, hold onto hate, and harbor acrimonious feelings. The only remedy is letting go, and being willing to forgive. Resentment is a habit and habits take a long time to change. Sometimes we need to forgive without reconciliation: forgiving for the purpose of forgiving. Certainly, what we strive for is to reconcile all conflicts, to clear the air, and to understand one another. But there are times in which this is impossible: with a parent who has passed away, with someone who has wronged you and is long gone, or with someone who is unwilling to communicate. These are the times when we must go deep into our own souls and see if we are willing to forgive anyway. Many of us keep on thinking of those who wronged us. We dream about them, we see them in every person we meet; some of us know them by name and even description. Even the slightest resemblance of them turns our stomachs into a knot.

84 Martin Luther King, Jr., sermon, 1960.

Weeks, months, and years pass. We continue asking ourselves, "Was I never to be free of this person? I can't go on like this."

The conflict between two individuals or two groups can cease, but often the seeds of future conflict are there, ready to germinate at the first opportunity. Without forgiveness, we achieve only a surface calm, not a reconciliation that is the foundation of true peace. Endless rage, resentment, guilt, and anger drain the life out of everything we do. My dear sons and daughters, the wronged individual must first uncover his or her anger by recognizing how resentment and obsession is affecting his or her life. As you give yourself to the other, you are the one that is healed. The reason is, we are not at peace with others because we are not at peace with ourselves. When a person forgives, he or she incorporates the virtue of kindness, respect, generosity, and moral value.

Thomas Szasz once said, "The stupid neither forgive nor forget; the naive forgive and forget; the wise forgive but do not forget."[85] Much of the time, we choose not to forgive because we believe the other person doesn't deserve our forgiveness. Remember, humility will continue to struggle until forgiveness is carried in our hearts. God wants to be our leverage in living, empowering us to feel better about ourselves, more excited about our future, more grateful for those we love and more enthusiastic about our faith. He made a personal relationship possible between each one of us and himself through his Son, Jesus Christ.

Forgiveness is the act of compassionately releasing the desire to punish someone or yourself for an offense. It's natural to feel angry, to say, "I'm not going to let him or her get away with this," whatever "this" is. However, revenge reduces you to your worst self, puts you on the same level with those spiteful people, increases stress and impairs your health and immunity. Forgiveness does not necessarily mean reconciliation with the person who upset you or condoning his or her actions. What you are after is to find peace. Forgiveness is the peace and understanding that come from blaming that which has hurt you less, taking the life experience less personally and changing your grievance story.

Unconfessed sin in our lives comes between us and damages our relationship with the Lord. "Behold, the Lord's hand is not shortened, that it cannot save, neither his ear heavy, that it cannot hear: But your iniquities have separated between you and your God, and your sins have hid his face

85 Thomas Szasz, *The Second Sin* (New York: Anchor Press, 1973) 51.

from you, that he will not hear."[86] Not only does unforgiveness come between us and God, it also breaks our relationships with others.

My sons and daughters, God will wipe away the tears of anguish, and remorse, and the fear and guilt. Jesus promised, "Peace I leave with you, my peace I give unto you: Not as the world giveth, give I unto you. Let not your heart be troubled, neither let it be afraid."[87] I urge you to keep a place in your heart for forgiveness, and when it comes, welcome it in.

May the guiding Spirit lead you into forgiveness. Amen.

86 Is. 59:1–2.
87 Jn. 14:27.

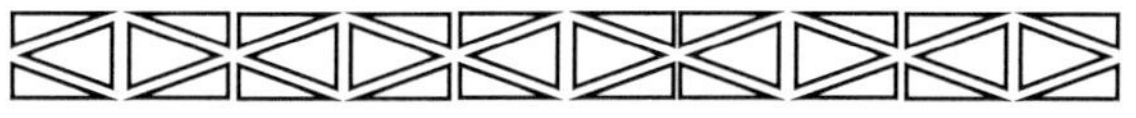

Funerals & Memorials

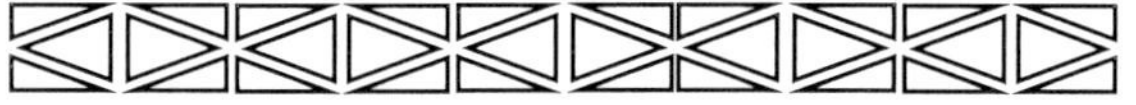

ADDRESS
at the Memorial Service for the Late Bishop George

Church of Saints Raphael, Nicholas, & Irene,
Thogoto, Kenya,
July 24, 2010

Reverend Fathers, Deacons, our Guests, the Relatives and Members of the family of His Grace, the late Bishop George, from the bottom of my heart I greet you all in the Name of the Father, and of the Son, and of the Holy Spirit.

"JESUS WEPT" is the shortest verse in the Bible.[1] But although it is the shortest verse, it carries the most important message for us Christians today. Christ Jesus did not weep because he could not do anything to help Lazarus on his death; he had all the powers bestowed on him by his Father to make his friend not face death. He could have just said one word and Lazarus could not even have come close to his death. Christ wept because his close friend had died. In his human nature, he felt that it was not necessary that Lazarus should have died; he felt mercy, he felt pity, and he was sympathetic and saddened by his friend's sudden death. As a man, he

1 Jn. 11:35.

felt the real pain of losing a close friend, and therefore could not control his tears; he wept. We are all humans and we could not have behaved any better than Christ if Lazarus had been our close friend. We could all weep and remember the good deeds that our friends used to do.

It is through Christ that death is defeated—and we no longer talk of the person being dead but asleep—because a time shall come when this person shall be awakened from his sleep and be with God in his Kingdom. If this person is sleeping, we ought not to weep but celebrate, because this person is not dead but sleeping. Today is a special day for us as we celebrate the memorial of our sleeping brother and friend, His Grace George Arthur Gathuna, who was the founding father of our Orthodox Church of Kenya.

Saint Paul writes to the Romans:

> For none of us liveth to himself, and no man dieth to himself. For whether we live, we live unto the Lord; and whether we die, we die unto the Lord: whether we live therefore, or die, we are the Lord's. For to this end Christ both died, and rose, and revived, that he might be Lord both of the dead and living.[2]

In these verses, we see very encouraging words about our Lord and Savior Jesus Christ; it does not matter whether we are dead or alive as long as everything is done because of our Lord. It adds that those who live should live to the Lord, while those who die should die to the Lord. Our Lord Jesus Christ defeated death by death, and was resurrected so that he might be the Lord of both those who are dead and those who are living. This assurance should motivate us to do good deeds which will make us be remembered when our own time to sleep comes. This will also act as a good sign that Christ will be our Lord even when we are dead. We should always live to Christ; we should all be his friend like Lazarus was, so that when we die, Christ will realize that we have fallen, and he will come to our rescue when the appointed hour comes.

Brothers and sisters in Christ, our gathering here is historic and it raises several questions that are related to the history of our Holy Orthodox Church. Our Church is a historic church, meaning it has derived its holy teachings and liturgical services from the first church of the apostles of Christ. So Christ becomes the cornerstone on which our Church has built its foundations. A question that one of you might ask: "Is there any need of studying church history? Is it really important in strengthening

2 Rom. 14:7–9.

our Orthodox faith, especially for us, the modern faithful of our beloved Church?" To both these questions I would answer in the affirmative.

I marvel at the fact that one of the remarkable aspects of Orthodox Christianity today is the seriousness of studying the history of our religion. My dear brothers and sisters, today I would term the story of the history of the Orthodox Church as a drama, a very powerful drama. But we ask ourselves: if it is a powerful drama, then why study it? The answer to this important question is that it gives us the understanding of how we got where we are, and, in the long run, it will make us wise. Church history introduces us to new friends, who are the saints and martyrs. This marks the importance of our great gathering today to commemorate our friend and brother in Christ, His Grace George Gathuna. He was our friend and still remains our friend, though he is not with us physically.

My fellow believers, when we take some time and look at our Church's history, we are often reminded of the price that was paid for us by Christ himself, and his apostles, saints, and martyrs, who suffered and died for us that we might enjoy the freedom of worship that we witness here today. Brothers and sisters in Christ, we often enjoy the experience of triumph when we live a Christ-like life, but end up forgetting the fact that we are not immune to the temptations and pitfalls which are brought by the devil in order to make us fail. This is where knowing our Church's history becomes handy. Church history enlightens us and fills us with new energy and makes us avoid pitfalls and landmines. From a careful look at the life of our fallen hero that we are commemorating today, we find several important historical lessons. We can be very affective ourselves if we emulate his example—that is, the way he lived his life, what really worked, and what was affective. The courage of His Grace George Gathuna has enhanced our endurance in the challenges that have faced our Orthodox Church to date and filled us with new energy and zeal to continue with the mission of Christ.

Today, my dear brothers and sisters in Christ, as I stand in front of all of you, I can say that the history and the works of our fallen brother, His Grace George, have become an inspiring part of my mission work here in Kenya. Though our brother met some pitfalls and temptations, which are quite normal for any sojourner in Christian life, he managed to keep the Church together. That's why today I can say that his is an inspiring history. It is said that information can guide you, but inspiration keeps you going; that is why today I keep on going in the mission of Christ and his Church.

Hopefully, the history of our brother will continue to be an inspiration for each one of us.

Most of us here today know that our Brother George died many years ago. In our Church, however, we believe that those who have died in Christ are alive in him, and will, on the last day, be raised bodily from the grave to new life, just as our Savior himself defeated death for us and was raised to life. This is the main reason why we commemorate our saints and ask them to intercede for us. They are present with us, not physically, but spiritually. It is important to state that our brother George is not dead, but he is with us here today. He is rejoicing with us, celebrating with us, and doing everything with us. We are here to talk about him, to marvel at his wonderful deeds just as an author said, "No one is dead as long as someone keeps saying [his] name or telling [his] stories." By talking about our brother, His Grace Bishop George Gathuna, he lives once again just as he used to.

Finally brethren, we pray for the soul of our beloved brother, His Grace Bishop Gathuna, that almighty God may grant him life eternal, and may his memory be eternal. We also thank His Grace for having stood with the Church in times of difficult challenges. We also ask him to intercede for us in our shortcomings and that God may enlighten us on proper channels to follow for sake of the continuity of the mission of our Church. I leave to all of you my paternal love and blessings. Amen.

HOMILY
at the Funeral of Papadhia Rahab Muongi

April 5, 2011

I greet you, Brothers and Sisters, in the Name of the Father, and of the Son, and of the Holy Spirit.

> The righteous perisheth, and no man layeth it to heart: and merciful men are taken away, none considering that the righteous is taken away from the evil to come. He shall enter into peace: they shall rest in their beds, each one walking in his uprightness.[3]

I DIDN'T KNOW where else to start concerning Mama Muongi, since these words from the prophet Isaiah really relate to her. For she was a faithful woman, full of mercy, and one who really loved the Church and the people. Today, she is not among us. She is resting; she has left us! For those of us who knew her, we are asking ourselves, why? I remember a few days before she passed away she had come to the headquarters, and she was well—whole, full of peace, and not sick at all. But, all of a sudden, the guest of death visited Papadhia's home. Death came for only one person: Papadhia. This is the way for all of us. Death will eventually visit each one of us each at his own time. Today you see me standing before you talking to you, alive and whole, but tomorrow I am no longer with you.

Think very carefully about this. Prepare yourself and be aware, "for the kingdom of God is at hand." The kingdom of God is with us now—not

3 Is. 57:1–2.

tomorrow, or the next year. It is today and now. There is no one standing here who doesn't have his own appointment with death.

It is an ultimate journey that each one of us will travel. These bodies we have today are just like tents, set up today and brought down tomorrow. Today we perform Papadhia's funeral service but tomorrow it is yours or mine. That is why in the funeral service we always ask: Where is the happiness of the earth, the riches and the beauty, where are they? These words are not for the departed; they are for us who are alive, to show us the vanity of life in order that you may prepare yourselves to enter into the eternal kingdom.

The hope of resurrection, as well as the joy of resurrection, is for those who are reconciled with Christ Jesus. We should therefore not fear leaving this life, because if you are reconciled with Christ, then you no longer die but only go to rest, in the hope of resurrection and awaiting the joy of the life to come.

There is a very wonderful church: beautiful, prepared, and surrounded with grace, an everlasting church. If only we could long for that church, our life would have a new dimension. It is not like any church you go to on Sunday. It is nothing like the church of today, full of conflicts and fighting; it is a holy church. This is where Papadhia has gone. She left this earthly church and entered into an everlasting, beautiful church, filled with grace—a church that is eternally praising and glorifying God.

Finally, beloved brethren, I exhort you, that each one examines his own soul. How is your life? When your time finally comes, will you die, or will you go into rest? When you finally leave this life, will you enter into the eternal Church or will you be thrown into eternal torment? What are you doing today that is preparing your soul?

I will leave you with these words from Revelation: "I heard the voice from heaven saying, 'Write, Blessed are the dead which die in the Lord from henceforth:' 'Yea,' saith the Spirit, 'that they may rest from their labors; and their works do follow them.'"[4]

May God bless all of you gathered here today. To all of you who have lost a mother, a grandmother, a friend, and a wonderful papadhia, may God remember you, may he wipe away your tears and may he give you exceeding peace in your lives. May he rest the soul of his handmaid, Papadhia Rahab where the righteous repose, and may he remember all of us when he comes in his kingdom, now and always, and to the ages of ages. Amen.

4 Rev. 14:13.

HOMILY
at the Funeral for the Son of Priest John Ng'ethe

July 8, 2011

I greet you, Brothers and Sisters, in the Name of the Father, and of the Son, and of the Holy Spirit. Amen.

IT IS A PITY THAT DEATH is the only sure event that takes place in our lives. To us all, death is imminent. It is like an appointment that we are all sure of; it will arrive eventually, in God's own time. For Orthodox Christians, there is the hope of resurrection and life to come, yet as human beings we still fear and really don't want to imagine ourselves in such situations. It is a reality that, even though we know too well it will happen, we wish not to think of it or even remember it.

Today we are all experiencing a great loss by the death of a young person. All of us, especially the parents and the relatives, are asking, "Why?" It is only human to ask ourselves that question, but we should expel that fear and really convince ourselves of this reality, whether we like it or not. A time is coming for all of us to take that unknown journey to eternity.

While we know of its reality, death is still a mystery. It is actually not something that God created, and even he even does not desire for it to happen. Since we are all sinners, death is the reason that God calls us all to repentance, since it is contrary to God's nature that he should take pleasure in the sinner's death; his benevolence forbids it. He takes infinite delight in the happiness of his creatures, and, therefore, cannot take delight in their misery. It is the reason that in our Church, we overcome the fear of death because we know where we are going. For us, there is a concrete way out of that situation. The Orthodox Church is like a medical center, in reality, where somebody is called to cure his passions and weaknesses, and where his relationship with God is renewed. Orthodoxy is giving the necessary medicines that are needed for our way to eternal life.

How we prepare ourselves is on us. Our God is merciful, loving, and forgiving, and it is our prayer that our resurrection is sure. It is actually a dogma of our faith—bringing the divine economy toward the salvation of mankind.

Therefore, concerning the eventuality of death, the question should not be "why," but rather, "are we ready?" for that unknown journey, which is always coming and will arrive abruptly. Therefore, we are called not to ask "why?" or "when?" but to know that we all need to prepare while we are still here on earth. The life to come is the greatest truth in the life of the Orthodox Christian. Jesus Christ and the apostles testified to this, as it is evident in many passages of Scripture.[5]

We should not be anxious; neither should we listen to the words of the contemporary world, because they are contrary to the words of the teachings of our Lord and of the apostles. Remember, "For yourselves know perfectly that the day of the Lord so cometh as a thief in the night."[6]

My final message, brothers and sisters, is that God really desires that each and every one of us receive that great gift of salvation. Confession and repentance is the most secure way of conquering the heavens. In other words, let us put ourselves in the position of the thief on the Cross in that wonderful conversation between himself and God. "And Jesus said unto him, Verily I say unto thee, To day shalt thou be with me in paradise."[7]

Since we are all very much concerned about our resurrection and the life to come, let us lift up our hearts and our eyes on high, and let us become imitators of the great army of holy men and women of our Church. Let us have that hope that we will be citizens of the Heavenly Jerusalem.

What a great thing, what joy, what beautiful melodies, what grace, what light. It is what we see in that hope of resurrection. Let us therefore rejoice in this knowledge and sincerely give thanks to the Lord for the life and the

5 See Luke 8: 54–55; Jn. 11:11–13; 11 Cor. 5:1; 1 Cor. 15:12–14.

6 1 Thess. 5:2.

7 Luke 23: 43.

work of our brother, who I am sure is hearing the voice of the Lord and responds, “Yes I am coming to you, receive me, I have the ticket to eternity and the doors of heaven are open to me.”

Let us therefore pray for the repose of the soul of our brother. May he rest in peace. May his memory be eternal and may his soul come to the attainment of eternal life through the saving grace of Christ Jesus. Amen

HOMILY
at the Funeral of Papadhia Hannah

Church of Saint Mammas,
August 2, 2011

Reverend Fathers, the bereaved Family of the late Fr. Iannikios and Papadhia Hannah, beloved Brothers and Sisters in Christ, I greet you all in the Name of the Father, and of the Son, and of the Holy Spirit. Amen.

I WISH TO QUOTE a verse that we always read during such a service as we are having today, one that mentions the departed person, yet it concerns us more—we who are left behind in this life.

> But I would not have you to be ignorant, brethren, concerning them which are asleep, that ye sorrow not, even as others which have no hope. For if we believe that Jesus died and rose again, even so them also which sleep in Jesus will God bring with him.[8]

Saint Paul clearly saw the fear and ignorance associated with death. He also saw the uncertainty of the afterlife, which was clearly manifested in the Church of Thessalonica. His message, through this second letter, was aimed at easing that uncertainty and instilling a sense of hope in the believers. It was centuries ago when this message was written, yet we are finding ourselves in this same situation each day that we are faced with death.

8 1 Thess. 4:13–14.

We are always living with the fear of death, more so because we love the life we have here on earth. Why do we fear this occurrence of death? We are always struggling and trying to acquire many things here on earth. We desire to have a beautiful house, a good car, a wonderful family; we want this and that, whatever can make life more comfortable. Yet all of this is vanity—"vanity of vanities"—as the preacher in Ecclesiastes puts it.[9]

Our life here is so temporary. Today, I am here with you, speaking to you, but tomorrow I will not be here; I will be gone. We should be living with this reality every day of our lives. For this reason, we have to prepare ourselves. How are we going to prepare ourselves? The message of the Bible is very simple. The message of the Bible is love. Can you love? Can you forgive? Can you accept one another? Can you embrace one another? I am sure many of us will say, "No!" Or worse still, some will say, "Never—it's not possible!", simply because we are humans and we are quickly angered.

Brothers and sisters in Christ, let us at this moment and at each moment of our remaining lives, think deeply about our going out of this earthly life. We are not permanent citizens. Our eternity was not meant for this life; it is in the other life. Yet, we need a V.I.P passport to this other life in heaven. How do we get that passport? It is through our life and deeds here on earth. Let us, therefore, change our lives today, and not fear this kind of situation, but be ready to go and meet our Lord Jesus Christ, to see that heavenly reality.

Today, we have come here to celebrate and thank God for the life of our dearly departed Papadhia. Many times, whenever I preside over a wedding, I always tell the couple how much their unity is paramount in completing and supporting each other in life. They are united both bodily and spiritually. Today, as we are speaking about Papadhia and Father Ioannikios, we ask ourselves: what is the role of a papadhia in our Church? I remember Father was traveling those days so much for the sake of church mission work. There were very few priests in the Church then. So Father was absent for many days on end. Yet, the Papadhia knew that it was her duty to support Father; she therefore never complained at any given time. She was a very strong lady.

This I put forth as a challenge to the new generation of papadhias, the young papadhias. It is their duty to support the mission work of the priests. It is their duty to stay close to the priests to support them and ensure that their mission in God's vineyard is successful. Look at the full life

9 Eccl. 1:2.

that Papadhia has lived; even after the repose of Fr. Iannikios she was still strong and always working for the Church and for the glory of God. Such humility and selflessness is a sure pathway to eternity and sainthood. The saints of our Church acquired the crowns of sainthood through such humility. This, brothers and sisters, is our V.I.P ticket to the next life.

Let us aspire, therefore, to live a full life in Christ, working for Christ and always putting in our minds that this is a temporary stop-over. Our destiny is eternal life with our Savior, Jesus Christ.

Finally, I wish that all of us would reflect on the words of Christ to Saint John during his Revelation on the Island of Patmos:

> And I heard a voice from heaven saying unto me, "Write, 'Blessed are the dead which die in the Lord from henceforth. 'Yea,' saith the Spirit, 'that they may rest from their labors; and their works do follow them.'"[10]

Let us pray that the Lord grants Papadhia eternal rest where the righteous repose, and that he remembers all of us when he comes in his Kingdom. Amen.

10 Rev. 14:13.

HOMILY
at the Funeral of Mr. William Muhoro

November 24, 2011

I greet you, Brothers and Sisters, in the Name of the Father, and of the Son, and of the Holy Spirit.

> The righteous perisheth, and no man layeth it to heart: and merciful men are taken away, none considering that the righteous is taken away from the evil to come. He shall enter into peace: they shall rest in their beds, each one walking in his uprightness.[11]

These words from the prophet Isaiah are really far reaching, especially when I think about our dearly departed brother, Muhoro. These words really relate to him. I say this because after we leave this place, many of us will forget him; only a vague memory will remain of his doings and his work, and maybe only the family will be left feeling the magnitude of their loss. My condolences go to the family and friends. They truly have been left by a great man—a man full of mercy and who really loved the Church and the people. Today he is not among us. He has left us, and he is resting!

Beloved brothers and sisters, while we are lost in the loss of a loved one, I would not wish that we be lost from the reality of the afterlife. For none

11 Is. 57:1.

who is righteous is really ever lost from us. To us, death is just a transition into the next life; a life of promises fulfilled. Just as Saint Paul says, "But I would not have you to be ignorant, brethren, concerning them which are asleep, that ye sorrow not, even as others which have no hope. For if we believe that Jesus died and rose again, even so them also which sleep in Jesus will God bring with him."[12]

Saint Paul clearly saw the fear and ignorance associated with death. He also saw the uncertainty of the afterlife, which was clearly manifested in the Church of Thessalonica. His message through this second letter was aimed at easing that uncertainty and instilling a sense of hope in the believers. It was centuries ago when this message was written, yet we are finding ourselves in this same situation each day that we are faced with death.

We are always living with the fear of death, more so because we love the life we have here on earth. Why do we fear this occurrence of death? We are always struggling and trying to acquire many things here on earth. We desire to have a beautiful house, a good car, a wonderful family; we want this and that—whatever can make life more comfortable. Yet all of this is vanity—"vanity of vanities"—as the preacher puts it in Ecclesiastes.[13]

Think very carefully about this. Prepare yourselves and be aware, "for the kingdom of heaven is at hand."[14] The kingdom of God is here and now, not tomorrow or next year. It is today, here and now. There is none standing here today who doesn't have his own appointment with death. Our dearly departed brother knew this deep within his heart. His goal, therefore, was to first acquire the kingdom of heaven.

I met Muhoro thirty-five years ago, and since then we have been very close friends. He was not only a devout Orthodox Christian, but very active in youth matters. I actually met him in the International Syndesmos. Thirty-five years, a person attending the Syndesmos Conference had to be really integrated in youth affairs. That, brothers and sisters, described brother Muhoro. He loved the youth and worked hard to see the youth flourish. He saw the future of the Church in the youth of his day. He worked to see that future fulfilled. I later met him when he was admitted to the hospital, and he was still firm and strong in the Orthodox faith.

Those of us who really knew him will testify to these words. For the life that we are called to live is such that when we depart, those around us may

12 I Thess. 4:13–14.

13 Eccl. 1:2.

14 Matt. 4: 17.

bear witness to our actions, as the Epistle to the Hebrews clearly states: "Wherefore seeing we also are compassed about with so great a cloud of witnesses, let us lay aside every weight, and the sin which doth so easily beset us, and let us run with patience the race that is set before us."[15]

Lets us ask ourselves how our exit from this life will be. What works are we leaving behind, what legacy will bear us witness at the mercy seat of Christ? Will it be love or hate, peace or turmoil, acceptance or prejudice? Let us therefore lead a life worthy of the kingdom to which we are called.

May God grant our brother rest where the righteous repose, and may the Lord bless us and remember us all when he comes in his kingdom. Amen.

15 Heb. 12:1.

ADDRESS
at the Twenty-fifth Memorial Service of Bishop George Gathuna

Saints Raphael, Nicholas, & Irene,
Thogoto, Kenya,
July 29, 2012

To know the canonicity of an Orthodox Church, one can simply listen to the name of the bishop, metropolitan, or patriarch commemorated by the celebrating clergy in the litanies. During the Divine Liturgy, after the diptychs, which is a list of commemorations, the clergy also say the following: "Among the first, remember O Lord, our Metropolitan [NAME], and our Bishop or Archbishop [NAME]. Grant them for thy holy churches ..."[16]—that is, they commemorate the bishop of the region, or if in a hierarchical liturgy, the celebrating bishop commemorates the primate of his Church. In our case, it is the Patriarch of Alexandria. While this may seem like just an obvious action in any Orthodox worship gathering, allow me to remind you all that this is a very deep part of our faith. This is because the commemoration of a particular bishop in a worship gathering defines not only the liturgical correctness required of the celebrants, but also their canonicity—that is, the correctness of their existence according to the church laws and guidelines; their catholicity—their being part of the one universal Church; and their apostolicity—that is, they possess a direct connection with Christ and his apostles through apostolic

16 *Hieratikon*, vol. II, 137.

succession. As a whole, the commemoration of the bishop grounds their ecclesiology—what defines them as the Church.

The fifteenth canon of the Synod of Constantinople demonstrates the importance of this event:

> What has been ordained for presbyters and bishops and metropolitans is to a much greater extent befitting to patriarchs. So if any presbyter, bishop, or metropolitan dare to secede from communion with his own patriarch and does not mention the latter's name at the place appointed and ordained in the divine mystagogy … the holy synod has declared him to be utterly alienated from any priestly function …[17]

Thus, not commemorating a bishop in an Orthodox service is a very serious offense. It means the lack of all aspects of unity with other Orthodox Christians, and thus, the lack of unity with Christ and his apostles. This disunity only means one thing: to be outside the Church. The same case of being outside the Church goes for all non-canonical churches, that is, some "orthodox churches" claiming to be true churches, while they lack a connection with the authentic Orthodox churches in the world that have the characteristics defined earlier.

The Church operates in a way that is similar to African society. As we all can bear witness, in African society, the family is very important in the life of any person. A person alienated from his or her family lacks so many important features of who they are, and, sooner or later, becomes an outcast. The principle, "No man is an island," works for the Orthodox tradition, too. All these principles were well understood by Bishop Gathuna and his counterparts.

There were five characteristics—liturgical, canonical, catholic, apostolic, and ecclesiological—for which our late Baba Gathuna was searching on behalf of the Church of Kenya. Without these aspects, he knew that he and his flock would not belong to the One, Holy, Catholic, and Apostolic Church. For Bishop Gathuna, the only place for his flock was in the Church. The only way to get in the Church was to be under a canonical Church, and thus he and his Ugandan counterparts searched for this canonical Church.

To look for a canonical Church was not an easy task in their day,

17 Canon 15 of the Synod of Constantinople, AD 861. *The Rudder* (New York: The Orthodox Christian Educational Society, 1983) 470, 471.

considering the ongoing second world war and colonialism, but they still persisted in their search. They could have chosen to stay under the pseudo-orthodox bishop they had inherited at their first attempt, or to join an existing denomination, or even to form a denomination of their own. But their desire was to be a part of the universal and apostolic Church. So, being led by the Holy Spirit, they worked hard, and persevered, and waited for the right time to come.

"Wherever the bishop appears, there let the people be; as wherever Jesus is, there is the catholic Church."[18] Through their bishop, a church is renewed and growth is promised, a fact witnessed by the expansion of our diocese. A church can only expand if she has workers—that is, clergymen. In the Orthodox Church, only a bishop can perform sacraments, along with those whom he has ordained and permitted to do so, and thus, where there is a bishop there is the Church through his power to administer sacraments and to appoint co-workers in his ministry. A church without a bishop will have no ordinations, and a church without ordinations will have no workers after the existing ones leave office, thus causing it to die. All clergymen work in harmony under their bishop's guidance and instructions. This is the reason that dioceses are created under a bishop, who is not only the father and overseer of his flock, but also the Eucharistic President. Bishop Gathuna wanted a canonical church that would continue and expand throughout the country. We are a result of his contributions and efforts toward this end.

> For we being many are one bread, and one body: for we are all partakers of that one bread ... For as the body is one, and hath many members, and all the members of that one body, being many, are one body: so also is Christ. For by one Spirit are we all baptized into one body ... For the body is not one member, but many.[19]

Through the bishop, a diocese is also connected to the greater local Church. In our case, the Orthodox Church in Kenya is connected to the Patriarchate of Alexandria through our bishop. Through this connection, Kenya is united with all other churches in Africa, not being a Kenyan Church only, but also an African Church. When the Patriarch of Alexandria is celebrating the Divine Liturgy, he commemorates in the diptychs all other

18 St Ignatius of Antioch, "Epistle to the Smyrnaeans". *Early Christian Writings* (New York: Penguin) 103.

19 1 Cor. 10:17; 12:12–14.

bishops who are heads of independent Orthodox churches as he is: for example, the patriarchs of Constantinople, Antioch, Jerusalem, and Russia; and the archbishops of the churches of Cyprus, Greece, and others. The bishops commemorated by the patriarch are only those with whom his local churches are in communion. This act, in itself, unites the Church of Alexandria and all other canonical Orthodox churches in the world; this makes the African Church not only African, but also universal. So, the Metropolis of Kenya is both Kenyan and African. At the same time, it is a universal Church. The catholicity that we enjoy today in the life of the Kenyan Church was a great dream that came to exist through the wisdom, efforts, and leadership of the late Bishop Gathuna. And, we recall the words of Christ's great prayer to the Father in the Garden of Gethsemane:

> Neither pray I for these alone, but for them also which shall believe on me through their word; That they all may be one; as thou, Father, art in me, and I in thee, that they also may be one in us: that the world may believe that thou hast sent me.[20]

Another important item that an Orthodox bishop carries with him is apostolicity. Apostolicity can only be acquired by a bishop ordained within a church that is accepted as canonical; that is, a church living within the boundaries of the right traditions and administration. The Patriarchate of Alexandria is universally accepted as an apostolic Church because, first among other things, she has her roots in the apostolic ministry of Saint Mark the Evangelist. The present Patriarch of Alexandria is the 124th successor of the apostle and Evangelist Mark. Through Saint Mark, who was the first bishop of the Patriarchate of Alexandria, all the bishops in Africa have a connection with Christ. The Orthodox Church of Kenya gets her apostolic continuity through her bishop, who is connected to the See of Saint Mark. Today, Deacon Kallinikos David Kinuthia has received this apostolic succession through me, his bishop. Therefore, the people whom he will serve as a clergyman will always be under this apostolic blessing. The people that receive sacraments from a clergyman of a church with legitimate apostolic succession receive the same blessings as Christians of the early Church.

The Patriarchate of Alexandria waited over a decade to come and see the flock in East Africa that wanted to join his patriarchate. But time was

20 Jn. 17:20–21.

not an issue for Bishop Gathuna and his team. They waited and, in 1942, met the Alexandrian envoy of Metropolitan Nicholas Abdullah of Axum. His Eminence saw the dedication and zeal of the leaders of this African church. Hence, Bishop Gathuna's dream that Kenya be a part of the Universal Church was realized. "So we, being many, are one body in Christ, and every one members one of another."[21]

What we are talking about today is, from the Orthodox perspective, what must happen for any group of people to be considered members of the Church. This is what makes us unique and different from other Christian faiths. This is the reason we consider ourselves the only true Church. This is what our Father, Bishop Gathuna, was looking for when he and others contacted the Patriarchate of Alexandria through Father Nicodemos Sarikas. He wanted the union of his flock with all other flocks of the Church of Christ existing in different parts of the world, as one flock with one Shepherd. Uniting with the Church of Alexandria was, and is still, the only door to all these. "That there should be no schism in the body; but that the members should have the same care one for another."[22]

Bishop Gathuna searched for unity with the One, Holy, Catholic and Apostolic Church, the locally and universally united Church. Today, many things have happened within this Church, but luckily we are still here and continuing the works of our forefathers. We also are grateful to God that we now have the reunion of the Church in Kenya since the year 2004. The unity, catholicity, apostolicity, and canonicity of our Church are no longer problematic. Thanks be to God, to Bishop Gathuna, and all stakeholders of the reunion, we are enjoying unity today after several decades of divisions.[23]

However, are we really united with one another? Do we love one another like brothers and sisters in Christ? Do we still have differences within ourselves? Are we one, like the body of Christ that we have received from the same cup today? Are we living the kind of life that our forefathers

21 Rom. 12:5.

22 1 Cor. 12:25.

23 A schism occurred within the African Orthodox Church of Kenya in 1979, when Bishop George was defrocked by the Church of Alexandria and later joined an Old Calendarist group. This schism was healed in 2004 and Bishop George was posthumously re-instated into Orthodox communion in 2006. See Evangelos Thiani, "Call for ecclesial recognition of Bishop George Arthur Gatungu Gathuna," in *Ortodoksia*, vol. 59 (University of Finland, 2019).

worked so hard to achieve, a life in which the Church is united and so are her members? Saint Paul reminds the Colossians:

> And let the peace of God rule in your hearts, to which also ye are called in one body, and be ye thankful. Let the word of Christ dwell in you richly in all wisdom; teaching and admonishing one another in psalms and hymns and spiritual songs, singing with grace in your hearts to the Lord. And whatsoever ye do in word or deed, do all in the Name of the Lord Jesus, giving thanks to God and the Father by him.[24]

As we celebrate the life of our departed father, brother, and concelebrant in Christ, Bishop George Arthur Gatung'u Gathuna, let us honor his efforts and those who were with him by uniting as persons, as brothers in Christ, as children of one father, as worshipers of one God, and doing everything in the Name of God with love and unity.

May the memory of Bishop George Gathuna be eternal and may his spirit of unity continue springing from each of our hearts! Amen.

24 Col. 3:15–17.

HOMILY
at the Funeral of Papadhia Leah Njeri Gakera

Parish of Saint Eleftherios,
Rironi, Kiambu County, Kenya,
November 19, 2013

Reverend Fathers and Papadhias, beloved Brothers and Sisters in Christ, I greet you all in the Name of the Father, and of the Son, and of the Holy Spirit. Amen.

DEATH IS ALL AROUND US. Wherever we turn, we always encounter death and the news of death. In the family and in the community, there is always the issue of death. Death is a visitor who comes uninvited and unexpected. We are greatly afraid of death. Yet, however, today I wish to tell you that we should not be afraid of death anymore. We are expecting to see the life to come. Death will come and the truth of the matter is that no one can run away from that. Whether rich or poor, whether high or low, nobody can run away from death. We shall all follow that same road. But we should follow that road with hope!

"Blessed is the way which you shall follow today." We sang these words today for our beloved. And I know how each and every one of us is feeling concerning her departure from this life. Reading through her biography, it shows that she was one of the pioneers of the Orthodox Church. It is actually by the hands of the late Bishop Gathuna that she was baptized into the Orthodox Faith. We glorify our God, because we have seen really that the Holy Spirit directed her deeds as our Lord desired. She later met the late Father John Gakera, and together they made a wonderful home. Together they have dedicated their lives to the Church in Kenya. We remember those days when they were strong in the faith and they gave their lives and time for the glory of God and his Church.

Today we are gathered here to acknowledge the work and life of Papadhia Leah. I am sure the young papadhias, who are here and those who are absent, have a person to emulate. We all like to emulate the life of Jesus and the saints of our Church, knowing that they were human as we are, but through their dedication they were able to attain holiness. Today we see them in this church and in our churches. I feel that Papadhia Leah was a very good example, since she was following and emulating the deeds of our Lord Jesus Christ and his disciples. So, we are acknowledging her dedication and her faith, as well as her dedication in cultivating the Orthodox faith in this area and all other places in which she has lived.

There is one thing we should remember, brothers and sisters in Christ. We have in front of us the wonderful picture of the coming of our Lord Jesus Christ on earth. We know that he appeared here two thousand years ago to save mankind. He brought that message of salvation. He commanded his apostles to take forth that message of salvation because that message was bringing to the people peace, love, and obedience. Those of us who have decided to follow Christ, humble and unworthy disciples as we are, should try always to live our lives actively fulfilling the wonderful ways of Christ.

If we look closely, we realize that we are different from the people next to us. Each and every one of us has his own gifts and weaknesses. At the same time, we are all given the same opportunity to become holy. Standing here today, we are listening to the very words of our Lord Jesus Christ, and we are sure that this is not the end of the life of Papadhia Leah, but it is the beginning of the real, true life. So, if each and every one of us wants to inherit that everlasting life, we should implement the teachings of Christ in our lives.

Sometimes we complicate our lives because we like to criticize others. That tarnishes our lives and the lives of others, too, because we are all images of Jesus Christ. Each and every one of us represents an icon of Christ. So the message is very simple. We don't need to speak philosophically concerning the wonderful Gospel of Christ. Are we able to accept one another, to honor each other, to listen to one another, to embrace one another? If we are able, know this for sure, that when the time comes to depart this life, we will be rejoicing. We should rejoice always because in Christ Jesus there is joy. When we are united with the sacraments and the life of our Church, then at the end we shall inherit the Kingdom of God. In that Kingdom of God, there is no pain or sorrow, but everlasting joy.

So, today, Papadhia Leah is resting. I am sure she is rejoicing, because she has fulfilled her work on this earth. She is finally reunited with her beloved husband, Father Gakera. Together they will rest until the day we go to meet them again. She is sleeping and resting peacefully. Let us accept that for us there is no death. There is the life to come. Eternal life is the true life.

Brothers and sisters in Christ, rejoice always in the Lord, and I am sure that when we all meet on that day, we shall glorify God. Let us stay united, humble, and loving toward one another. That love of Jesus should never depart from us, but rather always unite us. In this way, we shall always glorify God.

Let me take this opportunity to console the family of the late Papadhia Leah, and to tell them that the Church is together with them in this difficult time. Let me acknowledge once again that the Church recognizes her work and dedication. She will be eternally remembered.

May she rest in peace. Amen.

HOMILY
at the Funeral of Subdeacon Simon Kanyingi

Church of Saint Nectarios,
Maai Mahiu, Kenya,
November 26, 2013

Reverend Fathers and Papadhias, devout Deacons and Subdeacons, Brothers and isters in Christ, I greet you all in the Name of the Father, and of the Son, and of the Holy Spirit. Amen.

Mũrĩ ega? How are you?

I WISH TO SHARE with you and speak about a famous quotation of one of the saints of our Church. I want to talk about Saint Silouan the Athonite. I trust and believe that he is well-known by some of you. Many years ago, when I was bishop of Riruta, we managed to translate many of his writings. The reason I decided to speak about him today is because he had a very beautiful quotation: "Keep thy mind in hell, and despair not."[25]

These were actually the words of the Lord himself to Saint Silouan. One day when Saint Silouan was praying in the mountains, some demons appeared to him and disturbed him a lot during his prayers. According to his description, there was one huge demon and some small ones surrounding

25 Arch. Sofrony, *The Undistorted Image* (London: Faith Press, 1958) 200.

him as he prayed. Therefore, the saint asked the Lord why the demons are disturbing him as he prayed. This is actually a real story. I have an explanation from a spiritual son of Saint Silouan, who was my spiritual father, Saint Sophrony.

So this message is: keep your mind in hell—attach your mind to hell and do not be dismayed or disturbed—and finally you will be saved, as I interpret it. All of us sometimes find ourselves in hell. We even use these phrases when we are talking and we say to one another, "Go to hell" [*i.e.*. abusively]. This is because hell is a terrible place and we would not want to go there. There is, however, a very deep spiritual meaning to this phrase: keep yourself in this place, for by doing so, you will teach yourself all the things needed to uplift you spiritually. Saint Silouan is known to have gone to heaven and not hell by the end of his life; he was canonized because he implemented that phrase, which he received as a vision from God.

When I was young and very enthusiastic, I loved myself very much. I was thinking very big things about my life. I was telling myself that soon I would be a very famous professor. My spiritual father, however, narrated to me the story of Saint Silouan. Since that time until the present, I changed completely. I am sure that if each one of us were to implement that phrase, to keep our minds in hell and not be disappointed, we shall be saved. What a wonderful message for all of us, because when we are thinking about hell, the mind goes very far. The same happens when we are thinking about death. This is—according to us—a terrible condition. But it is not really so, because there is something else coming for us. If we humble ourselves and dedicate ourselves to God, if we become people of forgiveness and love, then we overcome our difficulties.

Brothers and sisters in Christ, as of late, I have been doing many funerals. This is the reason I want to emphasize this for both you and for me. This is our time. There is no delay. Put your mind in hell and do not give up. Struggle, however, to be humble, and you will reap wonderful gifts from the Spirit.

Brothers and sisters in Christ, we thank God for the life of our brother, Subdeacon Simon Kanyingi. Simon is traveling along that journey which all of us will face one day. It is a wonderful journey, a beautiful journey, if without doubt we remain faithful to the work of God. Are you ready to travel this eternal journey? I am sure we would all say no. We all perceive this life as a wonderful life. We therefore fail to perceive the afterlife. It is there and it is real. Let us therefore prepare to leave this life for the next.

Simon Kanyingi was a wonderful man. He loved his work. He loved his family, and he loved the Church of Christ. His wife, children, and grandchildren equally loved him. It is, however, important to realize that this life is not ours; it is God who prepares this life for us. It is therefore important to do those things that are pleasing to God. We should not fear when we think about death. We should rather become very spiritual. Our brother was dedicated to working for the Church through his profession. He has constructed very many churches, this being his last work. This beautiful cathedral will be admired by generations to come. As a catechist and a reader he loved the services. His words were always words of advice. Even though I myself was his bishop, he came to me, and the things he spoke were things I should follow in my life. His humility was an example. We should thank God and not accuse anyone. We should only thank God for the wonderful work our brother has done for the Church.

I wish to thank the wife of the late subdeacon, Mama Karugi, for her love and support for her husband. I am also thankful and appreciative of her, since on this day she did not adorn herself in black, mournful attire. She instead adorned herself in white, which shows she is not mourning but rejoicing—rejoicing as on the day she married the late subdeacon. You had a wonderful husband, who, I am sure was a blessing to you, your children, and your grandchildren. I am sure every one of you will be remembering him and will teach each other to follow his example.

There is so much to say about Simon since he was a good example. I urge all of us to always remember Mr. Kanyingi, and not to think of ourselves as righteous. Let us think about death, so that we can focus on life and live in a humble way, the way taught by Saint Silouan.

So, brother Simon, go in peace. Take with you all the beautiful memories and all the good work you have done for our Church with all the beautiful services you have loved so much. Rest peacefully, knowing that as we stand in this very beautiful church, which is the work of your hands, because of this you will be remembered. We are all sure that we will meet you again in the second coming of our Lord.

In the meantime, be united in Jesus Christ with that hope of the life and resurrection to come of our Lord Jesus Christ. Amen.

The End

ADVENTURES IN AFRICA
was typeset in Garamond Premier Pro by
SAINT TIKHON'S SEMINARY PRESS
and printed by
SPENCER PRINTING,
Honesdale, Penn.

Glory to God for All Things